Feminism in Community

INTERNATIONAL ISSUES IN ADULT EDUCATION

Volume 16

Series Editor:
Peter Mayo, *University of Malta, Msida, Malta*

Editorial Advisory Board:
Stephen Brookfield, *University of St Thomas, Minnesota, USA*
Waguida El Bakary, *American University in Cairo, Egypt*
Budd L. Hall, *University of Victoria, BC, Canada*
Astrid Von Kotze, *University of Natal, South Africa*
Alberto Melo, *University of the Algarve, Portugal*
Lidia Puigvert-Mallart, *CREA-University of Barcelona, Spain*
Daniel Schugurensky, *Arizona State University, USA*
Joyce Stalker, *University of Waikato, Hamilton, New Zealand/Aotearoa*
Juha Suoranta, *University of Tampere, Finland*

Scope:
This international book series attempts to do justice to adult education as an ever expanding field. It is intended to be internationally inclusive and attract writers and readers from different parts of the world. It also attempts to cover many of the areas that feature prominently in this amorphous field. It is a series that seeks to underline the global dimensions of adult education, covering a whole range of perspectives. In this regard, the series seeks to fill in an international void by providing a book series that complements the many journals, professional and academic, that exist in the area. The scope would be broad enough to comprise such issues as 'Adult Education in specific regional contexts', 'Adult Education in the Arab world', 'Participatory Action Research and Adult Education', 'Adult Education and Participatory Citizenship', 'Adult Education and the World Social Forum', 'Adult Education and Disability', 'Adult Education and the Elderly', 'Adult Education in Prisons', 'Adult Education, Work and Livelihoods', 'Adult Education and Migration', 'The Education of Older Adults', 'Southern Perspectives on Adult Education', 'Adult Education and Progressive Social Movements', 'Popular Education in Latin America and Beyond', 'Eastern European perspectives on Adult Education', 'An Anti-Racist Agenda in Adult Education', 'Postcolonial perspectives on Adult Education', 'Adult Education and Indigenous Movements', 'Adult Education and Small States'. There is also room for single country studies of Adult Education provided that a market for such a study is guaranteed.

Feminism in Community

Adult Education for Transformation

Leona M. English and Catherine J. Irving
St. Francis Xavier University, Canada

SENSE PUBLISHERS
ROTTERDAM/BOSTON/TAIPEI

A C.I.P. record for this book is available from the Library of Congress.

ISBN: 978-94-6300-200-4 (paperback)
ISBN: 978-94-6300-201-1 (hardback)
ISBN: 978-94-6300-202-8 (e-book)

Published by: Sense Publishers,
P.O. Box 21858,
3001 AW Rotterdam,
The Netherlands
https://www.sensepublishers.com/

Printed on acid-free paper

ADVANCE PRAISE FOR
FEMINISM IN COMMUNITY: ADULT EDUCATION FOR TRANSFORMATION

Feminism in Community: Adult Education for Transformation is an essential addition to an already significant book series, International Issues in Adult Education. In putting feminism at its heart, it not only fills a deep gap in much work on community and adult education, it ignites new ways of dis/covering transformative practices. The authors have built on their critical engagement with feminism, community and social action to develop a new call for the creation of change, doing 'community' differently and raising global issues about transformation. This book is a must read for all of us concerned with putting gender at the heart of these debates and seeking not only to develop new perspectives, but to go beyond this and move ideas into actions. *Sue Jackson, Birkbeck University of London*

Calm and fire; resistance and defiance; creativity and hope; dialogue and listening; the concrete and the virtual; spirit and embodiment; critique and empowerment. These are but a few ideas that come together in this pivotal, internationally focused compilation by Leona English and Catherine Irving on feminist adult education and learning. It is a stellar addition to the field and a must read. *Darlene E. Clover, University of Victoria, Canada*

Leona English and Catherine Irving's book on feminist adult education and learning emulates a partnership discourse; it is about women and for women, and supports women's voices and leadership in academia and beyond in formal, nonformal and informal settings. The authors identify critical issues of women's struggles to move beyond safe and supportive spaces to a more critically engaged pedagogy. By naming diverse forms of resistance and subversive strategies for change, they lead women into emancipatory and freeing positions for exercising power. This insightful text urges citizens to engage in reimagining an alternative and sustainable future. *Dzintra Ilisko, Daugavpils University, Latvia*

This is a skillfully and passionately written book that amplifies feminist (adult) educators' contributions to the description and explanation of women's oppression, and their strategies for women's empowerment and liberation; strategies that are rooted in learning within groups and communities, and learning towards group and collective transformation. It calls for naming, learning and action. *Olutoyin Mejiuni, Obafemi Awolowo University, Nigeria*

All adult educators who work with women as learners should read and savor this book. It is about igniting the fire of learning, or examining how the lives of women so ignited have changed the world through their spoken and unspoken feminist efforts.

It draws on the multiple dimensions of their teaching and learning—the cognitivie, the affective, the creative, and the embodied and sacred domains—whereby they learn not only to critique systems of power but to create and make change in the world. This is a landmark text on women as learners and change agents in the 21st century world. *Libby Tisdell, Penn State University, USA*

This book is unique in reminding us that if we forget our social justice roots then progress is undermined. This is one of those rare and exciting books that really helps its readers to think differently about the need for continued engagement with feminist and adult learning, and I highly recommend it. *Lyn Tett, University of Edinburgh, Scotland*

TABLE OF CONTENTS

ACKNOWLEDGEMENTS

We would like to acknowledge the able assistance of Peter Mayo, Professor of Education, and editor of this series, for working with us to completion. His unwavering belief in our project has made it possible and his insights have made our ideas much clearer and sharper.

We would be remiss if we did not acknowledge our colleagues in adult education who share our passion for feminist research and who are truly committed to transforming the world in ways that are imaginative and creative. We thank Shauna Butterwick, Paula Cameron, Erin Careless, Maureen Coady, Darlene Clover, Patti Gouthro, Dzintra Ilisko, Sue Jackson, Nanci Lee, Olutoyin Mejiuni, Angela Miles, Carole Roy, Nancy Taber, Lyn Tett, Libby Tisdell, and others too numerous to mention for their insightful writing and collegiality, which have made this work on feminist transformation possible. We hope that we have engaged with their ideas and writing it in a way that is fruitful and faithful to their intended meaning.

In a special way, we acknowledge the feminist contributions to transformation shown by our late colleague Susan Eaton. We admire very much the way she lived out her commitment to a transformed world for women.

We are grateful for the editing work of Wendy Kraglund-Gauthier and Ashley Pettipas in the preparation of the manuscript, and we acknowledge the Coady International Institute and St. Francis Xavier University for their support of this project.

FREQUENTLY USED ABBREVIATIONS

AAWORD	African Association of Women for Research and Development
AHL	Adult health learning
APC	Association for Progressive Communications
AWID	Association of Women in Development
CAL	Coalition of African Lesbians
CEDAW	Convention on the Elimination of Discrimination Against Women
CREA	Creating Resources for Empowerment in Action (India)
DAWN	Development Alternatives for a New Era
ESL	English as a Second Language
EU	European Union
FEMNET	African Women's Development and Communication Network
GAD	Gender and development
GDP	Gross domestic product
ICTs	Information communication technologies
INGOs	International nongovernmental organizations
LGBTQ	Lesbian, Gay, Bisexual, Transgendered, Queer
MDGs	Millennium Development Goals
NAC	National Action Committee on the Status of Women (Canada)
NGO	Nongovernmental organization
OBOS	Our Bodies, Ourselves
OECD	Organisation for Economic Co-operation and Development
OISE	Ontario Institute for Studies in Education, University of Toronto
PAR	Participatory action research
PB	Participatory budget
PLAR	Prior learning assessment and recognition
SDOH	Social determinants of health
SEWA	Self-Employed Women's Association
STEM	Science, technology, engineering, and math
UNESCO	United Nations Educational, Scientific, and Cultural Organization
UN Women	United Nations Entity for Gender Equality and the Empowerment of Women
VAW	violence against women
WALL	Work and Lifelong Learning Research Network at the Ontario Institute for Studies in Education/University of Toronto
WCTU	Women's Christian Temperance Union

INTRODUCTION

All summations have a beginning, all effect has a story, all kindness begins with the sown seed. Thought buds toward radiance. The gospel of light is the crossroads of – indolence, or action. Be ignited, or be gone. (Mary Oliver, 2005, p. 59)

In the spirit of Mary Oliver's words, this book is about igniting: igniting learning, igniting hearts, and igniting citizens to learning and action. Our particular focus is on adult education for and by feminists in the community; and in writing this book, we want to share the flame many feminists have for creating change and the world we want.

Over the past 10 years or more, we have been engaged in critical scholarship on gender, feminism, and social action, with a particular focus on the nonprofit and grassroots spheres. In this book, we draw from those writings and studies in which we collected and analysed data and wrote about feminist adult educators. Our focus then, as now, is on how feminists have negotiated identity and learning in international contexts or multisector environments; struggled to lead, learn, and participate in nonprofit organizations; and enacted a feminist pedagogy through arts processes, Internet fora, and in the community. Though our varied research projects had different emphases, they were united in their focus on facilitating, negotiating, and strengthening women's lifelong learning for change. For us, they had a particular strength in highlighting the complexities of identity and practice of the feminist adult educator, and we would like to explore some of that complexity in this book.

Other themes that emerged in this research were the tensions inherent in discussions of identity formation and flux, spirituality and religion, resistance and participatory democracy, informal and nonformal learning, social media networking, indigenous knowing and worldviews from the Global South. These themes are explored in various chapters throughout this text. The themes, while diverse, are tied to recurring interwoven issues and contexts. We will make a deliberate effort not to simplify or conflate the issues but rather we will engage them in the level of complexity that is appropriate to them. Writing some years ago, feminist theorist Patti Lather (1996) decried the addiction to accessibility and clarity, a move that she saw as having a politics of its own; it dumbed down serious and complicated ideas and robbed them of their robustness. We think Patti Lather had a point.

This book grew out of our observation that there is an increasing gap in the literature on women and learning, especially from a critical, political and engaged perspective. These issues still matter, and a book with a deliberative focus on women, gender, and learning is a way to fill this void. As authors and feminists, we were formed in second wave feminism with its stress on equality and structural change, and later informed by the third wave's integration of poststructuralism and diversity. And, as adult educators, we were both influenced by a number of writers and books in our own field: *Women's Ways of Knowing* (Belenky, Clinchy, Goldberger, & Tarule, 1986) as well as the specifically adult learning-focused book by Elizabeth Hayes, Daniele Flannery, Annie Brooks, Elizabeth Tisdell, and Jane Hugo, entitled *Women as Learners: The Significance of Gender in Adult Learning* (2000). This latter book has been helpful over the years for those of us who teach in adult education in terms of its reference for pedagogical strategies and approaches for women and learning as well as its representation of both significant authors and issues relevant to women doing formal teaching and learning in higher education. Additionally, there is Jeanie Allen, Diane Dean, and Susan Bracken's (2008) examination of the experience of female students in higher education. Here in this book we continue those conversations, applying lenses of social science theories as heuristic devices to better understand how adult learning occurs, what the contextual factors are, and how power and resistance are implicated in the adult learning process. We bring a decidedly critical and theoretical perspective to explore issues of race, class, and gender in an international context.

Some of the work published in the past few decades on feminist adult education in the community has been formative and has influenced the creation of this text. In 1996, South Africans Shirley Walters and Linzi Manicom edited the collection *Gender in Popular Education: Methods for Empowerment,* which brings to the fore many feminist-informed methodologies for doing popular education in community contexts around the world. Recurring themes and analyses—gender and race, globalization, and development practice—were updated and reframed in their 2012 edition (Manicom & Walters). Contributing authors in that 2012 collection explore popular education practice in diverse spaces such as theatre, prisons and online, and integrate current thinking on colonialism and political repression. Also, Angela Miles' (2013) edited collection, *Women in a Globalizing World*, provides solid sociological analyses of many complex development issues for women, and like Manicom and Walters, highlights the diversity of the spaces claimed by women to promote learning and action. While Allen et al. (2008) are strong on educational processes and institutions, Miles' (2013) authors put considerable emphasis on women's engagement with community development. Similarly, the various articles in Nancy Taber's (2015) special issue of the *Canadian Journal for the Study of Adult Education,* have a strong emphasis on feminism and the community. What these publications have in common is a continued interest in how women's ideas and practices are intricately connected and how they work toward collective change.

Feminist theorizing has also contributed greatly to our understanding of women's learning and activism within the larger international development sphere, and the role of public policy. Two major events—the International Women's Year in 1975 and the subsequent Decade for Women culminating in the Third World Conference on Women in Nairobi, Kenya—enabled feminist theorists, researchers, and practitioners from the Global South to play a role in policy discussions. The 1970s–1980s were significant decades when activists were raising awareness about the implications of ignoring women's lives or making assumptions about women's contributions to economies and societies. Women in Development (WID) became the catchphrase to ensure women were not forgotten in policy decisions and program plans. Different camps debated on the best ways for integrating women's participation in the development discourse, and critics contended that the prevalent top-down approaches being offered did little to change the system that was inherently discriminatory. The term Gender and Development (GAD) describes the next stage of the process to increase women's involvement. Key contributions of GAD were its focus on (a) research to gather details about women's participation, and (b) gender training activities at varying levels, from international agencies to grassroots organizations. The implementation of training, research, and programs to integrate women into development helped build women's organizations to increase learning and participation activities to connect the grassroots with international policies.

Organizations such as Development Alternatives for a New Era (DAWN) arose, and today continue to represent women from many countries to identify how development initiatives addressed or ignored women's work and lives (Sen & Grown, 1987; Sen & Durano, 2014). Their critical work shatters the old myth that feminism is nothing more than an agenda of Western countries. Researchers at the University of Sussex and its Institute for Development Studies in England have written extensively on gender and international development through a decidedly feminist lens. Their theoretical contributions are helpful for adult educators who are bridging local and international issues in development practice and community learning. For example, the work of Andrea Cornwall, Elizabeth Harrison, and Ann Whitehead's *Feminisms in Development* (2007), as well as their *Gender Myths and Feminist Fables* (2008), address contradictions and challenges in development (see also Cornwall & Edwards, 2014). The various conversations in these collections inform our discussion of education, pedagogy, and learning in settings as varied as community, international nongovernmental organizations (INGOs), and higher education and the state.

These examples of feminist writing aside, the early 21st century has been challenging for those pursuing a continued interest in women and adult education across the spectrum. Sociologist Margrit Eichler, Patrizia Albanese, Susan Ferguson, Nicky Hyndman, Lichun Willa Liu, and Ann Matthews (2010) point out that adult education has not had a strong emphasis on women and learning, and we certainly have noted the waning of women's voices and concerns. Eichler (2005) herself sought to correct the androcentric bias of the field by examining women's housework as a site of informal learning. Concerned by the fact that corporate concerns are guiding adult education, she countered with her own studies on the value of learning housework and called for even more attention to the everyday nature of women's learning. Eichler's (2005) particular concern with housework came from her sociological observation that housework undergirds and indeed makes the market economy possible.

Our book is somewhere between the approaches examining educational processes and those highlighting community engagement. We bring a focused energy to the topic of women and adult learning within the community and, though we build on work of theorists in feminist community development, we make an explicit attempt to integrate the insights of pedagogy and theory-informed practice. Drawing on local and global examples, we are interested in exploring the adult learning and teaching theories and practices that make development possible. We continue these popular education conversations and bring a strong adult education focus built on theory, practice, activism, and community, highlighting teaching practices and contexts where adult educators themselves learn informally and nonformally. Current issues such as social media, the insights of poststructuralism and postcolonialism, and work on organizational structures and processes are also given attention.

Most of all, we want to draw attention to the identity and practice of the adult educator teaching and learning with women as a distinct category and group. A particular concern is the focused attention to gender mainstreaming in the past 20 years or so that obscures women as a discernable category in many arenas of practice. We are not alone in making this observation. Jenevieve Mannell (2012) pointed out that after Beijing World Conference in 1995, there was a deliberate effort to mainstream women's issues (and not separate them out), which often led to the inclusion of women becoming little more than a technical task—one more box on a checklist to be filled in to show that one was diverse and inclusive. Rosalind Eyben (2014) describes the continued tension between "working within existing paradigms or changing them" (p. 160), which sounds a lot like the criticisms of a few decades ago done to make issues identified as "gendered" fit into the existing system, rather than addressing the inherent inequalities.

This mainstreaming, though well-reasoned normalizing process, sometimes resulted in the undermining of the hard work of studying the persistence of gender disparities and of developing strategies to effect change. This normalizing process has also obscured the distinct contributions of feminist educators and practitioners. In adult education, we have similarly subsumed the category of women's learning and the goals of feminist pedagogy into depoliticized good teaching. There has been a glut of books and studies on interdisciplinary approaches such critical and cultural studies and global studies, which presume inclusion of women. We are neither post-women's learning nor post-feminist learning, as there is much to be done and we are definitely not post or past the issues. Uncritical inclusivity runs the risk of papering over differences rather than addressing them.

Such misconceptions, additionally, create challenges for working on the ground to overcome oppression. Joyce Green (2007) notes the arguments of those writers who dismiss feminism as representing the worldviews of colonizers. Green's collection demonstrates, in contrast, examples of how Aboriginal feminism brings together key ideas of feminism and anti-colonialism to deepen awareness of the intersection of race and sex oppression that Aboriginal women face. Opportunities for alliance building with other social justice advocates have been key in achieving changes to discriminatory laws.

When one looks at continued violence against women (VAW) or women's underrepresentation in politics and institutional leadership, and the indications that they are slipping further in these contexts, it is clear that mainstreaming and interdisciplinarity are not always the best options. Terms such as *feminism*, *community*, and *women* need to retain their political and deliberative place alongside other additions and approaches. And, it seems obvious women have to reclaim terms that have been confined to the personal realm and which have lost agency and purpose. Margaret Ledwith (2011) pointed out that concepts such as empowerment have become synonymous with "self-esteem at a personal level" (p. 13), and the more politically charged meaning has become lost. That is unfortunate and all too obvious in the explosion of self-help and me-first thinking.

The use of the term *gender* itself has contributed to the problem. Global agencies such as the UN and the World Bank have deliberately embraced the term gender (not women) so as to make explicit links between men and women in the struggle to address domestic violence, hunger, reproductive rights, and economic rights. These are legitimate causes, and the rationale is indeed clear, yet its use presents a dilemma. We hold with the Association of Women in Development (AWID), a global feminist organization, which uses the term "women" in its name, as it is a specifically feminist organization. When we use the term gender and more particularly *gender relations*, we do so as a category of sociological analysis that points to how we are gendered or socialized into roles, and sometimes how this limits our agency and societal expectations. This is further complicated with increasing attention to those who are transgendered or who are pushing for greater understanding of sexual identity beyond the binaries of female or male.

The urgency of referring to feminism and women is underscored by developments at the UN level, which we explore further in Chapter 11. As Nellie Stromquist (2013) has keenly observed, while UNESCO's fifth international adult education conference, CONFINTEA V in Hamburg in 1997, had gender as a central notion, CONFINTEA VI in Belém, Brazil in 2009 shifted considerably its language and priorities away from women. Indeed, the sixth conference managed to drop deliberate and separate references to women and empowerment. Of the seven lines of recommendations resulting from Belém, gender is not mentioned directly but has a minor role to play in one of the recommendations, namely "participation, inclusion and equity" (p. 32). If even UNESCO is de-emphasising gender—its synonym for women's issues—we know that the time is time is right for putting women and feminism back on the table in INGOs and community-based spaces where women's education and learning are directly affected and involved.

Despite the global issues for women, and the progress that is both debatable and hoped for, it is also apparent that the term feminism, though quite established, is problematic for some younger women. Professor Susan Bracken (2008) sees this often in teaching young women in adult education programs. Unlike Women's Studies students, whom she also teaches, women in adult education classes are sometimes loathe to see feminism as relevant to their context or their situations. Women's advances in the 20th century aside, the term feminism is still plagued by stereotypes of divisiveness and radical action that make some wary. There is a range of feminist perspectives, that respond to time and location, running the gamut from advocating for pay equity right along to radical forms agitating for fundamental societal shifts, yet all hold a political intent of change.

A contributing factor to the backlash against feminism and to a certain reticence in using the term is the mistaken belief that women have already attained equality. Western media is preoccupied with portraying women through self-focused practices such as yoga, relaxation, and self-reflexivity (sans the critical) and as having reached the top rung of corporations. Our Western popular press is so besieged by discussions of women attaining Fortune 500 status while struggling to balance work and family life that one can be forgiven for thinking that it is 1950 and not the 21st century. The danger of such thinking, of course, is that it is "nostalgia without memory" (p. 30) to use anthropologist Arjun Appadurai's (1996) phrase for one of the cultural dimensions of globalization. We forget that we are global citizens and that our struggles are not over; indeed, we can also forget that there was a struggle and that it was hard fought. Western privileging of the "self" hides the collective intent of feminism to rout out discrimination in its many forms, whether or not we, as individuals, experience them a daily basis.

In her brief primer, *Feminism is for Everybody*, bell hooks (2000) notes that ever since she became a feminist she had wanted to write a little book that would explain clearly what feminism is and why it matters, why it still matters. She calls for more continuing feminist education for the survival of the movement. This rings true for people in other movements who connect the slippage of education to the decline of their movement. It is no wonder that we are seeing the return of feminist battles from the 1950s–1980s that were confronted and won. Gendered stereotypes that were once thought to have been debunked are re-emerging in many spheres ranging from children's toys to popular psychology. Gina Ribbon calls the practice of characterizing certain abilities to female or male brains as "neo-phrenology" that impose gender stereotypes rather than explore the elasticity of human thought and behaviour (cited in Healy, 2014).

In many ways, feminist conversations—in the West, at least—have turned inward and not outward. When Stephanie Coontz (2011) published her retrospective on Betty Friedan's (1963) *The Feminine Mystique*, she noted that women readers of the now-famous book, often seen as a touchstone in the Western feminist movement, saw it as a liberating force in their lives, pushing them to self-fulfillment and awakening. Some 50 years later, Coontz is critical in her commentary, arguing that Friedan's version of feminism was less radical and more personal than it has been purported to be. Coontz's critique of the focus on the self-echoes Barbara

Ehrenreich's (2009) dismissal of the *Relentless Promotion of Positive Thinking* and how it has done a hatchet job on efforts to achieve equality, which particularly affects women and distracts them from real action. Women, like everyone, are caught up in individualism, a lack of systemic challenge, and a focus on "what I can do for me."

A more recent example of such "me-first, positive thinking" for women is Facebook executive Sheryl Sandberg's (2013) *Lean In*, which contains the message that career women can make it if only they work hard enough—the emphasis is on the liberal goal of encouraging women to think and act differently to increase their participation in the existing system. Sandberg's feminism is what bell hooks (2013) calls "faux feminism"—a narrow focus on women's self-defeating behaviour that overlooks the decades of feminist theorizing connecting gender, race and class. High achieving women including Sandberg also reflect bell hooks' (2000) earlier description of "power feminists" (p. 45)—the realm of white, wealthy, professional women who perpetuate an inherently hegemonic, patriarchal system, and who identify more with white men of privilege than with oppressed peoples. Katha Pollitt (2013) has also expressed disappointment with this book and its neoliberal agenda of individualism and corporatism.

In both the West and Global South, creeping neoliberalism has had profound implications on public services and on the survival of women's organizations. Whereas in the 1970s there was considerable growth of feminist organizations, today we have cutbacks and shifts in funding priorities that have challenged the sustainability of women's organizations. Gita Sen, a key figure in the analysis of WID and GAD in the 1980s, recently reflected on the changes over the past 3 decades and the implications for feminist organizing today. She and co-author Marina Durano (2014) have charted the erosion of the "social contract" through such factors as the domination of market economic ideology, religious fundamentalism and environmental degradation. They call for a reinvigoration of human rights to be at the centre of the development debate. Similarly, Linda Carty and Chandra Talpade Mohanty's (2015) study of feminist activists highlights the effects of the present dominance of neoliberalism on theory and practice and the need for feminists to renew solidarity across cultural, national and economic lines.

In thinking about feminism and adult education today, we wondered how a truly intersectoral analysis that prioritizes feminist learning concerns might work and how we can include more than white women in this discussion, rather than avoiding the "other others" (Ahmed, 2002) which refers to the many groups of difference that are precluded from many North American discussions of feminism. Apart from some more critical race studies that bring in an intersectoral analysis (Smith, 2010) and some publications focused on women and learning, there has been an absence of a more complicated reading of women in this place and time. There is also a need for a stronger international discussion about women and women's issues. In response, our book is about these learning tensions, national and local, and international, and how they are worked out globally.

As we think of the global questions around education and learning for women, we must think of the places where most of this learning occurs, especially for women. The questions for adult educators here are drawn from the foundational work of Griff Foley (1999) who used them as a tool for understanding the dimensions of radical adult education. Though Foley was not writing specifically about women, some of his questions are useful in guiding our examination of learning and teaching for and by women, in contexts such as community based organizations, nonprofits, higher education, the home, the public sphere—indeed, in any place that learning occurs. He asks:

> What forms do education and learning take? What are the crucial features of the political and economic context? How do these shape education and learning? What are the micro-politics of the situation, the places in which adults live and work? What are the ideological and discursive practices and struggles, of social movement actors and their opponents? To what extent do these practices and struggles facilitate or hinder emancipatory learning and action? What does all this mean for political education? What interventions are possible and helpful? (Foley, p. 10)

Foley's (1999) questions keep us focused on learning, the core element of effective development, even if it has not always been recognized. We also must look at the importance of sustained learning in social movements—successful social action does not mean the learning can stop. Classic adult education and development initiatives such as the Antigonish Movement highlight the primary role of continuous education and learning. In writing about the Movement, economists Santo Dodaro and Leonard Pluta (2012) emphasise that from the early days in the 1930s, study clubs were the local mobilizer for reading and discussing ideas and became a cornerstone of planning for action through member-owned forms of organizing. Adult education was always at the centre of the Movement's "Big Picture" or plan for development. They note that problems arose when, as economic organizations formed as a result of the study club activities, a sustained interest in education began to wane. When the co-operative movement neglected ongoing educational efforts, people began to lose a connection to the underlying philosophies of co-operative principles providing a people's alternative to corporate power. This disconnection, in turn, weakened the commitment to this alternative economic form, and contributed to the failure of the co-operatives that had been created. When citizens do not see co-operatives as distinct from other economic models, nor see their own roles and responsibilities in the life of the co-operative, the sole focus is reduced to the bottom line, with other priorities and players lost in the shuffle. This dynamic plays itself out again and again in various realms, including feminism. Progress is undermined when our social justice roots are forgotten or ignored. As adult educators involved in many of these issues, we want to keep learning front and centre.

Much of women's learning is done collectively and often informally. As bell hooks (2000) recalls that feminist consciousness grew through women learning in groups before there were formal women's studies programs. The growth of feminist research and study in the academic context provided theory and analysis that furthered women's understanding of conditions they already knew and experienced at very personal levels—experiences which they came to understand to be felt by women on a larger scale. Notably, hooks emphasises the importance of continuing feminist education for the survival of the movement. This rings true to people in other movements who can identify the slipping of education to the decline of their movement, as is the case with trade unions or with the co-operative movement as noted above. Such education must span all sectors of society including the community level, and must take on a variety of forms including expression through popular performance such as music. hooks is adamant that education was and is an integral part of sustaining feminism: "Most people have no understanding of the myriad ways feminism has positively changed all our lives. Sharing feminist thought and practice sustains feminist movement. Feminist knowledge is for everybody" (p. 24).

The issues are clear and the need for continued engagement with feminist and adult learning is equally clear. Following this introduction, in Chapter 2 we focus directly on leading and learning in feminist organizations in the community, the primary location or context for adult education. In these organizations, the links among and between feminism, learning, and the community are being negotiated constantly. Though they are often glossed over in related discussions of development and community empowerment, we see them as integral to discussions of feminists and learning. In Chapter 3, the community is addressed as a site of informal and nonformal learning about the social, cultural and economic determinants of health. We invite readers in Chapter 4 into a conversation about how to use the arts and creativity to foster learning about crucial issues. In Chapter 5, we concentrate on social movement learning as a way for feminists to work with other social movements to effect change, including the ways ICTs are used for learning and activism. In Chapter 6 we highlight the complexity of change in light of religious and spiritual difference and dialogue. In Chapter 7 we examine the ways in which feminists in the community negotiate and learn from community research partnerships that contribute to new knowledge and insight. Chapter 8 contains an overview of feminist pedagogy, and in Chapter 9 we explore fundamental social transformation. In Chapter 10, we delve into the all-important issue of power and resistance in informal learning, and Chapter 11 we review international policies and practices on feminism and adult education. The book closes with Chapter 12, which contains our critical appraisal of the foregoing conversations as well as insights for practice and research.

All through this book, our critical commitment is to the educator who works in the community to foster adult learning and activism and to negotiate creative ways of leading and working in organizations for change. We have drawn on our own experiences and past work in weaving the different strands of experience, theory, and issues. As we developed the book, we came to see that some issues such as the place of the body in women's learning might have deserved their own chapter. The body is a particularly feminist focus of inquiry through the physicality of emotion, health, embodied learning, and artistic expression and in the tension of physical or virtual presence online; yet, because of space constraints, we decided to weave this discussion throughout the existing chapters.

A final note about style. We chose to privilege women's names and identities in our text. Following the insights of Valerie-Lee Chapman (2003) and Susan Tescione (1998), as much as possible we refer to female (and many male) writers by their full names, which standard social science styles such as APA do not. This text politicizes further the place of women in society and serves as a resistance to a predominantly male-by-default worldview by making visible the many female writers and contributors to our thinking.

FEMINIST ORGANIZATIONS

Leading and Learning

The Red Thread Women's Development Organization was formed in Guyana in the mid-1980s by seven activists in response to the country's political situation. Nurturing women to become politically engaged was, in their minds, a way to oppose factionalism and repression. Initially, the group of women worked in the community, providing basic education to women in craft design and production (hence the name Red Thread). Slowly they became more engaged in dialogue about the many issues at play within feminist organizations. For them, the traditional use of crafts such as embroidery provided a practical income generation dimension, but it also created a space for collective learning and analysis of their lives. Over time, Red Thread became more intersectoral by emphasising the necessity of working across divisive lines of race and class, maintaining a delightful subversiveness as evidenced by their politically suggestive name. Learning and action form the core of their work. In chronicling The Red Thread story, Kimberly Nettles (2007) observes:

> The embroidery itself, formerly a craft of middle-class ladies, was redefined in this context as a revolutionary art form. It was used as a vehicle to teach the community women about the economics of production – specifically in terms of assessing the value of their labor. ... [Red Thread] created a space where women could talk and learn about each other's lives. (pp. 72–73)

In Nettles' (2007) view, the Red Thread collective was part of the founders' vision and a practice to embody a struggle to recreate the country and to re-envision its future. The members became researchers, publishers, educators, and entrepreneurs. They were all engaged in naming and resisting their oppressors—a resistance movement challenging the overarching class and gender divides in the political struggle of Guyana. The Red Thread organization created a very politicized place, both literally and figuratively, in which women could gather to create and sell craftwork, as well as to mobilize politically. And, like many organizations, there were a variety of groupings of women within Red Thread, including the resource women who were the founders and the community women who joined them. Their products were both sources of income generation through the selling of their crafts and deliberate statements of empowerment by their very existence. The significance of Red Thread and other feminist movement organizations to create an expansive view to promote women's well-being, advancement, and safety is no surprise to most readers. Similarly, Mala Htun and Laurel Weldon's (2012) review of the importance of 4 decades of movements shows that they are the single-most effective factor (not governments, economic prosperity, documents, or INGOs) influencing change, especially with regard to VAW.

CENTRES OF LEARNING

Feminist organizations such as the Red Thread, through purpose and necessity, have always been centres of learning. The suffragists of feminism's first wave raised women's awareness of democratic participation. Consciousness raising groups of the 1960s and 1970s supported women to start with their lived experiences to uncover the causes of the inequalities they faced. Beyond the topics discussed in these collectives, the organizational forms that emerged became increasingly more politically oriented. Feminists reinvented the organizational structures and practices that they saw as inherently patriarchal and hierarchal, the very antithesis of feminist collectivist action. Collective frames working towards consensus became essential to living out feminist principles in organizational form. Yet, it is not always clear how leaders emerged in these organizations or how they were sustained in their positions. The forms of leadership were as varied as the organizational structure.

What Are These Organizations—What Do They Look Like?

Feminist nonprofit or civil society organizations share much in common with all community-based organizations in that they have a list of tasks or a mandate that is specific to each entity. Irish community development researcher Andrew O'Regan (as cited in Donnelly-Cox, Donoghue, & Hayes, 2001) names these common organizational tasks as:

- Delivering services, often in partnership with the state
- Identifying and addressing new social needs
- Maintaining and changing the values system in society
- Mediating between the individual and the state
- Providing a forum for the social construction of the individual. (p. 197)

O'Regan notes in the original work that these five tasks are interrelated functions as most organizations and leaders wear multiple hats and perform many tasks on a daily basis. All of these five functions may or may not be present in one group, as each organization, given its mandate and constituency, emphasises different aspects or roles. Depending upon its size and scope, an organization may be able to work at multiple tasks with multiple partners, or may be preoccupied with the delivery of services and lack the capacity to expand beyond that. Yet, as we will explore further in Chapter 11, there is a push and pull from the grassroots through to political and bureaucratic levels. It is noteworthy that adult education of members and the community is a hidden value in each of these named tasks. To supplement O'Regan's list, feminist organizations have additional roles, the first of which is related to their *raison d'etre*, to be a political actor on behalf of women in the public sphere. As well, feminist organizations are engaged in a constant process of formal, nonformal, or informal learning, either through deliberate teaching of classes or through the active engagement of women in learning politics and policies. Their learning and teaching agenda, implied or articulated, may include the learning that occurs when doing the jobs of an organization, whether it be managing personnel issues, bookkeeping, communicating, negotiating difference, budgeting, or fundraising.

At the community level, feminist organizations range from women's resource or drop-in centres, anti-violence agencies, transition houses for victims of violence, to agencies providing women-specific health, counseling, or training services (see English, 2011). Often, these organizations are intersectoral and they address disability, immigration, poverty, and race, since the reality is that most socio-political-cultural issues are multifaceted. The people in these agencies observe the common causes of the myriad symptoms they deal with on a daily basis. An awareness of the interconnected sources and products of oppression often leads organizations to take a similarly intersectoral approach to match their services to the issues. We follow Kimberle Crenshaw (1991, 2010), Audre Lorde (1984), bell hooks (2001), and many others in acknowledging the convergence of multiple issues in feminist work. Women in grassroots centres themselves have long recognized and dealt with these multiple issues and partners, especially with the need for education around key concerns.

As a particular kind of community organization, feminist NGOs pay special attention to the external inequalities women encounter—violence, poverty, literacy, childcare—sometimes to the detriment of internal relationships and to their members' learning and organizing, which admittedly are thorny, but vitally important, issues. A tension thwarting the more inner/reflexive process has been the wariness to reveal inside weaknesses when faced with perpetual concerns over funding and anti-feminist backlash policies or activities (English, 2005a). Women's organizations, as a result, often struggle alone with their organizational challenges.

Of course, not every feminist organization operates in the same way since each is situated differently and has its own mandate. Yeheskel Hasenfeld and Benjamin Gidron (2005), for instance, observe that third-sector or community organizations are typically viewed from one of three vantage points, and theoretical and research traditions. They may be seen as one of "civil society," "social movement," and "nonprofit sector" organizations. In this context civil society is rather narrowly defined to represent the voluntary sector. The authors add that such distinctions are often not clear cut in reality, and offer a description of hybridity that reflects the actual work of those dealing with inequality. The first focus, civil society, is on autonomous volunteer-run associations characterized by citizen participation and horizontal network relations (e.g., social clubs, mutual aid associations). The second refers to social movement organizations such as Greenpeace or AWID, which use political strategies and actions. The third, nonprofit sector organizations, are formally organized and granted charitable status. According to Hasenfeld and Gidron, this isolation of research traditions and the clear-cut distinctions that can be made among them escapes the fact that there are indeed many hybrid organizations that reflect the evolution of social action, such as protest groups forming organizations, or charities that engage in research to engage in policy change. Many feminist organizations, especially those that are locally based and established to meet myriad community needs, are hybrid organizations that include all three traditions. The advantage of applying Hasenfeld's and Gidron's multiple lenses to feminist organizations is that they help to articulate their unique nature as both addressing needs and having a social movement agenda. In embodying a philosophy and politics of feminism, feminist organizations are forced to move beyond nonprofit goals of care and service and toward social transformation. This cross-sector understanding captures the multiple purposes of feminist nonprofits.

Who Leads a Circle?

To lead a feminist organization, to manage the dual tensions inherent in dealing with the state and in building an organizational structure that reflects feminist values, is a contradiction, especially in Western culture where traditional hierarchical ways of leading are the norm. Organizations such as Red Thread in Guyana are meant to be collective and to work as an organic unit. The paradox is rooted in the constant tension that exists between collectivist and bureaucratic aspects of leadership, a theory that was well developed by Joyce Rothschild-Whitt in her classic 1979 article on women's and feminist organizations that were negotiating the tensions from ideals of the original organizations in the 1960s and 1970s. One of her insights is that an organization often morphs from a free flow event into a more structured entity by the very fact of maturing, strengthening, and growing. This bureaucratization happens with an increase in members and the need to be more structured in order to lobby agencies and governments, organize for action, and collaborate with other organizations. It would be difficult to apply for a government grant, in Canada at least, without indicating an executive director, assistant director, and treasurer, and showing a strong framework and slate of officials.

Yet, dynamic and charismatic leadership is often the driving force behind successful feminist organizations. Running a nonprofit organization like a women's centre or shelter draws upon incredible fortitude and political savvy of the individuals involved, not only in terms of managerial skills but also in terms of negotiating with the various external partners and with the internal members, not to mention the broader advocacy and policy work required to overcome gender discrimination in its many forms. Alejandra Scampini (2003), for instance, notes that feminist and education issues were prominent at CONFINTEA V largely because of coordinated efforts of women's organizations at that conference. Similarly, feminist issues receive attention at various levels of government because of coordinated action. The creativity and agility required to work in a neoliberal climate of perpetual scarcity and ever-increasing bureaucracies involves intense but often unrecognized learning on the part of many feminists. If leaders of feminist organizations say they are open to change and to ideas, they actually need to model this in the workplace by exploring ideas and working collectively to frame and reframe them.

The promotion of circles, egalitarian governance structures, and consensus decision making bears witness to feminist commitments to voice and to experimentation with structure. However, these strategies can create their own issues, especially if they do not align with how the organization is really operating. The discourse of "horizontalism" (p. 13), as discussed by Gerbaudo (2012), is reflective of the language of consensus and flat decision making to which many feminist organizations aspire. Yet, by virtue of size, complexity, and funding mechanisms, many organizations have difficulty in practising in ways other than hierarchy. In some cases, there is a false perception that all members are equal and have equal say in all matters, large and small. There is a point at which feminist leaders need to be honest about circles and structure and operate in concert with our reality. This honesty and malleability neither diminishes authenticity nor the future of the feminist movement.

Skills That Need to be Learned in an Organization

Feminist organizations, especially those that are nonprofit, may be viewed in the public as bleeding hearts adverse to profits, inherently weak, and less efficient than their competitive counterparts in the for-profit world. Or, if they serve a publicly-funded role of providing services, they may be seen as a misuse or waste of taxpayers' money, labelled as "special interest" groups with the attendant insinuations that they do not serve the public good and are creating duplicate programs available more economically elsewhere. Even researchers have tended to look less at nonprofit organizations as they are usually outside the for-profit realm and are less likely to attract research funds. Yet, in any of these feminist organizations, the same leadership, education, and managerial skills need to be learned and practised to make them viable. In fact, the history of feminist organizations shows they can be very effective, incredibly well run on shoestring budgets, leading changes that later become commonplace or taken for granted. Grassroots training, office and financial management, policy work, public education, and advocacy are all skills that, for the most part, were learned hands-on at these many community sites of social change. Although we can quibble that training is not a valid adult education function, Holst (2002) has shown that skills training is a time-honoured tradition in social movements. Adult educators have a proud history of training members in activist skills and practices—indeed, it is a strength of our field.

Some of these activism skills evolved through more formal programs or activities that attracted women's participation, where the seeds of collective organizing were planted. The classic adult education examples include the largely female Chautauqua in New York State, which started as a training centre for Sunday school teachers in the late 1800s and became an important alternative education program for women who could not afford the more traditional route of attending college. Simultaneously a school and organization, Chautauqua became the central starting point for subsequent temperance and violence prevention programs (Kilde, 1999). Notable among the attendees were suffragette Susan B. Anthony and Jane Addams, founder of the Chicago settlement community for immigrants, Hull House (Addams, 1910/1912). Chautauqua served as an inviting place for women as it allowed them to speak to men and women and to cross traditional boundaries of separate sphere thinking. An incubator for women's causes and concerns over its extensive history, Chautauqua continues today, though in a more traditional liberal arts mode.

For feminists, much of their skill development in nonprofits involves organizational management, political organizing, community development, governance, and communication, some of the same skills that Chautauqua helped to build with women. Although skills training is largely defined as employment training, nonprofit work at the community level can be seen as requiring no skills or no particular educational preparation. Yet, there are many acquired skills that can be learned, including governance procedures and policies that are integral to organizational life. Effective organizational leaders in the for-profit or nonprofit worlds learn these skills through experience, though the learning process is often not visible. Over time, organizations naturally become more structured and institutionalized, in part because funders demand it of them and in part because they need to get things done, making it essential to have executive directors, boards, bylaws, minutes, accounts and audits, not to mention tax returns, bank accounts, and standardized operations and procedures.

Yet, the tools and rules come with cautions. Audre Lorde (1984) reminds us that using the master's tools is not enough to change how things are. "What does it mean when the tools of a racist patriarchy are used to examine the fruits of that same patriarchy? It means that only the most narrow parameters of change are possible and allowable" (pp. 110–111). Lorde speaks of tokenism, of adding on different perspectives in order to check off the required boxes, and she cautions that tokenism does not tear down the walls but it might just replicate the models of oppressions and cause more problems. Simply replacing men with women in positions of authority, for instance, will not alone remove discrimination. A more meaningful dialectic, as Lorde says, is needed. That said, it is still important to know what tools are used by the masters, to learn their skills and abilities, but also to keep pushing the boundaries, finding other tools, in order to dismantle patriarchy.

While feminist organizations operating in a multi-stakeholder environment are compelled to take on bureaucratic requirements, they need to do so with critical awareness. Feminist leadership programs that draw uncritically on the tricks of the trade of the mainstream business schools and overlook the strength of finding different ways to lead, manage, and collaborate will not achieve the change desired in any substantive way. Patti O'Neill (O'Neill & Eyben, 2013), who has worked as a gender advisor in the Organisation for Economic Co-operation and Development (OECD), has come up with her own twist on Lorde's "master's tools" when she considers the work of feminists within bureaucracy working for transformation: "I think you *can* use the master's tools to *renovate* the master's house" (p. 89, emphasis hers). She warns that it is not an easy process and the tools must be handled deftly, requiring ongoing reflective practice regarding the trade-offs or compromises that may be made along the way. O'Neill works with her networks to develop the language they need to speak to the economists, or those in trade or security. Yet, the nagging question remains: are renovations enough and will they result in sustained, long term change?

To their credit, feminists have often resisted adopting organizational forms that reproduced the patriarchal structures they were up against—a resistance that has spawned a wide range of experiments in alternative ways of collective action. These struggles and experiments have, for the most part, been played out at the grassroots level, as the concept of formal leadership training remained primarily the realm of training for the corporate sector. Yet, recently the idea of feminist leadership training has come to the fore. CREA, a women's human rights organization in India, became concerned that the burgeoning of "feminist leadership" programs did not attend adequately to the history, theorizing, and lessons of feminist organizing.

Srilatha Batliwala (2011), who is affiliated with CREA, conducted a comprehensive survey of what is meant by the term *feminist leadership* and how it has evolved internationally in recent decades. Batliwala's findings are insightful. She concludes that feminist leadership is *not* the style promoted in the corporate sector that is more accurately described as "feminine leadership" that reinforce gender stereotypes. The image and exemplar that immediately comes to mind is of a boss whose shoulder you can cry on. In an effort to find a place for women in the boardroom, supposedly inherent female traits of collaboration and nurturance help to promote a perceived kinder managerial approach. The flipside of the caring feminine leader is the stereotype popular in the management discourse of the "queen bee"— female managers who bully their (usually female) subordinates or who are accused of such behaviour if they do not live up to the expectations of the caring stereotype (Drexler, 2013). In any case, the model of making women fit in masculinist-defined organizational structures leaves the climate ripe to perpetuate gendered perceptions that undermine women's expertise and authority. This argument echoes the concerns of Hasenfeld and Gidron (2005) about viewing third sector organizations from only one lens. Feminist organizations have a unique ideology and politics that demand a particular, hybrid approach to leadership, organization, and research; one lens simply will not do.

Organizational Learning within the Movement

A feminist organization is often the most visible sign of a movement; it is formed when the movement becomes more institutionalized over time. Usually, there is a natural progression from idea to structure, and can be found with most ideas like peace, which has spawned such organizations as Peace Brigades International; anti-nuclear protests and environmental awareness that arose thanks to writers such as Rachel Carson's (1962) *Silent Spring*, that evolved into organizations like Greenpeace, the World Wide Fund for Nature and Friends of the Earth; and the women's movement became organizations like DAWN and AWID. In some cases, the institutionalisation is quasi-government or funded by governments. Some organizations, such as Greenpeace for example, exist outside nation state support, cautious as they are to avoid the strings that inevitably come with such alliances.

In this complex funding climate, especially in social democratic contexts, as we will discuss below, it is no wonder that it can be difficult to articulate what women should learn to be effective leaders, how this learning might occurs, and who might participate in the intricate process of creating new visions of leadership that more accurately support the social justice goals of feminist organizations. Srilatha Batliwala (2011) reminds us that feminist leadership is inherently tied to the values and practices of the feminist movement, and that it ought to push back against neoliberal frames of so-called inclusion based on reinforcing sexist gender roles. This is not a "one-size-fits-all" approach to leadership development. Those interested in promoting feminist leadership through education must understand the ways in which their practice is informed by feminist theory and the history of the women's movement. The skills to be learned relate more to deepening analysis and reflexivity than to the confidence-bolstering coaching strategies and self-help guides popularized by management gurus that populate the shelves of bookstores.

Batliwala (2011) notes the issue of leadership has always been discussed and debated at the grassroots, though these analyses have been underrepresented in mainstream academic literature. Evidence of this evolution, where it exists, resides in the reports, minutes, and other documentation from women's organizations, which are now held in various archives or the personal papers of lifelong feminist organizers. Batliwala traces some variances in emphasis or process between Western feminist organizations and those of the South, but most share a developing understanding and critique of power.

Given the focus on power, the central forum for learning for feminists in community-based organizations has been through active hands-on engagement in organizing and activism. This informal learning can happen in the everyday and can be influenced in a variety of ways for women, including in an embodied way—learning through the body and actions on and through the body. As Tracey Ollis (2012) details in her work, an embodied pedagogy can work through the activist's body and, by extension, through any feminist body. It can also happen through emotions and relationships, which are very important for women and learning. Important here are the facilitators and barriers to this learning. These barriers may be constituted of resistances that arise—the resistances, tensions, and everyday disruptions that constitute human interaction, and these resistances may arise as nodules or points of power. To every capillary of power, there is a resistance (Foucault, 1980).

Indeed, the key to the success of many feminist organizations, such as Red Thread in Guyana, is the broader learning, awareness raising, and critiquing made possible among the community women. Their learning is hard to quantify—or, to use the language of adult education and training, prior learning assessment and recognition

(PLAR)—and is often recognized only after years of reflection, consolidation, and integration.

The focus is on how women in organizations learn to do more reflexive work—the work of integration—to understand the gaps between values and practice. This is especially important, as it has been identified for a long time the subversive dynamics or "deep structures," particularly in purportedly non-hierarchical settings, is where hidden power resides. This is where the important drivers of transparency and internal accountability are critical (Batliwala, 2011), and where women in these organizations need to learn how to identify destructive dynamics. That said, there are practical skills too that need to be learned, but they need to be learned in a way that reinforce, not undermine, feminist values (Batliwala). Women taking on leadership roles is a potentially transformative action, "enabling deep-seated changes in the self that have resulted not only in a sense of self-awareness, empowerment and liberation, but in new ways of acting for change in the external world" (Batliwala, p. 59).

Learning in the feminist movement and in organizations occurs formally, informally, and nonformally (Coombs, 1973) and as Michael Newman (2008) has pointed out, learning of any kind is an innate part of life. For feminists, some of this learning occurs in courses and programs they complete before they join or work with an organization. In an organization, they can learn nonformally by attending short courses and workshops, engaging in informal learning through everyday interactions and being on boards, being involved in meetings, watching how the media treats women's issues, and networking in person and on social media sites. For instance, a local nonprofit organization may be networked with others in the nation or internationally for the exchange of ideas and strategies.

New movements or activities in which feminists have participated, such as the Occupy Movement (see Rebick, 2013), draw new members who may only participate for that one time; Ollis (2012) calls these circumstantial members and uses the term lifelong to refer to those who continue in activism over the long haul—both groups of members are engaged in social transformation activity and learning. The Indigenous movement for rights and self-determination in Canada contains both types of activists as seen in their Idle No More campaign that emerged in 2013, that has included marches, flash mobs, and protests to draw attention to such issues as land rights, housing, poverty, and education challenges on First Nations reserves (Nanibush, 2013). This campaign was marked by peaceful witnessing and ceremony as ways to speak truth to power and to reclaim rights and responsibilities, including women's place and leadership prior to European contact. The public protests created an opportunity to build alliances with other movements (Coates, 2015)—both those groups who shared concerns, such as the environment, and those who wanted to show support for Aboriginal rights. Circumstantial members, drawn into the immediacy of First Nations' plight, were fortified by contact and learning from those who have long experience in cognate movements such as feminist and environmental movements. Expertise among members of different movements is often shared online, in person, and through media. Facebook, Twitter, and various social media supported, engaged, and furthered this movement, attracting young people into this "aboriginal concern" for housing, adequate living conditions, and safety.

Idle No More began as a response to changes in legislation brought forward by the Canadian government, but evolved to become attached to a wide range of concerns such as Indigenous land claims and resource extraction. It is a movement with a strong female leadership presence, even if that presence is not always obvious to the public; the Idle No More (2012) website has recognized the four women who initiated the protests that grew to become this ongoing campaign. Idle No More was not a singular action. Leaders have emerged who are now working to strengthen education and learning about First Nations' issues and how to agitate for change. Much like the citizenship schools and other training done within the American civil rights movement in the 1950s and 1960s, with the help of the Highlander Folk School in Tennessee, there is an initiative to have teach-ins and "summer sovereignty schools" to help strengthen the knowledge of their core activists. The Idle No More website also provides a space for other action groups, such as those demanding action to address violence against indigenous women.

Media portrayals of actions such as Idle No More can sometimes have a tendency to celebrate the large scale activism and learning that women engage in and to diminish the everyday heroism of women whose activism within a variety of organizations has been sustained over time. As we often see, once the media spotlight dims, it may be assumed that the activism has also dimmed. This hides the reality that sustained activism involves long stretches of quiet, behind-the-scenes organizing. For example, Canadian and Australian scholar Elizabeth Burge (2011) has profiled the lives of 27 women activists in Atlantic Canada, telling their stories and highlighting the ups and downs of their campaigns for change. One of the observations to be made on these profiles is that the women learned much over a lifetime of facilitating change and mounting resistance, often working quietly and persistently, often through faith-based, craft, and otherwise "benign" organizations that nurtured very political goals. This is in contradistinction to the resistance that comes to mind for most international activism which is usually very visible, very public, and very loud in terms of protest. The women in Burge's (2011) study were engaged in long term change projects and were less likely to be involved in heroic change; we might term this a *post-heroic* and *post-activist* position (see Fletcher, 2003). They went about their work in low profile ways by building consensus and through nurturing community, rather than seeking the limelight or staging mass protests. They exercised this form of leadership in their towns, small groups, and organizations; furthermore, the activism is collaborative and in some cases, not related to an actual organization. Yet, it is sustained over time. Burge (2011) profiled promoters of French Acadian rights, leaders within political parties, and champions of trade unions. The learning and the activism has been adapted to the scale, intensity of the local environment. Their learning has partly been about patience, collaboration, and the long haul.

From Movements to Institutions

Organizations that build around one issue often grow in other directions or become ensconced in other movements, forming bridges and alliances with partners, for example, the environmental movement, animal rights, human rights, and literacy. This occurs for a variety of reasons, including the insights of new members, the availability of funding for these cognate issues, and the ways in which the media shape public perceptions and concerns. For instance, violence against women has become one of the major issues in women's organizations, even in places where crime is diminishing, in part because we live in a fear or "risk society" (Beck, 1986). Yet, the risks faced by the most marginalized populations, such as Aboriginal women, do not garner sustained mainstream attention or support. What politicians and mainstream media highlight as threats to our security, cynics would charge, reflect political self-interest more than concern for the voiceless and collective wellbeing.

Women's learning and activism have become deepened, tied to, and supported by women's resource centres. They were often formed as safe havens for women to converse, learn, and collectively challenge oppression. These now-institutional spaces, still perceptively tied to second wave feminism, face the challenges that feminism itself faces: of being misunderstood or overlooked. Sociologist Sylvia Walby (2011) claims the perceived waning of the term feminism is partly a consequence of feminists and their organizations participating in the broader civil society sector in which the explicit terminology of feminism may be subsumed within other social causes. Taking an explicitly political stand, which these resource centers do, is challenging in socio-economic environments where funding is scarce and priorities are placed on "getting along" through partnerships and collaborations with donors and other stakeholders. There is a renewed need to increase engagement, awareness, and participation in the face of the shrinking, contested civic space through privatization, downsizing, and offloading of state roles to the voluntary sector.

As centres that once were activist hubs become established service delivery agencies, we might ask: How and where are the critical spaces recreated and maintained? What does this mean for women's learning and activism? What do collective learning spaces look like? What are the collaborative processes to design such spaces, both formal and informal? Even funders who may potentially support citizen-engaged learning for social change demand demonstrated impact and effectiveness that can be hard to capture beyond individual learning goals (Mayo & Rooke, 2006). They want these institutions to work and be accountable.

Feminist citizen learning in these resource centres, as in all feminist spaces, involves the ways people come together in the learning to claim and open up spaces for participation and to change power relations. A related challenge is the capacity of activist organizations to document and preserve their work and collective knowledge (Choudry & Kapoor, 2010). Women's centres have historically played a key role in this important documentation work, a role that is a challenge to maintain. Community educators know that a focus on action, and a collective history of activism, that involves co-learning and co-knowledge is needed: "if local people are engaged in using their own knowledge then they can develop a capacity for self-determination" (Tett, 2010, p. 51), as well as claim the political space for conversation and activism.

One question is whether these spaces can also exist in the same robust and vibrant way online, in chatrooms, forums, or online activist sites like GuerrillaGirlsBroadband (see http://www.ggbb.org/), which fights sexism and racism in the art world. This is an offshoot of the Guerrilla Girls who, since the 1980s, have used street performance, graffiti and posters to ridicule museums and galleries who ignore women's contributions to the arts. The evidence of this group shows that a great deal of organization can happen in a wired world to combat these issues, as we will explore further in Chapter 5.

Arguably, a movement would die out without attachment to an organization that has a focused understanding and mandate for change, and the capacity to see it through. Witness the rapid rise and fade of the Occupy Movement, which for a short time captured widespread media attention as protestors drew attention to the most privileged 1% of the population (Young, 2012) Occupiers' reluctance to formalize as an organization or to align themselves with political parties stands in sharp contrast with the Tea Party in the US, which emerged as a conservative protest group in 2009 and has grown to work with and influence the Republican Party They remain vigilant in their scrutiny of Republican politicians who drift left of their brand of social and fiscal conservatism (Skocpol & Williamson, 2012). This relationship of an idea to a party is, of course, often problematic, but the Tea Party has gathered momentum, gained adherents and continued to thrive with its linkage to the Republicans, as their most viable option to influence public policy.

ISSUES IN THE MESHWORK

Susan Bracken (2011), in her insightful ethnographic inquiry of women's organizations, reports on one of the key skills needed to work in these organizations: program planning. Her study, in which she logged more than 400 hours, led her to conclude that what we need are fewer prescriptive lists of how to lead and plan, and more "specific strategies or pitfalls associated with everyday power and negotiation practices" (p. 135). Bracken's data show that the interactions are complex and necessarily disorderly, as they involve the negotiation and strategic planning that must occur for decisions to be made and for the unfolding process of feminist processes to occur, that is, "an evolving process that takes on the challenge of negotiating power and interests as both a feminist growth process and a feminist goal- or outcome-driven process" (p. 136). Bracken is interested in the everyday ways that this planning occurs, how it involves exercises of power, and how the participants negotiate the inherent challenges. This daily negotiation of interests, beliefs and practices, she notes is preferable to an interpretation that sees women's organizations as places of strife and turmoil where nobody gets along.

Funding

One attribute that feminist and community-based organizations in much of the world, and certainly in social democratic states, have in common is their interdependence on government or public funding—either through direct support or through contracted provision of social services. Government regulates organizations through laws governing how they may form and operate, taxation (such as charitable status) and defines the scope of what organizations are allowed to do. "By means of coercion and incentives, government cultivates, constrains, regulates, directs, and supports the entire range of institutions and associations that comprise social life" (Rosenblum & Lesch, 2011, p. 286). As strong as they might be on their own, they rightly call on the government support to fulfill a wide spectrum of services and activities to society in tandem with government responsibility and collaboration with community. The neoliberal turn to divesting the state from support of groups such as women is clearly problematic. As Kalpana Wilson (2008) points out, "Within the neoliberal discourse of development, the agency and empowerment of poor women has been increasingly conceptualized in terms of the withdrawal of the state from social provision" (p. 86). This neoliberal approach has led to increasing expectations of women's organizations and NGOs to fill the gap, again framed in terminology that made this sound empowering, "freed to exercise their agency" (p. 86). The offloading of social services to women's organizations, in fact, reinforce gender stereotypes since women are expected to step in and care for their communities.

One of the challenges in receiving public dollars is the restrictions that often accompany the funding. The perceived hands-off approach that neoliberal governments tout may mask increasingly strict regulatory frameworks dictating what organizations can or cannot do—those acts of coercion and incentives noted above. Whereas the state may see social service as a value, it is less likely, certainly in Canada and the United States, to want to see these funds used for activist training or protest, which in reality are important for open democratic engagement. Organizations may find themselves having to be careful in the language they use to describe their work. Yet, feminist organizations have a definite role in sparking and enhancing activist leaders who are needed to help strengthen and continue the feminist project: In the words of Penny Waterhouse and Matthew Scott (2013), "The role of the dissenting activist, of whatever form or style, has now become critical for our collective health and wellbeing" (p. 3). The challenge is that in the context of activist organizations that become service delivery agencies, the collective learning that was once so central to their formation runs the risk of being lost. The ongoing reflection, renewal, and critique required to maintain an effective activist role locally and beyond needs to be nurtured.

The precarious nature of funding for women's organizations causes grave problems and appears often to erode the solidarity and mission of feminism. Public funds, if available at all, can vanish with a change in government priorities. Securing private, corporate, or foundation funds result in a never-ending treadmill of fundraising, budget decisions, short contracts, layoffs, and board conflicts over spending. All the training in the world cannot sort out governance when there is no money to govern with, even if there is a commitment to implement employment to work programs, educate about violence prevention, or provide support to those with literacy challenges. In many places, funding to women's programs has been diverted to issues that affect women but not necessarily only women. The Millennium Development Goals (MDGs) (Sachs, 2005), for instance, have drawn attention to the need for maternal child health, which is an issue that affects women, but it also diverts funds from women's political activity which might address the root causes of threats to maternal and child health (Batliwala, 2012). The MDG goal calling for girls' primary education leaves educational access at higher levels on the back burner for governments, and consequently for those seeking funding to support such initiatives. The so-called problem of women's issues purportedly is being addressed, but scratching beneath the surface reveals this is not actually the case.

Part of the conflict in the allocation and use of funding is caused by the constant erosion of the nonprofit organization's mandate or initial mission to be political and to do advocacy. When the whole organization, in order to get funding, is doing service work, then it is hard to continue with the multiple other issues and concerns about the movement. One cannot possibly change the government or civil society while writing funding applications to run programs such as computer training. This is further complicated by the need to establish partnerships to solicit funding for programs. Furthermore, nonprofit organizations are more likely to make strategic partnerships when their funding is threatened, that is, move to partnerships with those who can have success with funders and not necessarily those who have shared vision and values, such as other likeminded organizations in the community. The situation also provides challenges for organizational capacity to respond to emergencies or to take advantage of openings when international attention to a problem arises. One only has to think of the situation in India where a woman is raped every 22 minutes yet it was one high profile gang rape that launched street protests and opened up public discussion (Ayed, 2013), to realize the role of mass mobilization and international pressure on such egregious situations. The organizations on the ground must have the ability to respond. Advocacy partnerships and national partnerships, not to mention international ones, are important if issues such as women's safety and equality are to remain on the table once the media attention fades.

Internal Governance and Learning

Another topic in feminism is the debate over what actually works in these nonprofit feminist organizations and how the usual model can indeed support the prevailing philosophy, be it neoliberal, liberal, radical, postmodern, or environmental (Calas & Smircich, 2006). It takes a lot of time to sort out structures, and it takes sustained energy and attention from leaders to help facilitate the discernment around learning from experience. This echoes Batliwala's (2011) concern noted earlier about the failure of too many training programs to learn from the past. At the heart of the issue is the ability (i.e., time and energy) to name one's dilemmas, positions, and goals, a luxury that organizations engaged in advocacy or politics may or may not have. Part of the issue is, as Bernedette Muthien (2006) asserts, that the whole movement needs a focus on the internal life of the organization as a place not just to win battles, but also to nurture a creative and politically alive space that allows women to explore, challenge, and nurture political ideas. How to create this space in an organization that needs to appear acceptable to funders, meaning worthy of funding, is a challenge. Funders may not want to pay for ongoing staff development and learning, and organizations may not want to admit they need this development if they are seeking contracts for projects. The tension between egalitarian organizations and efficient ones is very hard to establish, and without funding it is hard to take the time to focus on learning how to strengthen the organization, negotiate competing priorities, or engage in activism. A culture in which members are constantly putting out fires and struggling to survive does not allow much space to look at how the organization is or should be evolving.

Supporting voice in a place that needs funds is at all times difficult. Supporting the learning that nurtures voice is next to impossible to fund when there is a focus on negativity. This is doubly troubling when the feminist organization itself is focused on the people who "need help"—those who are impoverished, illiterate, living in crisis. Not only are the leaders in the organization not able to focus on their own internal structures, they are constantly forced into service provision, at the expense of education.

A prevalent question is how to negotiate the tension in women's groups in the nonprofit sector between old and new. We witness the old diehards who founded the local nonprofits and then the insurgence of younger women who want a say. Often, their voice will not be heard because the founders who have been around for a while have decided, often for good reasons, what is going to happen and when. Founders Syndrome has been studied in business organizations (Block & Rosenberg, 2002), and has also been identified in the feminist realm (English & Peters, 2011); it is very much an issue in all places. English and Peters complicated the survey-like work of Block and Rosenberg, who named the problem but did little to break it down and analyse it. While founders might be a problem, the issue is not as clear cut as getting rid of the older or founding members, many of whom are needed to actually do the work that a more employment-challenged, underemployed youth group cannot do (English & Peters). Simultaneously, founders are expected to both be a leader and let others take the lead. In English and Peters' study, founders reported that they struggle with the tension between allowing new people in and accomplishing important organizational tasks. Nor are younger founders immune to this take-charge imperative.

The ideal collective organization rarely exists. More often we have a hybrid mixture of forms in which governance is shared, and is, at times, hierarchical. The ideal is impractical and worse yet, unfundable, as many feminist organizations have come to acknowledge. In addition, these organizations are intended to be lifelong learning organizations that support the goals of feminism and encourage learning about feminism, its history, its intents, the way in which it has evolved, and its relevance. As Batliwala (2011) sums it up, feminist leadership is about advancing social change and is not an end in itself; leaders are not created just to be leaders of any generic institution. They are to engage in social actions to overcome gender discrimination. Feminist leaders, with their experiences and analysis, are in key positions to effect changes that other forms of leaders do not (see Batliwala, 2011, p. 13).

Working Inside or Outside the System

At a certain point, a feminist has to make a choice about whether to achieve policy and political change from inside or from outside the system. Those who work within large organizations (e.g., donors, government, INGOs) may call themselves *femocrats* in reference to their positioning within a bureaucratic structure (Manuh, Anyidoho, & Pobee-Hayford, 2013). In many cases, they have experience in a grassroots organization or in the nonprofit sector, so they would likely be familiar with the working of these smaller organizations. Whereas the community-based organizers can indeed work with, network with, and identify allies on the inside, it is the femocrat who helps them, who is sympathetic to the cause, and who knows the ways and means of achieving change. Femocrats, for their part, may be seeking legitimacy and possibly meaning-making by directly contributing to work on the ground. A femocrat can be a valuable ally in identifying shorter routes to funding, other allies in the system, and resource people. Although the discourses and operational procedures within large bureaucratic structure may be hard to navigate, an insider can make that happen.

Takyiwaa Manuh et al. (2013) observe that a disjuncture can occur when a femocrat tries to mainstream gender ideas and feminist notions within a bureaucracy. If the technocrats do not have a strong grounding in "potentially transformative discourses and strategies" (p. 45) that are common to civil society, then there can be conflict and the ideas and processes may never be fully understood or followed in the organizations. Manuh et al. are clear that the knowledge alone is not sufficient; one has to understand and imbibe the ideology and accompanying politics. Feminist ideas and human rights may be approved in principle but neglected in action as a result. When the state is involved, misunderstandings and lack of analysis can become more pronounced in that government departments and ministers may have competing notions and priorities for promoting women's empowerment. In a federal Department of Labour, for instance, a notion of women's empowerment might be oriented to jobs, training, and microfinance to support entrepreneurship.

In a provincial Department of Community Services, aid to women might consist of providing immediate band-aid solutions to managing household finances. The frequent lack of connection between departments causes misunderstandings and may result in a less than cohesive approach. Of course, the political climate of the government will affect all decisions in a bureaucracy.

Policy Work

One of the key roles for an NGO—especially one that operates at the global level—is to work toward policy development and to contribute to international dialogues on rights, actions, and capacities. Often, organizations including the UN agencies, state aid agencies, and INGOs have internal gender experts who do training, policy analysis, and organizational change work specifically focused on gender (Prügl, 2013). This is important work, as we recognize the role of these large agencies in global policy development. In describing some of the training manuals that gender experts have developed, Elisabeth Prügl notes that in institutionalizing or normalizing gender expertise the possibility exists that they lose some criticality and ability to challenge systems of oppression. That said, gender policy experts serve a valuable role in dedicating time to the integration of gender agenda, including an increase in attention to women and peace at the United Nations. Through major conferences such as the 1995 World Conference on Women in Beijing, they have been able to demand inclusion in global justice. Yet, for every advance, feminist goals appear to be thwarted elsewhere, as we discuss further in Chapter 11. As well, women continue to be under represented at the UN. Yet, those feminists who work within these INGOs as gender experts, members, and leaders still push the feminist policy agenda forward.

Future of the Movement

Given the challenges of feminist organizations and movements, the question of long-term viability remains. We look around and ask, "Whither a women's movement?" The challenges come from many quarters: the ongoing anti-feminist backlash that invokes a culture of self-censorship to deflect criticism, the blending of women's issues into diversity studies, the use of ambiguous or often meaningless terms such as inclusion, or the further dissolution of feminism due to in-fighting and the alliance with more high profile and fundable issues such as the environment or health promotion. The discourse of collectivity and integrative feminisms that Angela Miles (1996) wrote about two decades ago has yet to be realized. Rather, we have the further bifurcation of women into discrete alliances with marginal issues that once again become tacked on as afterthoughts to other agendas.

Nonetheless, there are some feminist organizations that have been able to work across sectors and to continue to focus on and foster feminism. SEWA (Self-Employed Women's Association) has remained unapologetically feminist and focused on their all-female membership's priorities. This Indian organization started off in 1972 as a trade union to organize informal and home-based workers. It has grown to be multifaceted in order to meet the needs of women in India that are denied them in regular society. SEWA provides alternative co-operative banking and other services to support economic independence, healthcare, education, and training programs, as well as advocating for women's rights (Bhatt, 2006). The organization represents women who are self-employed and yet who form 93% of the workforce. SEWA was a labour movement that became a broad-based organization to sustain to rights of women workers and to provide tangible support of them, and is now widely celebrated in development circles for its multisectoral approach in promoting women's rights and security, that is, of embedding learning and activism in its everyday activities. Founder Ela Bhatt notes that they are constantly learning as they handle new problems identified by their membership.

It must be acknowledged, however, that SEWA is a large organization with a vast membership that can be mobilized when the need warrants. Small-scale organizations, on the other hand, are seen to be obsolete in a world where communities are called upon to provide their own local supports to care for their residents. The promotion of caring communities, as seen in the United Kingdom with David Cameron's attention to the Big Society (Scott, 2011), supports the notion that citizens will take care of each other if the government gets out of the way. For feminist organizations, this is especially insidious as women are perpetually stereotyped as the caring, nurturing volunteers who hold communities together. As services are withdrawn, more demands are made of women's generosity. "Why fund women's centres when women will do the work out of kindness?" is the assumption behind such rhetoric, which allows the government to walk away with a clear conscience, taking community resources and money with it, in effect divesting itself of responsibility while maintaining power and control (Kelly & Caputo, 2011). As a result, community members find themselves carrying more responsibilities with little say in the decision making process.

Alongside autonomous feminist nonprofit organizations, there often are feminist spaces within larger organizations. For instance, within the labour movement, women form groups and attend courses where they can explore ideas and work together to address gender discrimination in the workplace and within their own unions. They also try to support each other in terms of leadership within the organization, using the feminist cocoon as an incubator before they move to claim leadership spaces in the larger organization. In describing the Prairie School for Union Women, Canadian Cindy Hanson (2015) shows how women have carved out a place in the labour movement for themselves, not only a learning space but also as an organizing space. Spaces like these are vital to ongoing women's activism in fields where mainstream exclusion persists. Similarly, United States-based EMILY's List was created to mobilize funding to pro-choice female Democratic candidates as a way to connect them with the feminist machinery for election (Sawer, 1999). The organization has expanded to promote a range of social issues on health care and rights.

DISCUSSION

In some ways, engaging in issues that affect women, even those that integrate areas of difference such as disability, may indeed reinforce difference and cause further division. It may also perpetuate very dated stereotypes of the caring and relational women. By railing against the stereotypes laid before us—the nurturing, caring collaborative co-worker—are we saying that we do not want environments in which these ways of human interaction are not valued? Margrit Eichler (2005) has noted women do the bulk of the care work, and for many, their learning is closely intertwined with this reality. We perhaps need to look less at difference and more at our everyday practices. As feminists and researchers, we will want to avoid portraits that lead themselves to simplistic portrayals of women in feminist organizations as feminine and friendly or, worse yet, catty and confrontational. Avoiding such bifurcations is important as they split us and our organizational and governance work into categories of male and bureaucratic or female and collectivist. Indeed more significant is looking at the specific ways in which women are affected by their difference: how does disability affect women? How does immigration policy affect women? How are women's daily lives affected? How do feminist organizations learn from and respond to these challenges?

ADULT HEALTH LEARNING

For Women, with Women

A key area of work for feminists, both inside and outside of organizations, is to build broad-based support for women's health, often with the help of multiple partners and with a vision of health that transcends clinics and doctors. And, at times, this support has to be built in visible and provocative ways. When Theresa Spence, chief of the Attawapiskat First Nation in Canada, could see what the poor housing and infrastructure crisis was doing to her people, she knew drastic action was called for (Wotherspoon & Hansen, 2013). As a leader, she did not feel heard by the various levels of government, so she took matters into her own hands in 2012, staging a hunger strike near the national House of Parliament in Ottawa to show that her people needed help. This drastic act served as a visceral lesson in First Nations' angst, anger, and action. Spence's hunger strike was widely televised and tracked through Facebook and Twitter—it is a prime example of how one woman with race written on her body, could be a symbol and a living embodiment of protest for other Aboriginal women in Canada. Theresa Spence and the other indigenous women who have played major roles in these movements in the early 21st century that are collectively called Idle No More, were asking for respect and healing for their people. In the words of Wanda Nanibush (2013):

> Women who have worked at the ground level healing their communities from historical trauma, who deal with large socio-economic disparities and have counteracted cultural discontinuity—all brought on by colonialism and racism—bring a considerable knowledge base to the movement. (p. 504)

Deep within these words are a notion and a belief that a holistic way of looking at issues is important, and that it is not enough to focus specifically on First Nations' education or housing; healing, which encompasses all the issues that affect the community must also be a focus. This broad notion of what will make the First Nations strong again is reflective of the social determinants of health (SDOH), which the World Health Organization (2011) defines as:

> the circumstances in which people are born, grow up, live, work and age, and the systems put in place to deal with illness. These circumstances are in turn shaped by a wider set of forces: economics, social policies, and politics. (n.p.)

So, in addition to lifestyle factors and behaviours, adult educators working with First Nations' populations need to look more broadly at our full context, something the Idle

31

No More leaders have tried to do. This movement in support of First Nations' rights was criticized by some for lacking focus, but they have reflected the complexity of the multiple causes of the injustices First Nations face. No matter how many individual programs have been implemented to respond to individual crises, the root causes are not being fully acknowledged and addressed in the way that Idle No More activists call for. For adult educators, one of the key ways to support people's analysis of the complexities is to foster learning *and* education, both formally in schools and institutions, and informally in homes, communities, and groups (Coady, 2013).

CONNECTING HEALTH AND LEARNING

In the global sphere, adult health learning (AHL) has become increasingly important, both as a practice and as a lens for viewing social complexities and issues; however, the term itself is not widely used or understood. Simply put, AHL is a broad-based concern for learning and acting on the social determinants of health (English, 2012), and it pays particular attention to the ways that women are affected. AHL connects many other pieces to education, to the larger social context, and to the ways in which women live and learn about life. Indeed, the United Nations Decade for Women (1976–1985) tried to address many of these issues on a global scale, but most are still with us. When the MDGs were drafted, a deliberate effort was made to focus on select and measurable issues, which resulted in the decontextualizing of interlocking causes and decreased the potential for multisectoral approaches. Further, these MDGs are enacted primarily in the formal political sphere, where women's representation is marginalized (Cornwall & Edwards, 2014). Adult health learning goes much deeper to analysing the system and critiquing it, and finding alternate pathways for pressing for change.

Such a holistic approach to health learning is responding to growing critiques of the medical model. Mainstream health education following the medical model tends to assume the expert knower as lecturer, imparting expertise to the citizen as client of a system, and health as located in specialized medical facilities. For a long time, certainly for much of the second half of the 20th century, health was increasingly centred in the expertise of medical doctors, hospitals, and in the pharmaceutical industry. Women's reproductive health, for instance, was medicalized and child bearing was treated as an illness rather than a natural event. With increasing professionalization in many aspects of health care, it was common to see health as resting in the purview of experts, with citizens becoming more and more dependent on the knowledge and skills of a select few (Coady, 2013). With the growing attention to the social determinants of health, however, citizens have slowly taken back ownership of their health and their right to address and assess their broader interests in it. We see this in women's reproductive health initiatives, lobbying to legalize midwives and home births, and growing attention to the safety of the food supply.

While most of us know that the better our education and income the better our health, we do not often think about the fact that health is more than the absence of disease or the presence of adequate medical supports, in that it concerns itself with quality of health in the community, especially the health and wellbeing of those who are marginalized in some way. Integral to this is an understanding of the whole range of factors contributing to this health and wellbeing. Adult health learning brings a specific learning focus to this discussion that puts emphasis on the social determinants as important to understanding and addressing issues in our environment. It also stresses a more holistic and respectful approach to change and long term suggestions, of which Nanibush (2013) speaks.

For women, the stakes in being engaged in activities around the social determinants of health are high, given their history of attention to environmental, sexual, workplace, and other locations of oppression (see Miles, 2013). Multisectoral programs have responded by addressing multiple MDG priorities. For example, Olloriak Sawade (2014) describes a program working for girls' and women's education in which group leaders realized there would not be long term success until health challenges were addressed. What they call a "triangle of issues" involves access to education, gender equality, and reproductive rights. Their education work was strengthened by the perspectives brought to the group from the other sectors.

In being actively engaged in increasing learning about how we are affected by our communities of living, working, and earning, be it the rate of employment, the quality of our water, the dependability of our transportation system, the strength of our social networks, or our level of education, women are actively learning about health and ways to sustain it. For women, attention to AHL is crucial because they assume disproportionate levels of responsibility for caregiving and housework and bear the brunt of environmental changes, which directly and indirectly affect the lives of families. In order to support the wellbeing of their households, women need to be active in learning and teaching about the SDOH.

Yet, as much as we are aware of these determinants, we struggle to articulate and address them in a comprehensive way. It is difficult to work counter to systems that took hundreds of years to establish. As such, given its broad reach, adult education ought to be concerned with these social determinants, through a range of community-based practices that increase health. Community involves individual, domestic and local realms, though it is influenced by neoliberal policies and practices enacted at national and international levels. Some authors, including Alda Facio (2013a) have pointed out that the overriding emphasis of neoliberal globalization is on finance and profit, not democracy or change or freedom. Neoliberal globalization is designed by patriarchal leadership structures that systemically discriminate against women and has increased the effects of factors such as employment and transportation that affect health. It has created a consumerist society that makes us want more, to shop more, to attain consumer good, and in effect, to be slaves to the global market of "stuff." One only has to think of the growth in discount and bargain stores in the West that employ mostly women at low wages to hawk mainly Asian-made plastic and cheap consumer goods to Western society.

An economy that skews the value of goods to the point where it is usually less expensive to throw something out and buy anew rather than to repair it underlines the emphasis on cheap, supposedly "unskilled" labour. Apart from occasional news stories of factory fires, consumers may know little of the conditions the largely female workforces endure. These bargain stores' profit models are based on keeping wage costs low and on the Western addiction to stockpiling useless goods. The family, the home, and the market are linked in these stores, often in ways that are disastrous to our health and wellbeing.

Confusing the Issue

The Western media produces new medical studies literally every day, and there are entire sections of newspapers and websites dedicated exclusively to health. Often these sections focus on improving behaviour and lifestyle: typical items are dedicated to whether oat bran is healthy, or if a particular breast cancer test is working, or if hotel rooms are kept clean for travelers. Mothers' competencies are scrutinized among the experts lecturing on food shopping and preparation for healthy eating. There is a limited focus on the broader determinants such as a living wage or employment rates, which are determinants of health for the whole family and the population at large. Germs, exercise or diet, as individual-focused health factors need to be balanced in emphasis with pervasive conditions such as toxic work environments, low food security and climate change. Yet, we remain convinced that microscopic organisms will affect us most directly, and we are distracted from the core issues in society. Part of the problem is the way in which we have been coerced into reducing the larger and more important societal framework to single issues that are visible in our immediate environment homes, rather than seeing the global and interconnected picture of the determinants of health. Any education tied to it is then reduced to talking about distributing bottles of sanitizer and cleaning our homes until they are free of germs, as opposed to working on issues of climate, geography, and employment, which are more intricately linked to the health of the population. Reductionism and single issue thinking feed into a modern Western mindset that we can solve all problems, and solve them immediately, if only we take individual responsibility for our health and our illness. This masks the burden of responsibility for care, while facing eroded social services.

Complications from Adult Education

Adult educators have often been involved in the social issues that affect health—employment, labour, geography, literacy—but have not always connected these issues to health. And, all too often we have concentrated narrowly on education for individual transformation and growth to the expense of larger issues. One of our primary areas of study, transformative learning, for instance, has been largely constrained to talking about health as a series of individual choices and local conditions rather than as a venue for social transformation. Much of the writing on women, health, and transformative learning is focused on individual women in oppressive conditions (Meyer, 2009; Nash, 2007). For instance, researcher Jacquie

Hamp (2007) focuses on women who are struggling to make the transition from welfare to work, while Deborah Kilgore and Leslie Bloom (2002) are examining poverty and domestic violence involving women. While all of this research is helpful, it does seem to keep the focus more on negativity and individual experience than on social and environmental change, the determinants of health. The stereotyping of women's health issues and life situations as crisis ridden mires any discussion of their health in negativity and lack of possibility.

THE SOCIAL DETERMINANTS IN FOCUS

The social transformation perspective moves beyond the individual focus of most transformative learning literature, and encompasses the many economic, cultural, geographical and other factors that affect citizens and their health. These factors are particular to women because women are more likely to suffer negative health outcomes, and when racial and social class issues come to bear on their lives, they have even greater challenges. In recognition of these challenges, some researchers and facilitators have looked at how both race and culture can be integrated into a health awareness initiative. For instance, Melany Cueva and Katie Cueva (2008), in documenting their work with indigenous women in Alaska, point out that these women being trained as community health workers learned through dance and body movement. They learned to connect cancer education with not only their heads, but with their bodies as well. They brought together eight Alaska Native women of varied heritage including *Yup'ik, Inupiaq, Aleut, Tlingit,* and *Athabascan* women. When they studied the effects of dance and body movement on these women, through end-of-course written evaluations and follow-up written email correspondence, they found that "the expressive movements of dance as part of cancer education supported laughter, relaxation, fun, healing, learning, and deeper understanding" (p. 135). In many ways this is not surprising since we know that the body is an important part to learning and being, though it is much neglected in deference to the mind and the brain. Dance and body movement was an important way of connecting their own knowledge and know how, and the Western medical knowledge and medical education model was put in a context and not presented as the only way to learn and be. Moreover, medical knowledge was contextualized within their own ways of knowing and being and honoured their community and its past practice.

When we move away from the needs and concerns of white Western women, the connections of health to the broader determinants becomes clearer. The National Collaborating Centre for Aboriginal Health (NCCAH) in Canada (Nelson, 2012), for instance, has focused on race as a key ingredient in health. Writing about Aboriginal women, Charlotte Loppie Reading and Fred Wien (2009) noted that there are many factors that affect their health, including proximal, intermediate, and distal factors. The distal or removed factors such as physical environment, for Aboriginal people, include "to a large extent, colonialism, racism, and social exclusion, as well as repression of self-determination, act as the distal determinants within which all other determinants are constructed" (Reading & Wien, p. 20). It is precisely these distant or distal factors that adult health education is concerned with—how do we work with people who have multiple systems of oppression at play in their lives? Yet, for many of us, it is the immediate context that becomes the centrepiece of our work in adult health learning and education.

The factors described by Reading and Wien (2009)—proximal, intermediate and distal—are useful to reveal the varying levels of responsibility and agency for health. Such an analysis places the responsibility at the most appropriate level, in this case, naming the distal (we might also call these the social determinants). Yet, all three factors help us to see both the differences and the inter connections between the various ways we are responsible for our health. For Aboriginal peoples in Canada, the issues are both system-related (medical system) and systemic (colonialism and racism). The research of the NCCAH in Canada makes it clear that colonialism is an integral part of addressing Aboriginal health and wellbeing, and it will take more than immediate health interventions to create solutions. For women, the primary caregivers, the issues are particularly significant. This was certainly true when Peggy Gabo Ntseane and Bagele Chilisa (2012) wrote about the AIDS crises in Botswana, pointing out that understanding and educating about health is really about adopting an indigenous approach. As an example of using this indigenous knowledge in community-based work, Ntseane and Chilisa drew attention to the woodland plant bloodroot, an indigenous plant used in a variety of ways such as to treat cancer, dye clothes, and simply to enjoy.

Another key element in addressing issues that affect health is attending to social class or fully appreciating that corporate and political elites of the population are not forced to deal personally with the same issues and rates of food insecurity, preventable diseases or dangerous work conditions as poor people do. Furthermore, we need to identify the entanglement of social class issues with religious discrimination practice or international health policies that negatively affect women in the Global South. International health policy becomes a major issue, especially if it is prejudiced against women and their needs or does not substantially take women's needs and responsibilities into account. We are especially troubled by fundamental religious groups with outdated understandings of reproductive health that, in turn, have a major global impact on women's lives and the health of families.

Yet, for all the complications, it is sheer poverty that has the greatest impact on women's lives. As Andrea Papan and Barbara Clow (2012) note, the poor are especially hard hit by inadequate food policies and the effects of low social class. For the food insecure, in particular, there is a *vicious cycle* of poverty—and increased rates of obesity and chronic illnesses that are difficult to address. Nutritional deprivation, poverty, and obesity work together in a complex relationship that is exacerbated by stress, parenting challenges, and social isolation. Clearly, the provision of fresh fruit or vegetables is not the answer to these complex health issues; health requires multiple interventions and a comprehensive approach (Papan & Clow, p. 1).

ADDRESSING THE HEALTH ISSUES

One of the key decisions that adult educators must make is how they spend their time, whether they work on the proximal, intermediate or distal levels. At times, they work at each of them simultaneously, and not always in full knowledge of where their efforts are directed or taking effect. We look here at some initiatives for addressing the issues of women and health.

Moving to Action and Learning about Health

The history of adult education shows that women can address issues that affect them in their daily lives through learning and action, though not in the limited sense of each one learning and doing. They can work together not only to address cleanliness but also to tackle rather large societal issues that affect them. Rachel Gorman (2007) says that it is about the ability of women to "both *learn to engage in*, and ultimately *learn through,* collective struggles against oppression" (p. 185, italics ours). She posits three types of nonschool-based learning: survival, resistance, and struggle. *Survival* learning is how individuals develop strategies to cope in a world that has been constructed to exclude them. Individuals may figure out a coping strategy out on their own or may learn about it from other members of their community or social group. *Resistance* learning is how an individual or group develops strategies to resist the ways in which the world has been constructed to exclude them. *Struggle* learning is how a group develops an understanding of how their oppression has been constructed and reconstructed and how that group develops counterarguments and strategies to dismantle the oppression. When we used these concepts in our discussions about health, *resistance learning* refers to the ways women meet and oppose violence, poverty, and oppression as we encounter it in our daily lives, while *collective struggle* refers to the ways that women learn to identify and change the relations of oppression, which is the focus of adult health learning and the social determinants of health. We include an additional emphasis here that struggle is strengthened by *solidarity*, drawing on a shared vision for alternatives. The work of indigenous health centres invokes a reclamation and pride in culture as an integral component to healing (Atleo, 2012). This is not just a process of struggling against oppression, but of drawing upon and celebrating the strength within the group.

Rachel Gorman's (2007) typology is useful when looking at health in the community. Health for women involves survival, resistance and struggle, whether in dealing with actual disease, or the prevention of it, or even in trying to build a community from it. Learning in these circumstances is multilayered. Resistance, for instance, can refer to individual coping mechanisms and to protest inequitable policies or practices. Collective struggle in solidarity can apply to a group's efforts to develop strategies to confront oppression and develop alternative modalities. When a nonprofit organization is engaged in struggle, leaders sometimes forget to pay

37

attention to the need for learning. Social movement learning, as discussed elsewhere in this book, is about these large issues that have interlocking systems of oppression. It is also at this level, where alliances may be formed. The learning taps into the collective resources of the group including the traditional knowledge and strength of bonds that reinforce group solidarity.

Survival learning for health would be just keeping afloat in one's own house in terms of acquiring strategies to feed a family, cope with an illness, juggle meagre funds. By far, the greatest number of research studies on women are focused on survival needs. In earlier writings on transformative learning (see English & Irving, 2012; see also English & Peters, 2012), we noted that most of the articles on transformative learning, for instance, were really about how women survived amidst incredible odds, for instance, women attempting to escape from violent relationships. Examples of resistance learning would be neighbours fighting increase in taxes that penalize low income families, or the loss of publicly accessible parks and other spaces for free recreation. Struggle learning can be collective action to examine why the tax system privileges the wealthy or why a forest is being clear cut with no regard for where local residents source their water. While millions of dollars are available for a pulp mill or a shipbuilding enterprise, education, recreation, and agriculture face ongoing cutbacks. "Food deserts" describe urban environments where there are no easily accessible sources of fresh food which force people either to pay for transit, or rely on less nutritious processed products (Beaulac, Kristjansson, & Cummins, 2009). Food activists point out the futility of cooking classes to teach poor people to prepare healthy meals, when they live in neighbourhoods where healthy food is hard to find. If asked, women could tell many stories of the coping survival strategies they have developed or the rationale behind food choices that do not seem logical to a dietician. Community gardens, food co-operatives, and advocacy on food security are struggle responses to address food insecurity beyond the narrow focus on diet as an individual choice.

Resistance is a point of engagement beyond survival, and provides an opportunity for people to learn. Struggle in solidarity is goal where systemic change is enacted collectively for true change and revolution. This typology is about a feminist way of working because it engages groups of people in issues that affect them. Not only is there activity, but there is also reflection and analysis involved in the process. This kind of learning is meant to engage the community in very tangible and helpful ways.

In social movement learning theory (see English & Mayo, 2012; Hall & Clover, 2005) the concept of resistance is much more prevalent than the concept of struggle, because resistance often focuses on large global issues and concerns which are somewhat easier to identify and challenge. Much of this attention to resistance can be traced to Michel Foucault's (1988) popular idea that multiple pathways of resistance exist on equal and opposite vectors as the multiple pathways of power. In tracing resistances in an analysis of the social determinants, we can see the lines of power clearly.

One of the missing pieces in this discussion of social determinants of health is the actual effects of health in the lives of women and girls. It is true, as Paula Cameron (2011) notes, that women are intricately involved in the issues of health. They are more likely to be diagnosed with depression and more likely to access the mental health system than men are. Arguably men's mental health issues may show in alcoholism, violence, and abuse. Cameron notes that depression is the leading causes of disability for women and she points to depression and recovery for women as a site of transformative learning. Similarly, physician Gabor Maté (2004) notes that our bodies bear our hurt and bear our stress and that we need to listen to these bodies as they will do the speaking for us, difficult as it may be for us to hear.

Bringing Resistance and Struggle Learning into Health

In an interesting piece of work, Noelle Wiggins (2012) reviews the literature on the use of popular education as a means of empowering the health of communities. She works in Portland, Oregon and draws on creative ideas and practices from around the world to inform her understanding of how to educate for health, and move beyond traditional notions and ideas. She equates popular education with Paulo Freire and points out that it has been used in many places around the world to free people, yet it is not well known and practiced for health purposes in the West, in large measure because for want of specific strategies and techniques. As Freire and Myles Horton used the term, *popular education* refers to organization and initiative from the grassroots. Wiggins observes that popular education can include methods such as social learning games, social skits, brainstorm, simulations, and problem posing (p. 3), which have not traditionally been part of health education. She also notes the tie to the principles of the *Ottawa Charter for Health Promotion*, created at the World Health Organization's First International Conference on Health Promotion in 1986.

Heather Stuckey (2009b), in her study of how to use the arts in diabetes education, focuses on a group of patients and shows how in using coloured paper and artistic exercises she can help people pass beyond their first resistance and fear. Here is how she describes her process:

> The three sessions that emerged focused on exploring the meaning-making process using several forms of creative expression. First, we engaged in a creative process that focused on the body, through which images and metaphors of diabetes were constructed. Second, participants took pictures of images that reminded them of their diabetes and lastly, we discussed the metaphors and images through dialogue and writings. (p. 52)

This is a fine exercise that might have been extended by looking not only at how one makes meaning of being insulin dependent but also connects to the larger world of advertising for prepared food and looks at how women are affected by diabetes and caregiving. There is also room for looking at the proliferation of medical treatments

39

and machines that are individually financed and not available to women with low incomes.

Creativity is not a word to be constrained to the use of activities but rather to be applied also to imagination and larger ways of seeing the world and issues, as a gateway to systemic analysis (Stuckey, 2009a). As noted in Chapter 4, the arts are an integral part of increasing health for Aboriginal women, regardless of their health issue. Not only is their art production, whether it be weaving baskets, or performance, valuable in creating an increased sense of importance of their culture, it increases identity, self-determination, and sense of community. Art becomes an educational tool that decreases cultural isolation and which may increase health (Nelson, 2012).

The Boston Women's Health Book Collective demonstrates how women can work together in solidarity to take control of their health and information that affects their health, that is, to engage in learning through struggle and solidarity. Back in the late 1960s, numerous women came together to look at how they could take control of issues affecting their health, especially reproductive health (Birden, 2004). In the process, they began to compile their own guide to health. Their first guide, *Women and Their Bodies,* came out in a newsprint edition in 1970, with a formal published book known as *Our Bodies, Ourselves* (OBOS), published in 1973. Women are still working together to compile this guide, with the last count of authors being 300 men and women from organizations around the world. In 2011, OBOS was printed for the ninth time; it had been published in multiple languages in countries around the world, making it unique in production and distribution for women's health. Globally, there are people working in different countries including Tanzania, Serbia, Thailand, Turkey, Senegal, Israel, Russia, China, and many more, to create their own books on women and health, with more than 25 languages represented. These guides are culturally specific and oriented. This is a strong example of how a book presumably about reproductive health has branched out to global concerns and partners, and how it has drawn in more and more people to look at issues that affect women's health.

The ability to work around and beyond the medical model and to form partnerships and resistance to change in issues to affect health has long been a part of effective feminist work. Barbara Ehrenreich and Deirdre English (1978), for instance, were writing about women's health in the late 1970s and noting the long history of how women have been treated poorly by health care systems in the past. They provided a still timely feminist analysis of how women have been subject to the prevailing winds of the medical model, and how this has privileged Western masculinist knowing. Their point was to show how some women have been able to resist this model, but with difficulty. More than 30 years later, their analysis is still poignant: women's skills of traditional health knowledge abilities to maintain their health as in their use of herbs in healing was slowly taken over by a male model and devalued. Their work is still relevant in that women need to not only reclaim their knowledge of how to heal, but also to understand and critique the larger social and cultural forces that affect health. Such feminist historical analysis is very important for women as it names the past, uncovers the truth, and reclaims space that has been occupied. In short, it aids in the resistance process.

DISCUSSION

Much of our field of adult education, especially in North America, has been obsessed by a need for women as individuals to look at their own health and to take steps to change their food, their diet, their bodies, their homes, etc. Women have resisted such measures as shown by the Boston Women's Health Book Collective and by other actions to work collaboratively and in concert with their partners to address such issues and to work on policy and politics to effect change.

What becomes clear here is that the traditional modes of health education do not work. They may help women cope or survive, but they cannot help with resistance or change to any great degree. The journey through resistance, struggle and solidarity depend on a comprehensive adult health learning approach that refuses to be mired in individually focused solutions. It requires educators to be involved in change in the community, locally and globally.

ARTS AND ADULT EDUCATION

Adult educator Darlene Clover (2006a, 2007a) brought to international attention an arts in education project that took place at a family services centre on Vancouver Island, Canada. Called Sexual Exploitation Has No Borders, it became a communal quilting project for women who were victims of abuse and social workers who worked with them. The community arts project had a deliberative educational and learning agenda, and was used to process ideas and experiences of abuse. The artform itself, a quilt, highlighted the contrast between a traditional female craft of producing an item associated with comfort, but emblazoned with images and colours that conveyed the harsh realities these women were addressing. To expand the range of influence, the quilts were displayed in several international venues where they further facilitated the process of talking back and claiming power—as survivors and as artisans. Quilting and fabric arts by women are ways of reclaiming the social and cultural space that women traditionally have occupied but which served sometimes as oppressive. Quilting, from an arts-based inquiry perspective, is about turning that oppression into an imaginative and creative space.

It has become quite popular in adult education circles to talk about the use of art in education as if it were a new phenomenon and as if it were a new way to learn or as if art were a thing to be manipulated for learning. The reality is that art and artistic ways of knowing have always been an integral part of learning, education, and activism. Arts have been especially embraced by those educators working in local areas around the world and in popular education, as these forms transcend barriers such as literacy. One only has to think of Augusto Boal's (1974/1985) *Theatre of the Oppressed* in Brazil, which was used to engage local residents in drama to effect change in social and economic conditions, to realize that using the arts is an established and *bona fide* practice in adult education when the educational focus is social transformation and change (see Hoggan, Simpson, & Stuckey, 2009). Artist and educator dian marino (1997) integrated these two talents—arts and education—in her activism and political education with diverse groups such as factory workers, immigrants, youth, and First Nations. She was also involved, along with Budd Hall and others, in the development of participatory action research.

Engaging with art produced by others has also been a valued entry point to use creativity for learning. For example, Columbia University educational philosopher, Maxine Greene (1995), describes bringing her students to art galleries or to see polished theatrical performances in order to enhance their understanding of education. In her classes, she encouraged the reading of American literary classics

(*Huckleberry Finn, Scarlet Letter, Moby Dick,* and the like) as a medium to foster creativity, facilitate learning, and offer possibilities for education. This is the use of art in a "higher" art sense or art appreciation, a common use of art in formal education contexts. While it has the possibility to open minds and hearts, it has the dual goal of celebrating fine art and breaking class barriers to engaging with art that is still perceived as a luxury of the privileged.

Among adult educators, art creation is more common; we tend to engage our creative potential to move, create, speak, and write what *we know* in our bodies or our experiences. The art that is used and created is *by* the participants and *for* the participants. It would not be usual in these circles to engage with the great European artists as Maxine Greene (1995) did. When we learn through creating art, our whole being is integrated into the enterprise and transformation becomes possible. For many women, this type of learning, as we note in our chapter on transformative learning, is about honouring our whole being and of having an encounter with the content and the ideas. Such art is closer to Boal's (1974/1985) theatre work with rural participants, where spectators/audience members became spect-actors, and were invited to take part in the theatre show or production.

One of the challenges is the way in which the word creativity is usually employed and assigned to a particular kind of art—products that are salable and marketable. Creativity is often used synonymously with the word *artistic* to the point where there is considerable reticence for everyday people to engage in artistic ways of knowing, for fear of their efforts being judged as somehow not good enough. In contrast, the artistic way of knowing that we are celebrating here is available to all and does not refer only to fine art. We approach this from the perspective that everyone is creative, but we also acknowledge that here is still room for the profession of artist and for the space to perfect and practice one's art. In working with quilters, Darlene Clover (2007a) and her colleagues became aware of the importance of the craft itself—that the messages the women conveyed with their art depended, in part, on the development and demonstration of their sewing ability. Yet, they are disrupting gender stereotypes in the ways they use this artform, just as the women of Red Thread (Nettles, 2007) did with their embroidery. There is an aesthetic pride in the art form—it is not regarded as a utilitarian tool or as providing entrée to the "real" work of learning. Art in the sense that we are describing here may take a variety of forms to foster creativity and expression, and it can take bodily form (dance, theatre, sculpture), visual form (collage, painting, photography), auditory form (song, storytelling), and also audio-visual form (filmmaking)—the collective process is further facilitated by the potential of online collaboration.

Perhaps what is most needed is an understanding of how art is connected to democracy and participation. Aesthetic experiences are worthwhile, in and of themselves; yet, when linked to change and imagination, a link that Mae Shaw and Rosie Meade (2013) refer to as the creation of the "democratic imagination" (p. 197), these experiences can become catalysts for change. For Shaw and Meade, this imagination is cultivated by "community development practitioners in finding ways to enhance people's potential for democratic agency by helping to release or resource their capacity to be active and creative" (p. 197). Although Shaw and Meade are not referring only to women, and acknowledging the arts are not a female-exclusive domain, it is interesting to observe that the bulk of the writing on the arts has been from women (Butterwick, 2012; Cameron, 2011; Clover, 2010, 2012; Shaw & Meade) not because they are innately artistic but they seem to be effective in reaching women in a particular place, allowing them to release the democratic imagination, and to participate in acts of "subversion, opposition and resistance as much as by participation and consent" (Shaw & Meade, p. 197). These would seem to be the aspects of democracy that come closest to the community development realm.

The poetic arts also are used in social movements and activism. As Junko Onosaka (2006) notes, "Poetry helped conceptualize the women's movement, and moved with women" (p. 21). She cites such poets as Audre Lorde and Adrienne Rich, explaining that the new ideas bubbling in the women's movement often appeared first in poetry.

LEARNING THROUGH THE ARTS

As we discussed in the previous chapter on health, art is an integral part of knowing, including knowledge translation and mobilization around issues in health. Given its potential to draw people in, to attract the grassroots, and to transform, artistic ways of knowing have been used effectively in health settings to help people co-create and share knowledge. Within the Indigenous collective, the NCCAH, for instance, art is used in First Nations communities in a variety of ways including (a) art as therapy, (b) art as a protective factor, and (c) art as community building. Artistic ways of knowing are used in teaching and also in ancillary ways to increase knowledge and knowing around issues such as living with diabetes, restoring health, and challenging government structures that oppress health. Carl Grodach (2010) develops the *notion of community art,* observing that this art is less about art for the sake of art, and more about art as a vehicle for learning and exploration. Much effective adult education art is community art in this sense. Community art assumes the politicization and active engagement of public space, blurring the boundary of private and public, and allowing the creation of a space of potential in the community—things are happening and where action and development become possible.

For many of the groups discussed below, art is not new but it may need to be recovered since it has been disappeared. For the Aboriginal peoples of Canada, for instance, their artistic expression and know-how was suppressed by colonial regimes, and this affected their ability to be healthy. Recovering Aboriginal art and their artistic ways of being including drumming, basket making, and weaving is a way to restore health and to reconnect them with the land from which they were exiled (Nelson, 2012), as well as to build their sense of community with one another through ritual expression of the arts.

45

Rosanna Deerchild (2003) describes the art of "tribal feminist" Lita Fontaine who uses a creative approach to explore her Ojibway culture and mythology as well as to raise questions about women's place in society. Fontaine's installation piece "A Woman's Drum" challenges the sexism that has grown to exclude women from participating in drumming circles and her work serves as a reminder that the drum is sacred, evoking the heartbeat of Mother Earth. Fontaine uses performance and sound to tap into deeper emotional, embodied ways of learning and healing. Her tribal feminism seeks to understand and expose the ways patriarchal attitudes and practices have seeped into culture and ritual, such as drumming. Similarly, Zainab Amadahy (2003) describes a music workshop that highlights the spiritual connection and healing power of ceremonial music and drumming. The women who drum must overcome patriarchal biases that discourage or forbid them outright from drumming or singing in powwows. The women's very presence as drummers, artists, and performers allows them to reclaim an interest in their culture and way of being and helps resist the notion that the only valuable art is for marketable products such as baskets. Through their art they let it be known that the artistic process has the potential to increase a sense of identity and create cultural connections that enable authentic relationships. When alienation is lessened, as in this case, through art, there is a possibility for healing divisions and creating safe spaces for action.

Folk Art and Craft

And, of course, there are *community art spaces*, which are designated physical spaces in communities where art can be displayed and created with participation of the audience. The latter is one of the more transformative as it challenges notions of fixity and perfection in art. Art—visual, performance and other—can occur as people are engaged in the making of the art, whether on a small scale with women doing quilt making at a conference or in a public venue, such as the AIDS quilt, or on a large scale as with art creation spaces as in North Vancouver (see http://nvartscouncil.ca/).

The international AIDS quilt, NAMES Project–AIDS Memorial Quilt, a title often abbreviated to AIDS Memorial Quilt, is one of the largest community folk art projects in the world (see http://www.aidsquilt.org). The innocuous quilt, all 54 tons of it, has not only spread knowledge of AIDS-related illness but also has helped to transform an understanding of AIDS from a personal affliction caused by lifestyle to a worldwide issue that affects men, women, and children, and which has multiple causes and effects. The man credited with initiating the project was Cleve Jones whose Quaker background provided inspiration for the idea of quiltmaking as a way to make the lost lives visible (Brown, 1997). When one consider that women are the most affected by AIDS in terms of caregiving, it is appropriate that many of the hands that made the quilt were female. Quilting the issue brings attention to the ways in which AIDS is also a woman's affliction and increases awareness of the disease (Rhoad, 2012). The craft of designing and sewing the quilt transforms opinion, and demonstrates in a tangible way the complexity, the reach, and the problematic of the disease on an international level.

Puleng Segalo (2014) describes the use of "embroidery as narrative" using the analogy of this needlecraft itself in demonstrating how women who have survived violence in South Africa to "re-stitch their lives" (p. 44). This process involved the women working together to create the embroideries that depicted their lives and experiences of both repression and resistance against apartheid. The gatherings also gave them a safe forum to share stories of their experiences of racism, sexism, marginalization and silence that had been buried for years. In South Africa, where the process of truth and reconciliation has been widely lauded, this embroidery project is a reminder of the many voices who have remained silent, requiring new strategies to support healing.

It is not incidental that craft and folk art, the traditional medium for women's creativity and for bonding, are used by women to effect change. Craft becomes a medium for organizing, engaging creativity and the body, and allowing for the building of relationships. The links here are that the arts are both a medium for the building of community and also a means of expressing the energy and the ideas of the women who are gathered. The making of quilts and the creation of collective paintings brings women together to pass on their own knowledge and skills, all the while valuing alternative forms of knowing and expressions of knowledge.

Theatre for Transformation

Participatory theatre, such as with the form developed by Augusto Boal (1974/1985), drew inspiration from Freire's (1970) notion of conscientization to develop a theatrical methodology of working with participants to name their stories, enact their issues, and together find solutions to common problems. Educated as a chemical engineer, Boal left his technical world behind to work with citizens at the grassroots to have them engage their bodies and minds in movement and acting that privileged doing over talking, acting over speechifying, protesting over suffering, and helped inspire generations to work for change that was in their own interest. He even brought this notion of legislative theatre to bear on his later years as a city councillor. His notion of artistic ways of knowing helped advance the Landless Worker movement in his home country of Brazil as well as with all-women theatre groups in Bengal, India. Participatory theatre, especially street theatre, has been used in Vancouver by the Headlines Theatre Group to help participants in acting and producing theatre, engaging them bodily in learning for change.

Participatory theatre has enabled Northern Ireland women to enact their issues and responses to war, and to develop a sense of how their bodies are used. McWilliams (1995), for example, describes the women who formed a group called a Relatives' Action Committee to both protest and to create support for themselves, in a place where their brothers, fathers, and sons were engaged in a civil war. On one occasion they performed in the street about their troubles in the Troubles. They took their

47

theatre to a summer parade in Derry when they used a truck to display a pastoral scene of a woman at a cottage playing a harp. They then had the cottage slowly fall apart revealing 10 prisoners in jail (their family members) in detestable conditions symbolizing the "'dirty protest' in which Republican prisoners who were 'on the blanket' had begun to spread excreta over their prison cells as a protest" (McWilliams, p. 24). This provocative performance was a way of letting the audience know that women were there and were part of the protest. Drawing on feminist theologian Mary Daly, McWilliams describes them as "memory bearing women" (p. 17) or the women who took the lead in protest, in caring for families and agitating for change. Finding that they had no voice in the violence or its end, these women decided to protest in spaces that were available to them and where it was impossible not to see them. Street theatre as art became a public protest of the war in Northern Ireland.

Readers' theatre can be a way of using the arts to bring research participants into the center of the research, to have them come on stage to read their own transcripts, to tell the audience their opinions on topics such as health services, poverty, or abuse. Such arts-informed practices can be used to disseminate research findings so that the whole community can learn from the research, and also so the participants can have a role in creating the knowledge that has been learned. In terms of health research, for instance, women can tell how their lives in community are affected by the centralized medical system and how they have been demoralized because of the inhumane system. Readers' theatre provides research participants with a role in the knowledge dissemination process as well as in the data gathering phase. The audience then knows, feels, hears, and experiences the research in the same way as they might if they were in the room with the researcher and participants. Readers' theatre allows women to have a literal voice and to connect with the audience and other participants; it builds community and advances common causes (Walsh & Brigham, 2007).

Writing and Drawing as Artistic Ways of Knowing

Arts informed research is another way of talking about art that transforms and brings the knowledge from the community to higher education, in a reversal of the traditional flow of official knowledge. In *arts-informed research*, the knowing that comes from working in craft and in folk art or dance, for instance, is used to inform how research is done. Paula Cameron (2011) uses the zine, or the creation of an online book, to tell her story and that of her participants who have had mental illness and who have experienced it as a transformative event. The self-publishing and the self-creation, along with the drawing and writing, helped the participants in her study actively participate in their own recovery and to learn from it. The zine as an artistic forum is a way to help participants narrate a lived reality of an illness that women experience twice as often as men (Cameron, 2014).

Similarly, for her dissertation, Lynette Plett (2008) used quilts, craft, and other artefacts from her *Kleine Gemindi* upbringing to explore the Plett family story of being Russian immigrants to Canada who engaged in farming and who also made quilts as an expression of both religious faith and of self-identity. Quilt-making and crafting allowed the Plett women, who had no official role in the family or community, to have a voice, to express their wishes and desires. In telling their stories through quilting, Plett was able to break through her own past as a woman born into a culture and Mennonite community that seemed to restrict women to the home and to submissive partnerships. Again, the arts of crafting and quilting allowed generations of Plett women to learn from one another and to find a creative way to express themselves.

Likewise, popular educator Deborah Barndt (2011) relates how her five-country project of community arts and popular education brought together a transnational group from various parts of the Americas in a cross-border exchange of popular education practices. The arts employed varied from textiles, to community murals, to community television, to dance and song. What these projects have in common is their attempt to use the arts as a medium for social transformation and change. The commonality of the project is their willingness to be political, to use art for political reasons, and to be very deliberate in inclusion and movement for change.

Music and Film

There is a strong link between music (Wiessner, 2009) and civil disobedience and rights, as any follower of folk music knows. Music has the power to transform not only the musician but also the hearer who may experience the music in the body, the mind, and the soul. Feminist choirs are a prime example of an important venue for women to express themselves through music in solidarity with other feminists. They work through the body to build women's learning and to create a solid block of political support and solidarity. We need only look at the role political music played in Highlander Folk Schools programs for trade unions and the Civil Rights movement. In 1934, Zilphia (Johnson) Horton brought her training in music and theatre to Highlander's programs (McDermott, 2007). Participants wrote songs and plays to perform on the picket line or to use in union education. Zilphia encouraged them to share their own musical heritage which would have included spirituals, hymns and Appalachian folk songs, and by 1939, she had compiled a collection of union songs. The famous anthem *We Shall Overcome* was originally a Baptist hymn that labour activist Lucille Simmons crafted into a protest song for tobacco workers. At Highlander in 1947, Zilphia Horton, Lucille Simmons, and folk singer Pete Seeger reworked the lyrics to the form we know today (Lynskey, 2010). Another Highlander educator and musician, Guy Carawan, would later reflect, "Zilphia helped people feel good about themselves, their music, their communities" (in Lynskey, 2010, p. 45). The documentary film *Soundtrack for a Revolution* (Guttentag & Sturman, 2009) also highlights the vital role music played in the United States at this crucial time in its history, allowing voices of protest to engage the public's interest and support.

It is no accident that documentary film is often coupled with revolutionary music to create space and to encourage change. Adult educator Carole Roy (2009, 2012) has used film festivals as a means of creating and hearing local knowledge. In literally bringing these film festivals to the people who are directly affected by injustice, such as incarcerated women, Roy is able to engage their creative spirit in thinking about and naming the conditions of oppression and the possibilities of hope. When film incites protest, we are reminded that film is a very political medium; indeed, the visual representation of change shows us that film is powerful. A prime example is *In a Better World, d*irected by Susanne Bier (2010), a work that won the 2011 Best Foreign Language Film Academy and Golden Globe Awards. Bier shows the parallel journey of two men and their families in Denmark who become connected through their sons, and who together suffer a catastrophe that forces them to experience the continuum between pacifism and violence, and to contemplate and acknowledge the need for forgiveness. Films such as this challenge us to think of the potential for violence in human situations and encounters, as well as help change rigid notions and perceptions of pacifism and violence.

The creation of film is also of importance in this context. Participatory video has grown alongside the other participatory methodologies for learning and research. SEWA, for example, created their own video unit in 1984 (see http://www.videosewa.org).

Storytelling

Many of the forms of artistic expression we are exploring are ways of telling stories—through songs, images and performances. One of the key ways in which we learn and indeed create ourselves into being is through the telling of *our* story. In educational circles, this has come to be known as *narrative* and *narrative inquiry*, due mainly to the work of Jean Clandinin and Michael Connelly (2000). Yet, fables and fairytales, parables and memoires have been expressions of the human spirit since time immemorial. Newer, though, is the enabling and facilitating of storytelling in educational and learning venues so that participants can name their experiences and learn from them. Experienced educators know that allowing participants to move beyond sharing experience to creating and storying one's life is important for deep learning not only for the one telling the story but for the listener as well.

Once we bring our story to light, allow it to engage with other stories, and become a narrative for our time, then we are learning. Sharon Buttala (2004), a writer of memoire in Saskatchewan, explains that storytelling is crucial to how we live our lives, how we understand our past, and how we create our future. In remembering our own family's past, we can move things forward to the future. When one tells a story like Indigenous people have of their history of enforced residential schooling in Canada, citizens listen and are compelled to act, especially if the venue is public. First Nations writer and storyteller Thomas King (2003) speaks of the power of stories and reminds us: "Don't say in the years to come that you would have lived your life differently if only you had heard this story. You've heard it now" (p. 60).

The process of sharing stories and giving voice to individual experience can be used for collective and critical analysis to support social action. Margaret Ledwith and Jane Springett (2010) offer a concise overview of the ways story can be used in community development, and describe the process through a variety of perspectives and methods. The content of the stories may be expressions of individual experiences, or the content may take on creative forms such as poetry. Ledwith and Springett observe the confidence that can be developed when women writers come together in circles to tell and record stories; the writing circle they describe in the UK is an important early step for awareness and confidence building that can lead to more political forms of organizing. Ledwith and Springett's description highlights the equal importance of listening and telling stories, or engaging in collective learning. It is significant from the perspective of gender that these researchers closely identify the learning processes of the women in the writing group with the connected knowing phase identified in the work of Belenky et al. (1986).

While there has been a proliferation of the use of storytelling in such forms as town halls and public fora to provide alternatives to rationalist public discourses, there is still much to learn of its effectiveness. Additionally, one must ask what is done with the story once it has been told. Indeed, there may be expectations of what should be done that may undermine the impact of the story and the learning potential it holds. These are issues that interest sociologist Francesca Polletta (2006) who has studied the use of story in social movements. Her analysis is instructive for adult educators in developing ways to incorporate the use of story, as she explores the aspects that make story so powerful for awareness raising and mobilization. Polletta reminds us of the importance of the craft of creating and sharing stories and of selecting the stories that have the best resonance with regards to the issue and the audience. In Polletta's mind, the work of developing the story is the focus and it must allow for spontaneity; as with all good teaching, creating the space for spontaneity demands that the facilitator be very well planned and thoughtful. Stories can be seen as inspirational, representational, or deceptive; they are alternately trusted for putting a human face to an issue, or misrepresentative as when stories are trooped out uncritically and not explored deeper, as in the case of some politicians who rely on anecdotes in order to hammer home a point, not realising that the media will quickly dig a bit deeper to find how shallow or misrepresentative the tales are. No wonder people begin to get cynical.

Polletta (2006) provides what she calls a *sociology of storytelling* by examining how stories are used in social action, and how they are constructed in different cultures and contexts. This acknowledgement of difference provides great scope for adult educations to work with community members to dig deeper together to uncover, craft and share stories in a more meaningful way, as testimony or inspiration. Polletta strives to move past the perceptions of stories as being the opposite of intellectual discourse, of invoking emotion rather than reason. When one tells a story, one risks having it received as inspirational or not statistically significant. Stories too can be short bursts of action, snippets that speak for the whole, sometimes falling short of the larger issue, inadvertently hiding the long-term process which is the essence of activism. Citizens need to do more with the stories than just listen and appreciate them or sympathize with the storyteller—they need to be enabled to engage with the teller and the issues.

Polletta (2006) is not alone in raising questions about the use of story. We only need to think about the fact that storytelling is a popular method in management literature (see Denning, 2006), heralded as an instructional aid to provide instant connection to an audience and to transmit management concepts. Educators must remain attentive to story's potential for manipulation, a process that Cheryl Lapp and Adrian Carr (2010) call *storyselling* whereby stories are created to present a biased or uncritical presentation of a situation. Lapp and Carr challenge the teller of stories that cannot be interrogated and stories that must be believed, without question. The selling of stories to an audience undermines the genuine use of storytelling for community building purposes.

In a creative sense, we are speaking of a deeper process than using stories as instructional aids or as tools of manipulation for a neoliberal agenda. For adult educators, the process of creative expression, reflection, and collective building needs to lead to the ultimate goal of the story: critical transformation. We can keep asking the questions: Is the story a form of creative expression that helps to open up someone's thinking? Is it an entry point to deeper analysis and reflexivity, individually or collectively, as stories of different experiences are analysed together? Is it to craft a narrative as a representation of an issue to present to the world in a human way? This creative and transformative use of story that includes the process and the goal is far different from the rigid and neoliberal presentation of a narrative that is unchanging and unquestioned and in service of the market economy.

As adult educators, our focus in using stories encourages both reflexivity and critique. We have to work long and hard in many contexts to build the trust that many of our venues such as workshops do not allow. Trusting environments where participants can share stories of experiences, which can be deeply personal, need to be supported by authentically reflexive spaces. Barriers to trust or manipulation of participants and their stories will always deny potential and growth, or undermine trust. Adult educators have the challenge of ensuring safe spaces to allow difficult discussions.

Our field has a rich history of using story to help build community in a retreat-style learning environment. From the long admired traditions of residential education programs of Chautauqua, to settlement houses, through to the Highlander Folk Schools there was a recognition of the need to get away from one's daily context to find quiet space to reflect (English & Mayo, 2012). Staff at Highlander saw the importance of honouring and respecting people through collecting and sharing their stories in a residential setting. The emphasis at this school of rights and justice is on collective learning, education for group rights that leads to collective action. The residential setting is a time-honoured way of encouraging group story telling and bonding; through discovering shared experiences, confronting disjunctures, and walking in the shoes of the other social transformation becomes possible.

Along with group processes for action, our field has a tradition of participatory action research (PAR), which is people-centred and which has a strong aspect of telling stories, identifying needs, and coming to a collective approach to change. PAR employs skills that already exist as strengths in grassroots adult education. The rich data comes from stories not surveys, but they need to be explored and scrutinized to understand the discourses, contexts, and meanings. Like the chicken and the egg, it is a challenge to determine whether learning and researching by telling stories came before PAR or vice versa; perhaps they are one and the same. Myles Horton, the founder of the Highlander Folk School, noted that PAR "existed at Highlander all along, now it has a name... the Highlander idea of making people their own experts" (as cited in Conti & Fellenz, 1986, p. 5). PAR has also been particularly embraced and developed by feminists (Maguire, 1987).

And, of course, storytelling can be a participatory art forum, as with digital storytelling, which is more and more accessible as low cost recording devices become more available and the Internet makes broadcast space more widely available. Adults with low literacy skills can use digital storytelling to create videos to name their experience, bringing in images that are meaningful. Lise de Villiers (personal communication, September 10, 2014) at the local adult literacy centre talks about the digital storytelling and using video to capture the experiences of women living in poverty or homeless or energy-poor community residents. They need to have a way to recover their sense of self and their identity, which is in danger of overwhelming them as it stands now. Digital storytelling, de Villiers explains, involves the webcasting of learners' stories on the Internet and also includes a community education piece where they develop and distribute these homegrown educational packages to others. Such digital storytelling has the dual benefit of building learners' usable skills as they record and produce the videos and also for educating the public about what their living conditions and housing are. Digital storytelling has the potential to connect the individual story of women (and men) to the story of all the community, upsetting notions of what it means to live in a small rural town far removed from the tourist pictures of halcyon days promoted by government tourism boards. In the telling of our story, through videos, print, orally and in text, we raise the story to a public space where it can be examined, theorized and complicated for new learning and engagement.

Darlene Clover (2006b) recounts the use of cameras with the homeless to help them capture pictures of their environment, and how picture taking helped them gain some control over their circumstances. Clover (2007b) also describes a project called "Myths and Mirrors," situated in Northern Ontario, a region with a great deal of unemployment. In this project, women came together in a multi-art process that included "quilts, murals, mask-making, installation and performance art (i.e., stilt-walking and puppets), popular theatre, and drumming/music" (p. 515). A professional artist accompanied them as they used the arts to work though complex social issues that include unemployment, poverty, abuse, etc. Essentially, the art of Myths and Mirrors is a public representation of private grief and a way of bringing to life—a catalyst if you will— of all the ways in which we deal with many problems in society. As women come together, they deal with oppression and issues, and they confront them systematically.

However, not to be forgotten in the enthusiasm for creative expression is the caution that we are awash with recordings of stories and testimonies that will, for the most part, never be heard. Taping stories for the sake of it is not effective. What stories are captured and how they are used, again, is a critical element. Likewise, some uses of storytelling are very low key, but nonetheless effective. The Glasgow Women's Library (2014), for example, is gathering the stories of women's experiences of feminism through the gathering of badges from the women's movement in a program entitled "Badges of Honour." Badges have been used by women activists for generations, as we remember the small purple white and green badges worn by the suffragettes over a century ago and the more recent manifestations of "this is what a feminist looks like" or "I will be post-feminist in post-patriarchy." Women bring their badges, which are, in fact little pieces of tin or plastic that symbolize struggles, learning and empowerment. Wearing the badges make their politics visible, and the storytelling reveals the intense emotions of coming out, of confronting violence or prejudice, of gaining voice, and publicly declaring their politics.

DISCUSSION

Not every adult educator is an artist, nor are all artists adult educators. While we said above that the arts are not necessarily fine arts or only for professionals, there is the reality that some peole are more able than others to engage the arts and to use it for transformative purposes. It is also true that most of the examples we cited here are about the traditional and creative arts. Technology educator Virginia Eubanks (2011) provides a prime example of how the arts, and more particularly visualization, can be used artistically to theorize experience with technology. In exploring the notion of the Digital Divide with low-income women at a YWCA, she had the women depict their notions and experience of technology before they learned computer skills, thus helping disrupt the masculinist realm of computers and the Internet through the use of artistic ways of knowing.

We may also have to think about how we train the educator or, in this case, the artist as educator. As with any profession, educational ability—or an ability to teach what we know—is not a given, though it may often be assumed. We can benefit from instruction in how to teach, and how foundational models like Jane Vella's (2002) 12 principles of learning or even Knowles' (1970) set of principles about andragogy can help in this process when examined critically and adapted (see Groen & Kawalilak, 2014). We must also be aware of the discomfort people may feel in "performing" art and not too readily or uncritically assume its empowering or transformative potential for all.

We are moving from art as product to art as process, or to justice in the making. As women engage in art, they are enabled with good facilitation (the adult education role) to surface complex issues and to deal with them in a more supportive environment. The art makes it possible for them to be engaged with others, in a more collective enterprise, in a space where they can be supported and challenged on issues and more forward to changing their circumstances and possibly that of others. The issues then can be conjoined with others in a larger, possibly global, scale. In the words of one of Deborah Barndt's (2011) participants, "I hope you will say to yourself: 'I am not alone'" (p. vii).

CHAPTER 5

NETWORK FEMINISM AND
SOCIAL MOVEMENT LEARNING

The mass protests in Cairo's Tahrir Square during the 2011 Egyptian revolution garnered global media attention. The stories that received less attention were the incidents of harassment and abuse endured by women participants. To draw attention to the violence women faced then, and on an ongoing basis, one young woman, Nihal Saad Zaghloul, began connecting with others through social media. They formed a group called *Bassma* (Imprint Movement), raising awareness of violence in the Square and other public spaces, such as trains and buses. Collectively, they are taking action to reclaim these spaces for women to move freely (Reeve, 2014).

Members of Bassma organize patrols to help women who are threatened and work to bring perpetrators to justice. During these patrols, they also speak with people in the streets to raise awareness and to encourage them to take on mediation roles to help defuse potentially harmful situations. Men who have been witness to this violence have joined in solidarity, participating in the patrols to educate other men. The women of Bassma work with the male volunteers to discuss the causes of sexual harassment so that they can be effective advocates who understand the underlying power issues (Reeve, 2014). The women also work with another online activist organization, HarassMap (Zaghloul, 2013), that uses digital mapping to document instances of sexual harassment and violence in Egypt. The organized learning and activism among the women provides a base to share understanding with the broader community on the current conditions facing women, the actions citizens can take, and the legal supports required. This helps Bassma to develop advocacy strategies to educate others and extend their reach through alliances. The learning happens both within the group and throughout the community, providing a springboard to change.

ACTIVISM ON STREETS AND ONLINE

In the 21st century, it is difficult to speak of social movements without considering the impact of information and communication technologies (ICTs) as a way to communicate and mobilize people in a common cause (Foroughi & English, 2013). Definitions of ICTs primarily refer to the range of digital networks available to facilitate the sharing of information through the Internet, including email, social media, and other sites on the World Wide Web, and in some cases pre-computer technologies like community radio (Hafkin & Huyer, 2006). ICTs can also refer to the tools used to access these networks including computers, mobile phones, GPS and other handheld computing devices.

To consider the impact of ICTs, we need to understand not only the tools themselves, "but also the way these tools modify human actions and, in particular, what new actions they make possible" (Toboso, 2011, p. 111; see also Gorman, 2008). Bassma is one of a growing number of women's activist organizations that use ICTs to organize and advocate on incidences of gender-based violence (see FIDH, 2014). Their contribution to mapping VAW brings wider visibility to physical acts of violence.

The role of ICTs in work for social justice is also a growing source of interest for researchers and educators (Irving & English, 2009). ICTs provide a tremendous opportunity for nonprofit organizations active in advocacy, social movement learning, educational programming, networking, and fundraising (Kenix, 2008). Organizations that are not maintaining a vibrant online presence may find themselves at a disadvantage. That said, the work required to maintain that activity is immense and cannot be overlooked. Effective education and campaigning does not just happen by magic, or by the innate nature of the technology itself. Further, there are still many unresolved issues and aspects of learning to pursue in understanding the role of new technologies within our cultures and societies. Feminists, in particular, have drawn attention to the contested nature of the online world and of gendered understandings of technology.

Social Movement Learning and Documentation

Suffrage, temperance, and feminist movements of the 20th century were primarily conducted through in-person events and encounters such as marches, speeches, and other visual signs of protests. Our knowledge of these activities is largely drawn from the preservation of archival images and of the many pamphlets, posters, and manifestos created by these activists to educate the public on the injustices they hoped to overcome. Those archival images of women's mass demonstrations at parliaments or on university campuses still convey powerful messages of the physicality of women's public activism—a physicality that is still vital today despite the popularity of "online activism." For cynics, unfortunately, present day ICT activism evokes an image of a person changing the world from the comfort of an Internet café. Those who are critical of the potential of ICTs for social change use terminology such as *clicktivism*, denoting the ease with which citizens can profess to be engaged with an issue by signing an online petition or sharing news stories or videos on issues that catch their interest, without having to make any serious commitment of time, or risk to their privilege. Messages quickly get lost in the chatter of ineffective online petitions or shifting attention to the next big issue, when yesterday's issues are still unresolved. However, such criticisms risk overlooking the potential strengths of a variety of strategies to effect change. The activists of Bassma use technology to mobilize supporters and document offenses, but their on-street interventions are the actions that confront the violence head on.

There has been some attention paid to informal learning through the processes of participation in social movements, including participation mediated through ICTs. However, there is still much to learn about the intentional work of organizations to be strategic in their education role in the virtual spaces. The work of Bassma highlights the issues of gender within other social justice movements. Feminists working in solidarity with other activists have much to contribute, and both the women's movement and other movements are enriched by this collaborative learning (Bhattacharjya, Birchall, Caro, Kelleher, & Sahasranaman, 2013).

Technology-Mediated Learning in Social Movements

Most of the literature related to ICTs and adult learning focuses on the realm of individual learners (e-learning), or computing skill attainment, though social movement learning in this context is now emerging. We need more work on how ICTs are helpful in mounting social activism campaigns and drawing attention to how women adapt their collective organizing skills to the online realm when addressing issues that affect them. Women with disabilities, for instance, can use ICTs to participate in discussions on services and access. They can also use it to lobby for changes in policy and legislation. ICTs give them freedom from restrictions in accessibility and mobility—if, that is, they have the resources to do so.

REVISITING CRITIQUES OF TECHNOLOGY AND SOCIETY

This chapter revisits our earlier discussions of the use of ICTs by feminist organizations in the context of evolving theorizing on technology and society, the impact of ICTs in social movement learning and activism, and the relevance of these evolving understandings to women's learning and feminist organizing. The growth of new technologies has had a profound impact in many areas of society, and this impact has generated considerable critique and discussion. While some hail the democratizing power of knowledge being in control of the people, others fear for the cognitive effects of information overload and multiple demands on our attention, or the narrowing of interests to self-reinforcing online groups.

Debates persist in the role of ICTs to promote social change. Paolo Gerbaudo (2012) describes the "techno-celebrity discourse" (p. 6) referring to the veneration of the technology as the generator of change. He is critical of the reductionist descriptions of the Arab Spring uprisings as social media revolutions, making the point that this masks the real activism and physicality of mass social mobilizations and imparts the power of the movements to the technology in an almost deified way. In response to this reductionism, Gerbaudo revisits social movement theories along with studies of the role of technology to help contribute a broader understanding of how activists themselves use social media. Notably, Gerbaudo is equally critical of "techno-skeptics" who demonize the realm of ICTs with equal passion. It is this camp that questions the commitment of those "clicktivists" in the cafés.

This tension between champions and skeptics has been equally apparent in feminist theorizing of technology and society, echoing Audre Lorde's (1984) warning that the "master's tools" are imbued with the inequalities imposed by the masters themselves. Is it a matter of ensuring that women have greater opportunity to participate, or are the tools inherently flawed? Now in the 21st century, the argument almost seems to be moot as outright rejection of technology is a near impossibility. Yet, it seems to take so much of our time just to keep up with technological innovations to sort out what is a fad and what is a transformation that we are lagging in developing a deeper, reflective understanding of learning and action in this context.

At the heart of the matter is the reality that technology is created by humans; there are always opportunities for change if we have a clear understanding of the issues. Thus, while we may not be able to reject the presence of ICTs, we can, and should, pursue advances that are more inclusive. For our purposes, we focus on a few discussions within the realm of technology and society that have practical impact in community-based learning and activism. The issues focus on access, typically termed the "digital divide," women's experiences of technology, and women's learning in this context.

From Digital Divide to Digital Inclusion

Alongside the potential of computer technology, concerns about the inequalities that are created or perpetuated through technology have evolved over the past few decades. The concern expressed is that as human activity such as commerce, politics and education is increasingly mediated through technology, those who lack the opportunity for full participation in this realm will be marginalized. Since the 1990s, this concern has often been described as the *digital divide*. Critiques that initially focused on highlighting the regions or populations with or without connectivity (Shade, 1996, 2004) have evolved to integrate analyses of the persistent causes of a *deepening divide* (Van Dijk, 2005). This shift helped to show the related issues and implications for people marginalized by factors such as socio-economic conditions, gender, and disability (Jaeger, 2012). Those sectors of the population that already faced barriers to full participation were now becoming doubly disadvantaged. Critical discussions on ICTs are now reframing the focus from mere access and adaptability to issues of power and control (Eubanks, 2011). Recognition of these issues that extend beyond the technology itself have given rise to a shifted emphasis to "digital inclusion" (Selwyn & Facer, 2007) to stress the active social practices required to bridge the divide. For adult educators, this highlights the openings for learning that encompasses more than technology support or skills workshops.

Mario Toboso (2011) describes *functional diversity*, which places the emphasis on effectiveness rather than access, supporting citizens to make use of technology for their own goals. Toboso describes this in the context of citizens with disabilities, where the emphasis is on citizens appropriating technology to do what they want, instead of looking at it from the perspective of simply replicating the experience of those without disabilities. This requires fuller participation of people with disabilities in the development of technology, and a shift in thinking in a technology field still governed by certain standards of design (Toboso). What we are really talking about here is control.

Organizations working at the community level are very much aware of evolving digital disparities as they help citizens try to navigate social support services. Government bureaucracy has moved from local offices staffed by civil servants to online forms for everything from filing tax returns to seeking employment assistance or disability support. Another opening gap is due to the withdrawal of government funds for community access computer centres, based on the assumption that "everyone" has access, therefore it no longer requires publicly funded support.

Community organizations end up trying to bridge this gap by offering computer access—a particular challenge when the organizations themselves are working with shoestring budgets and inadequate equipment. Yet, these organizations do play an important role in understanding the specific priorities of these marginalized populations. For example, while India has a booming IT sector, many women continue to be marginalized from participation. This inequity highlights the importance of organizations at the community level, such as local health centres, libraries, or women's centres agitating to provide access and training that is actually accessible to women who may have limited mobility opportunities (Vivek & Antony, 2014). In addition to education and support to their clients, organizations are active as advocates. They can help give voice to these sectors that are denied other avenues to make their perspectives visible, and push back to policymakers who may not be aware there is still work to be done.

Gendered Networks: Feminist Issues and ICTs

Feminist theorizing regarding technology's impact and its potential for transformative social change has brought a significant, evolving critique (see Cooks & Isgro, 2005). Earlier theorists such as Donna Haraway (1985, 1991) explored the possibilities for technology to strengthen women's identity collaboration through her call for affinity grouping for women, rather than bifurcation into identity politics. *Cyberfeminism* denotes the theorizing and activities representing women who have claimed their place in using and defining the role of technology in their lives and work (Gajjala & Oh, 2012). The promise of technology to disrupt patriarchy has, however, been challenged by persistent barriers. Cyberfeminism has been criticized for overlooking the women who remain excluded from participation (Van Zoonen, 2001), and has been challenged to increase theoretical rigour (Rosser, 2005, 2012). The term is fading, but the enthusiasm of this theoretical work is still championed by those envisioning the full potential of technology-mediated forms of feminist activism. Analyses have been further enriched by recent studies exploring the rise of revolutionary efforts over the past 5 years and the role of technology in coordinating and mobilizing dissent. Focusing on the Global South, writers such as Ineke Buskens and Anne Webb (2009, 2014; also Buskens, 2013) have featured the use of technology for women's mobilization over the past decade in Africa and Asia.

The progress of the cyberfeminist vision is challenged by continued underrepresentation of women in leadership positions within the field of technology. This highlights the other main thread of critique and analysis that has focused on understanding the perpetuation of masculinist biases of technological innovations. While ICTs are still relatively new, the critiques of gender, technology, and society are not—intellectuals such as Ursula Franklin (1999) have long been asking us to look at the masculinist underpinnings of technology's role in society, and how women's contributions to technology has been largely unrecognized. Those in control of technological systems have all too often left women in end-user and lowly paid roles such as telephone operators and factory workers. Ever the optimist, Franklin maintains a hope that is still relevant:

> The great contribution of women to technology lies precisely in their potential to change the technostructures by understanding, critiquing, and changing the very parameters that have kept women *away* from technology. Only then do we have the possibility of changing the real world of technology itself. (p. 104)

Researchers continue to pursue women's participation and contributions in a technology-rich society. Virginia Eubanks (2011), for example, reports on a 4-year study of training she provided to working class women at the YWCA in Troy, New York State. Her observations reveal tales of the women's frequent engagement with and subjugation by technology—a critique echoing Ursula Franklin's (1999) earlier work on telephone operators and typists. As Eubanks notes, many low income women have extensive work experience with technology through jobs in call centres or as data entry clerks. They also experience the effects of dehumanized technology through their computer-mediated interactions with government departments and social service agencies. Participants in her study describe case files lost in the system, decision-making processes that appear to the client as having been made by the computer, and the acute awareness of surveillance mechanisms.

We still have much to study to see if Haraway's (1985, 1991) vision for increasing collaboration via ICTs has come to fruition. Sceptics would counter that technology's control and surveillance really just further replicates unequal power relations or isolates citizens within their small sphere of shared interests. Recurring studies showing steady declines in the number of women pursuing careers in technology fields. Attempts to explain the low rates include the usual suspects: gendered stereotypes regarding math and technology, lack of role models or mentors for advancement in the field, and the persistence of overt sexism.

However, finding alternatives seem to be harder to address. According to Statistics Canada's (Hango, 2013) tracking of gender and science, technology, engineering and mathematics (STEM), the women who do excel in these disciplines in school are still at a disadvantage compared to their male counterparts. Simplistic answers such as the stereotype of the technophobic female do not hold. Individual exemplars of achievement in the ICT field, including Facebook's Sheryl Sandberg (see also hooks, 2013; Pollitt, 2013), only serve to highlight how few women rise in the ranks of this new boys' club, members of whom are sometimes called "brogrammers" to highlight the masculinized culture that continues to thrive (Wohlsen, 2012).

The implications this has for women working in the community is highlighted by Katrina Peddle, Alison Powell, and Leslie Regan Shade (2012). They describe the field of ICTs, "community informatics" that works to integrate an understanding of the role of technology to support community development and activism. Peddle et al. trace the development of this field of practice and suggest that this field "would be strengthened by further acknowledging feminist contributions in science and technology studies...and by welcoming new feminist interventions in practice and evaluation" (p. 117). As this sector relies on awareness of the social context, feminists in the community are ideally placed to provide the critical analysis to contribute better understandings of inclusion and the potential of technology to promote social change.

More telling are the experiences of women who face the consequences of becoming tall poppies—daring to speak up and be noticed online. Female journalists and feminist organizations are now tracking the growth of cyber misogyny seen in the very gender-specific nature of hate mail, death threats, and other virtual attacks they have received as a consequence of their work and public presence. *Take Back the Tech* is an initiative of the Association for Progressive Communication that participates in the annual international *16 Days of Activism Against Gender-Based Violence* (November 25 to December 10). To raise awareness of this toxic online environment, their website includes a feature on addressing electronically-mediated forms of stalking and harassment (see https://www.takebackthetech.net/).

The mass collaborative online information source, "Wikipedia" has garnered scrutiny for its gender bias, as critics contend the content reflects the perspectives and biases of the majority of its contributors—primarily Western, white males. The underrepresentation of women, both as authors and as subjects of entries (Hargittai & Shaw, 2014), is being met with responsive actions such as "edit-a-thons" including one coordinated by the Royal Society in London, held, appropriately, on Ada Lovelace Day (see https://royalsociety.org/events/2012/wikipedia-workshop/). Feminist instructors have also been organizing class projects encouraging students to write entries by studying a little known woman in history and writing an entry on her. This helps address the imbalance in Wikipedia content, but also opens a space for students and researchers to further their own learning by exploring and documenting the history of these women's lives.

63

Women's Learning and ICTs

How citizens create online spaces to promote learning, awareness-raising, and alliance building to resist oppressive politics and policies is the question asked here. Arguably, as Cindy Royal (2008) says, the Internet is a "gendered space" in which gender-specific cues, images and other content are specifically used to appeal to their intended audience. As we observed in our survey of the websites of women's organizations (Irving & English, 2011), there is an abundance of typically feminine and feminist visual cues as the second-wave feminist colour purple, the iconic ♀ symbol, or stereotypic images of women, flowers, and children. This gendered way of being in cyberspace both helps women claim a space on the Internet but it also silos them as women. What are effective ways to create a vibrant learning space? For this, we need a better understanding of the actual contribution of ICTs to women's social movement learning, to the effective functioning of feminist nonprofit organizations, and about women's access to ICTs.

Relevance for Women's Learning and Action

Given the goal of feminist organizations and movements to promote informal and formal learning opportunities for women, the use of ICTs is integral to the field of adult education and of women's learning in particular. We need to know a great deal more about how the use of ICTs can promote learning, what the barriers are, and what needs to be done to further their supports for informal learning. We also need to assess ICTs' credibility as facilitators of learning.

Feminist nonprofit organizations are sites of informal and nonformal learning where citizens learn advocacy, literacy, and the practices of social democracy. Similarly, the movement promotes learning, though its form is more fluid. For both the social movement and the nonprofit organization, there is a frontline awareness of the relevance of the digital divide. Organizations that "know" their clients find ways to identify and challenge exclusion in its different forms.

A growing body of research highlights the implications for teaching and learning in our knowledge society, though much of the available literature focuses on formal learning environments, such as classroom technology or distance e-learning instructional methods. Incidental and informal learning among women working in the ICT sector has also been studied (Butterwick & Jubas, 2006). The representation of women as instructors has also been considered, as one study notes the reinforcement of gender stereotypes in programs where women may provide the introductory, supportive, experientially connected teaching, but the invited "experts" are still typically men (Vehviläinen & Brunila, 2007). Little has changed now, as creators and developers of technology primarily continue to be men who develop the software and hardware. As long as this imbalance persists, most women will continue to be the users of this technology with little opportunity to be the intellectual force behind its design. Studies tracking the women's participation in information technology programs over the past decade see a worrying trend of declining enrollments. The balance is not going to shift anytime soon.

Women who are educators in this field also require reflexivity to question biases they themselves may bring to the classroom. As Virginia Eubanks (2011) offered computer training for the women at the YWCA, she recognized a contradiction between what she thought they needed to bridge the digital divide and what the women themselves sought. Eubanks realized that the skills training that she was able to offer was not addressing the power imbalances that perpetuated inequality, nor did it acknowledge the women's existing knowledge and experience that had come through mistakes, low-waged jobs, and encounters with bureaucratic surveillance systems. Their prior learning about technology conditioned them to be skeptical of the technology and the potential of further training. Through her analysis of the working women's experiences with technology and power, Eubanks was able to see that a far better goal of these training programs might have been to cultivate what she terms "critical technological citizens" (p. 30). In some ways, this harkens back to the insights of 1970s' second wave feminism, which supported consciousness raising to understand and politicize personal experiences of injustice. Working within nonformal learning programs in community-based organizations, potentially allows for more responsive and creative approaches than programs that are more rigidly dictated for job training with measurable employable outcomes.

The effective and attentive training that Eubanks (2011) came to appreciate stands in contrast with short-track, predesigned programs which generally do not allow for careful digestion of information, questioning, analysis, and connection with previous experience and knowledge, nor do they create spaces to consider alternative plans for action. In short, speed bypasses the learning cycle, especially critical reflection. Missing also is the context and the socio-cultural aspects that are crucial to understanding events and their implications. Mulling over possibilities is an important activity, though it is often forgotten in an environment that equates speed with efficiency. The time between mulling and moving on, or acting, needs to be extended so that deliberation can do its work.

There is no doubt that teaching in an online environment can be challenging for those who normally work in a classroom environment. In writing of their experiences in learning to teach online, Wendy Kraglund-Gauthier, Ottilia Chareka, Ann Murray Orr and Andrew Foran (2010) write about the challenges the virtual space had on their assumptions about pedagogy. Their research anecdotes reveal a struggle in coming to terms with feeling a loss of the power afforded to them by a physical presence in a classroom and control over the physical space. The ability to control the medium in which learning occurs is lessened in online contexts. Yet, there are also opportunities for community-embedded learning that enables people to act on their learning in their work. Reflecting on a program with development practitioners, the lead facilitator found the potential of deliberation a strength of online learning, as participants were able to create their own private learning space (Lee, Irving, & Francuz, 2014), which provided a balance to the over-emphasis on group work or circle work that we note elsewhere. Online learning in this context, requires an understanding the overlapping spaces of people's presence online, in their homes, at their workplaces, and in their own minds.

Social Movement Learning

Mass protests and uprisings have shown the use of ICTs for awareness raising, mobilizing, and documenting social movements in action. Mainstream news abounds with stories of the role social media has played in demonstrations, protests and revolutions (Hall & Clover, 2005, 2006). We saw this with the fascination of the press in activists' use of Twitter during the 2009 political protests in Iran. This was a foreshadowing of the key role that social media would come to play in the Arab Spring. Millions around the world were able to follow daily actions as the 2012 revolution in Egypt unfolded. The use of social media to organize the protestors contributed to the media's nickname of the uprising as "the twitter revolution" (Gerbaudo, 2012). The state, aware of this phenomenon, strove to curtail access through blackouts and other forms of disruptive technology.

The tension regarding the risks of increasing reliance on technology for mobilization is expressed through fears of police surveillance, or of state crackdowns by disrupting or blocking communication networks. More recent discussions of similar state control in democracies have further heightened calls to track cases of censorship and other limits to freedom of information. Critics note that limiting access to information channels such as social media violates democratic principles— yet, while democracies are quick to criticize authoritarian states for jamming signals, they too are exploring ways to monitor and control communication when dissent emerges in their own land (Oyieke, Dick, & Bothma, 2013). Ignoring the influence of the Internet in the context of such state and corporate control is not an option, especially for marginalized, threatened, and politically disadvantaged groups who realize the need to have their voices heard and the need to use the Internet and other mobile devices for lifelong learning purposes.

Mainstream media's coverage of events has also dovetailed with international advocacy efforts to increase visibility of ad hoc campaigns, and garner global support for atrocities that may have once gone unnoticed beyond the community in which it happened. Witness the international pressure on India to address the systemic violence against women in the country following widespread outrage over the case of a woman on a bus who was gang raped and murdered (Ayed, 2013). Gahlot (2014) reports that real progress has been slow, but that action is more likely in cases that receive public attention. One of the most celebrated cases of the collaboration of media and activism is that of the 2014 Nobel Laureate Malala Yousafzai. Her activism began as a child blogger for the BBC Urdu Service describing the conditions schoolgirls faced in her region of Pakistan (BBC, 2012). Amidst growing international attention to her promotion of girls' education, she was shot by the Taliban (Yousafzai, 2013). This act effectively made Malala a household name around the world for those who advocated for girls' rights.

Yet, media profiles and awareness-raising are not enough. An umbrella organization in India, Women Power Connect (see http://www.womenpowerconnect.org/), provides the background and analysis needed to ensure that the awareness raised by high profile cases translate into in policy change that has effects beyond the individual cases. In this way, moving beyond the headlines of the infamous Delhi rape case, some real progress is being made. A comedy troupe in India became an online sensation with a video sketch they created to respond to prevalent "blame the victim" attitudes expressed following another high profile rape (All India Bakchod, 2013). The video presents disturbing images of bright young women using irony to expose the absurdity of victim-blaming language. Such digital advocacy tools can be used to inspire people in disparate regions who face similar situations and who can adapt such online evolutions of popular street theatre. While the medium of online video is still quite new, the use of drama and satire has a long tradition in activism to make messages engaging and memorable.

Youtube and other creative media have become familiar and helpful as teaching and learning spaces. TED Talks, for instance, have become a popular venue for learned people to talk about topics for an extended period, beyond the typical media sound bite. This format, however, is still a tightly scripted, lecture-based activity, leaving little room for learner engagement and critique, and there is growing criticism of this intentionally casual, though highly managed, style (Harouni, 2014; Romanelli, Cain, & McNamara, 2014). More grassroots are the lively responses to a European Commission initiative in 2012 to engage young women in science studies. The EU sponsored online video called "Science: It's a girl thing" received widespread ridicule because it seemingly reinforced gender stereotypes (Revkin, 2012). What was interesting was how quickly this critique expanded to stimulate an explosion of creative responses, also by video. Some of the videos parodied the original's content, while others documented real stories of how women saw themselves as scientists in field such as medicine or biology, providing a counternarrative to the stereotype. The use of ICT as an artistic medium facilitates a response that is instantaneous, global, and creative. The use of technology and the arts to change opinions, to challenge, is encouraging.

Idle No More, as we noted in earlier chapters, is an ongoing advocacy movement led by Indigenous peoples in Canada. The campaign began when four women in Saskatchewan initiated a protest against the federal government's proposed legislation that would reduce environmental protection of many waterways (Mann, 2012). The tagline "Idle No More" took hold and protests emerged across the country, initially in support of this issue, but quickly spread to encompass other longstanding grievances and issues relating to Indigenous rights, environmental protection, and awareness raising of endemic violence against Indigenous women. The online activity of Idle No More has ebbed and flowed over the past few years, in synch with degree of mobilization of the various groups that have formed across the country. As a process that has no clear organizational or leadership structure, the Idle No More tag is invoked by numerous individuals or groups affiliated with Indigenous activism when new protests arise in response to emergent political issues or acts of injustice or violence. Protests have taken on a variety of creative physical forms, including sit-ins, marches (Carleton, 2012), as well as an ongoing active online presence. Idle No More campaigners also have adopted an increasingly popular technology mediated street action: the "flash mob." Protesters will appear in a public place at a specific time, engage in a surprise public act, such as a dance or song, and then quickly disperse. The actors use social media to coordinate the physical action, and to share the video afterwards. While much of the mobilization occurs through dispersed groups connecting via social media, Idle No More campaign maintains a central website (see http://idlenomore.ca) that is now archiving stories, artwork, and other documentation so others can learn of their work and develop ideas for their own activism.

Learning and Activism in Feminist Organizations

High profile campaigns and "viral videos" aside, questions remain regarding the sustained ability of organizations to make effective use of ICTs in the nonprofit sector to further their goals of promoting social movement learning and activism. Working mostly in the community, feminist organizations typically represent socially and economically marginalized citizens and are often located in a marginalized space themselves within the nonprofit world, and, as such, have to use a variety of teaching and learning approaches. They provide educational programming; social movement learning about advocacy, change, and feminism; literacy services; and mentoring and coaching. They support informal and self-directed learning through literature and other media as well as casual conversation (Livingstone, 2012). And, they have had a long history of enjoining learning and education with political intent. Many feminist social action groups of the 1970s have formalized over time to create the well-established community-based women's resource centres, political lobbying groups, anti-violence agencies, and shelters that exist in the nonprofit sector today. Since the 1990s, feminist organizations have moved their visibility online through the creation of websites to ensure their presence in this vital realm.

Earlier studies on the adoption of ICTs by the nonprofit sector emphasised the importance for organizations to focus their attention on their online presence, citing their position of trust within the communities in which they work (Te'eni & Young, 2003). With the explosion of content available online in the decade since this observation was made, the ability to assess the reliability of information is every bit as important, if not more so. An organization's various activities in education, advocacy, networking, and fundraising all require a current and credible online presence to reach clients, supporters, and policymakers today.

The lack of physical presence, so integral to second wave feminism, diffuses a concentration of energy and time. In terms of the feminist movement, there was a time when groups met in the flesh and talked to each other; communication was enacted through the body, mind, and spirit. Now the online chats take the body out and serve as atomized spaces where different women do different projects, raising questions of a diffuse learning space that undermines the strength of earlier feminist organizing through collective meeting and discussion in resource centres or feminist bookstores (Onosaka, 2006). Also, meeting online further renders invisible those who are not participating. That said, a study out of Norway shows that the more the voluntary organization uses the Internet, the more it gathers people and participants together for in-person meetings that is making a blend of two styles of operation (Eimhjellen, 2014). This is not and cannot be an either–or world.

There seem to be innumerable missed opportunities for feminist organizations to share knowledge, engage in community-based learning, and give voice to the marginalized. Adult educators who work in the community sphere need not only to look at successful attempts to use ICTs for social movement learning and activism, but also to ways in which ICTs are not being used effectively. As our "classroom space" is much larger than a higher education classroom, we need to be aware of the barriers and enhancers to informal learning in the community, on the Internet, and in nonprofit organizations, especially those oriented to social movement learning. Our ability to keep pace with the use of ICTs for learning is a measure of our ability to address adult learners' needs. Yet, a large question remains about how technology-media learning works at the grassroots and how it moves beyond communication to community building, which is the heart of social movement learning.

In many ways, the real point of the discussion is that the issues are the same. Whose knowledge is valid, that is, who decides whose work is valid is the central question—whose knowledge is created, controlled, and shared? Much of the media is controlled by the corporate world, and that is still the issue for feminists worldwide. The creators of a great deal of Internet content are still men and the high end technology jobs are still filled by men. As end users of the technologies, albeit for highly political and organizing purposes, we still need to be critical of the technology, its creators, and its uses.

In an earlier study (Irving & English, 2011), we systematically analysed 100 websites of feminist organizations. We examined their activities of (a) promoting adult learning; (b) participating in awareness raising of issues and promoting advocacy; (c) demonstrating organizational transparency and credibility; and (d) promoting community building and engagement. As researchers, we were interested in implications for women's resource centres and issues of knowledge sharing, facilitation of adult learning, and networking in the broader context. We found that while many feminist organizations had a web presence, one third to one half of the websites were in disarray, making them ineffective for education or reliable information. It was clear these sites were not reflecting the active programming that was occurring on site. There was also little awareness of the potential of archiving their information that others could use for learning and research. Many organizations seem to have stalled in the cyberfeminist period of showing enthusiasm for the technology by developing an online presence and collaborating online, then lacking the ability to maintain it. One of the main issues that this study raised was the continued underfunding of feminist organizations. The inability to maintain a crucial communication link is as significant now as it was then. It likely serves as an indicator of all the other crucial tasks that the organizations have to downplay or set aside until more funding is available.

The sad reality is, that several years on, many of the centres included in our study, have closed their doors due to cuts in funding. Anyone engaging effectively online has to be tech savvy and dedicated to sharing timely updates—goals that can be harder than it sounds for thinly-stretched NGOs or volunteer-based community groups. Feminist organizations and movements have a particular interest in maintaining a vibrant virtual presence. Yet, beyond scattered case studies, little is known about how effectively these organizations utilize the Internet to accomplish their objectives, or how the use of ICTs could improve their sustainability rather than act as yet another strain on limited resources.

In their earlier work, Buskens and Webb (2009) described examples of "empowerment thresholds" which they explained demonstrated those actions that women were able to make substantive gains by making use of ICTs to support their activities. They emphasise that ICT use is but one component of a number of social, cultural, and economic factors that women mobilize to make a change in their lives. These examples provide rich opportunities for learning.

GenderIT.org, a branch of the Association for Progressive Communication (APC), advocates for women's rights regarding ICTs, and is proposing revisions to sections of the Beijing Platform for Action on communication, to bring it up to date with advances in technology over the past two decades. The key priority areas they identify include such issues as access, political agency, privacy, STEM, and addressing global issues such as the environment and violence against women, including cyber abuse (Association for Progressive Communication, 2015).

The Association of Women in Development (AWID) has developed a critical capacity to use ICTs to profile and challenge what is happening to and with women in the world, and to analyse how women are affected. They can, in fact, be considered a clearinghouse for global feminism. Their weekly email digests compile news stories, features, information sources, and action alerts from around the world, and particularly emphasise content from the Global South. They identify information sharing as an important component of their mandate, as well as the promotion of skillbuilding to support other organizations in their information exchange efforts. Policy level research is geared towards contributing to international decision making on development practice. AWID also places a strategic focus on young women's activism, both to ensure that issues of concern to young women are integrated into the overall work of the organization, but also to support the development of the next generation of feminist leaders.

Lessons on Learning

Selwyn, Gorard, and Furlong's (2006) finding that considerable informal learning is occurring on the Internet underscores the need to pay close attention to what citizens research and how. If adult educators located in feminist organizations want to ensure quality learning experiences with credible content, they need to pay close attention to how they are doing in this regard and to make learners want to access their sites. Considering the potential of ICTs to increase educational participation and outcomes, factors which Selwyn et al. emphasise, adult educators need to think a great deal about their content, their methods, their presentation, but most importantly, their clients and audience.

Here we make some suggestions for the use of ICTs and feminist movements and organizations. We see that women need to be vigilant about the content they access and distribute online.

There seems to be three main streams here: access, use, and sustainability.

Access and control. Access in this context looks beyond the numbers of handheld devices and Wi-fi hot spots, to consider the issues of inclusion, control, and power. Like the YWCA women of Virginia Eubanks' (2011) work, simply learning technical skills does little to overturn systemic discrimination. In the field of library science, user instruction was renamed years ago to "information literacy" to emphasise the importance of finding and making use of information. Information literacy is a necessary competency much like language literacy and numeracy. "Critical information literacy" like critical education, brings in the socio-political analysis of where information comes from and in whose interests it serves (Elmborg, 2006; Smith, 2013). Maria Accardi (2013) takes the process of critical information literacy a step further by integrating principles of feminist pedagogy in facilitating learning that overturns standard library instruction models. Given the speed and volume of material, of what people forward, tweet, and read on any given day, the need to hone critical skills is vital.

The changing nature of the digital divide should not hide the fact that it still exists, though in more complex ways. Until greater inclusion is accomplished, uncritical reliance on ICTs will continue to leave behind people who may not have money to buy these technologies, or the literacy to use them critically. How organizations work in continuing to address the pervasiveness of the digital divide in whatever form it takes is still a priority. This is a more complex issue than access alone. The Appropriate Technology movement of the 1960s–1980s may provide some suggestions in grassroots organizational responses. There was a great effort not just to make existing technology available, but to find local-level adaptations and support local-level inventions.

71

Design, use, and evaluation. The shift in emphasis from access to control prompts us to question whose knowledge is represented and who contributes to making information available to others. This is about design that reflects the user. In the corporate sector, much time and effort is put into design. News sites are replete with "click bait" to attract people to their websites. In the nonprofit sector, how much time goes into design, testing, and evaluation of websites is an issue. One size fits all templates do not work for organizations who draw their strength from local connections and knowledge of local communities.

Practitioner-researcher Jenny Horsman (2012) has looked closely at the role of the web in transformative learning for women who are both literacy challenged and affected by violence. Focusing on her own website learning, she points out that some women do not learn from the website, many do not use it, and many are resistant to it. So, in addition to posting articles and papers on women and violence on her website, she offers workshops and other educational experiences to assist women. In many ways this form of learning furthers literacy and women's rights and helps build the movement. Yet, Horsman questions if ICTs alone are enough to get a movement going, especially since most revolutions start out small, not large. Having organizations track their own webspace and be apprised of what is working and what needs attention is important work to do, but challenging.

Eimhjellen's (2014) research shows that engaged online activity of an organization has the potential to support or reinforce engaged in-person activity. Evidently, users can see beyond the technology itself to value the strengthening of human interaction, whether or not it is technologically mediated. That said, Eimhjellen's study did not show a high degree of two-way communication online between organizations and their membership.

A related issue involves evolving usage patterns by people. How organizations reach out into the online spaces where citizens are congregating is a priority for those trying to figure out where information is expected to be. When protests erupted following the police shooting of a youth in the United States in 2014, people were following the events as they happened using Twitter feeds. However, some noticed that Facebook was not keeping up with events, apparently because different algorithms were being used to record information. Facebook prioritizes information based on people's profiles and friends, while Twitter is more attuned to "trends," though how information is manipulated in these sites evolves constantly (Zerehi, 2014). The lessons are that citizens are going to the platforms they know to find information (i.e., their social media links rather than directly to news websites) and that they need to be aware of how information they receive is filtered.

The cases described by Anne Scott and Margaret Page (2001) and Bharat Mehra, Cecelia Merkel, and Ann Peterson Bishop (2004) provide methods and strategies for participatory website work. Although, these studies were written over a decade ago—a long time in the context of ICT development—participatory processes are adaptable to change. Organizations might also look internally at strategies for integrating their website into their overall mission for justice (Smith, 2007).

Sustainability: Documenting social movement learning. Activists in the midst of a social action may not think of their work in historical perspective, yet much of what we know of social movements is preserved in the material produced from their activities. It can be difficult for them to store and archive their activities for long-term observation and study of the movement (Choudry & Kapoor, 2010). In addition to the role of ICTs to connect people for mobilizations during the critical times of response to injustice, they are also vital for the preservation of the documentation of these activities. When Pierre Walter (2007) studied the Clayoquot Sound environmental protest in British Columbia, he based much of his research on electronic documentation from the environmental organizations involved.

Archives of women's social activism through the 20th century (Wieringa, 2008) are treasure troves of information documenting their ideas and activities through pamphlets, research studies, testimonies, posters, and a myriad of other artistic forms. Their work in producing handmade newsletters and pamphlets grew and formalized to become women's presses, which have been conveyers of women's ideas for centuries, a point stressed by bell hooks (2000). These publications, in turn, spurred the creation of feminist bookstores in the 1970s–1980s which became learning hubs for activists in the surrounding community (Onosaka, 2006). The popularity today of "zines" for activism, self-exploration and learning (Cameron, 2011) evokes the hand-made style and immediacy of these earlier print forms using art, collage, and poetry.

Over the decades, Guerrilla Girls, who work to expose gender bias in arts institutions in the United States, has grown from organizing visible street protest to making feminist issues visible online through their use of stunning images and sly humour. They still also rely on very visible physical spaces of street art and billboards (see http://www.interviewmagazine.com/art/guerrilla-girls#/). While some may say that this ICT venue is necessary for youth participation, even well-known elder activists such as the Raging Grannies also have stepped up to record and share their songs and street actions online (Roy, 2004).

DISCUSSION

This discussion is a reminder of the need to preserve e-histories of women's organizations, just as the early waves of feminism were documented through the preservation of leaflets, manifestos, badges, banners, posters, and related paraphernalia of protest. Questions arise about how present online actions will be preserved for posterity. Activist archivists claim that documenting and preserving the work of marginalized groups is a political act and are creating methods to support this work (Bly & Wooten, 2012). For example, archivists in the United States are identifying new ways to work with activists to preserve records from the Occupy Movement (Young, 2012). The Occupy Archives Working Group has worked to educate participants on the importance of archiving. They also realized the importance of institutional support to ensure archival material is accessible to the public for the long term (Evans, Perricci, & Roberts, 2013). The work can be tricky when the main actors are coming together from outside the context of formal organizations, and sustainability is a challenge if there is no large institutional collaborator.

Part of this process involves education regarding awareness-raising on the importance of documenting protest and activism, as well as practical guides on how to do it, including digital preservation tips such details as including text descriptions within digital image files and data storage to avoid what archivists warningly call a "digital dark age." This may be overlooked as public attention seems to focus on the hyper surveillance potential of digital media, that things cannot be forgotten with systems storing all of our digital activity. Long term preservation of what we want to keep is an ongoing concern.

RELIGION, WOMEN,
AND ADULT EDUCATION

Of all the factors that affect women's lives internationally, religious fundamentalism is one of the most serious in that it has implications for women's well-being and health and for the population at large. Given the influence that religions, especially fundamentalist factions, have in the fabric of societies worldwide, it is important to examine their place and their effects. An example of how seriously women's groups take religion is illustrated by the formation of the Coalition of African Lesbians (CAL), a resistance movement against homophobia. CAL brings together 30 organizations in 19 countries, all of which are fighting for the rights of persons who identify as lesbian, gay, bisexual, transgendered, or queer (LGBTQ). CAL's members have a strategic direction that involves careful and systematic analysis of factors such as religious and state fundamentalism, crises in democracy, capitalism, patriarchy, and militarism. CAL has determined that all of these factors contribute to a culture of violence, and they have put measures in place to address them. In particular, CAL is protesting a fundamentalist religious system that oppresses and endangers a significant portion of the population, especially women.

There is no doubt that women involved in adult education have had a troubled relationship with fundamentalist religions, in large measure because these religious groups are perceived to be oppressive in terms of their stance on reproductive freedom, women's equality, and the education of women (Harper, English, & MacDonald, 2010). Spirituality, too, has been dismissed, though it is clear that spiritualty differs from religious fundamentalism. Those who do take up discussions of spirituality are quick to distance themselves from oppressive religious groups, and indeed from most religious groups, choosing to make careful distinctions of meaning (e.g., English & Tisdell, 2010). Arguably, though, the use of distinctions is a luxury of Western women who can pick and choose allegiances and beliefs.

This chapter begins with the notion that it is difficult to challenge and analyse any system such as religion if its existence is not first recognized. It is equally difficult when the role it plays in many adult educators' lives, especially for women, it also not recognized. From a global perspective, religion is a force that needs to be met head on, especially when religion means religious fundamentalism or a rigid and strict adherence to religious beliefs, often as a reaction to liberal attitudes and change. AWID, for instance, has dealt with notions of religion and fundamentalism by launching a major international effort to highlight and exchange strategies for working on the ground to counteract fundamentalism in countries such as Mexico,

Indonesia, and Lithuania. In writing about this issue, Shareen Gokal, Rosanna Barbero, and Cassandra Balchin (2011) observed that AWID has reason to be concerned: its international research shows that 69% of activists from 160 countries surveyed "believe religious fundamentalisms obstruct women's rights more than other political forces" (p. 5). Gokal et al. are careful to note that while fundamentalism is a definite problem in development circles, religion is not necessarily so, as they see religiosity as widespread and having the potential to be a force for political and democratic rights, as well as a force for diversity and inclusion (p. 6). The challenge for practitioners and researchers, however, is that religion has largely been ignored or dismissed in discussions of development (Klassen, 2003; Marshall & Van Saanen, 2007; Nussbaum, 2000) with some exceptions (Audet, Paquette, & Bergeron, 2013; Berkley Center, 2011; Deneulin & Bano, 2009; Rakodi, 2011; Tadros, 2011).

Religion is a factor in policies globally. In a special issue of *Canadian Woman Studies* devoted to women and religion, writer Ann Porter (2012) observes that not only is the neoliberal agenda (e.g., market and economic stress) of the Canadian government being accentuated but also the pressure that come to bear to make it a neo-conservative (moral and religious overtones) rule. Since the current Prime Minister Harper's tenure began, we have seen an increase in the appointment of religious figures or people who have strong ties to evangelical, traditional family oriented values and to anti-choice perspectives. This is seen also in other countries with social democratic backgrounds where the traditional staid and regressive are being elected, who proceed to curtail progressive policies and programs in the name of fiscal responsibility. As Ann Porter demonstrates, neo-conservatism and neoliberalism go hand in hand and are at times difficult to distinguish, in part because it is convenient for the social conservative to hide behind fiscal policies framed as demonstrating fairness and responsibility. Indeed, that has been the case in Canada where funding for women's programs like the Status of Women has been cut. We see the government here as going backwards on women's issues, sometimes not naming the issue as women's but attacking benefits and rights that women need, such as employment assistance, childcare, etc.

We use the theoretical framework of hybridity and third space (Bhabha, 1994) to help understand the complexity of the lives of women who work with religious/spiritualty issues internally and in their adult education and development workplaces. As subject/actors in their own lives, women must negotiate boundaries of North and South, and North America and international identities. For those who have been nurtured by religious traditions, the challenges of working internationally can be quite complex. They usually are expected to move between cultures and states, as if unaffected and unchanged, as if notions of what it means to be a feminist or a believer do not matter to the work at hand. Those educators who travel to and from the South as itinerants in adult education and development work must constantly negotiate differences. While they negotiate internal struggles, as women who work for justice on a global scale, they also run the risk of attracting external labels and stereotypes such as Westernizer, proselytizer, and feminist.

This chapter gives voice to adult educators' stories and their political negotiation of identity and position, especially as it relates to religion. The space that is identified here is a third space, where, in Homi Bhabha's (1995) words, "an effort has to be made to live on the cusp, to deal with two contradictory things at the same time without either transcending or repressing that contradiction" (p. 82). As those involved in education work know, specialists may see the ill effects of religious fundamentalism but still have roots in religious traditions. Contradictions and resistances are at the heart of this third space discussion; when applied to women's relationship to organized religion, these contradictory issues are cast in sharp relief (Gokal et al., 2011; Mejiuni, 2012; Ver Beek, 2000). Examples include statements like, "I am a member of a religious group, and I resist many of the teachings" or "We consider ourselves spiritual and not religious, but I still identify as Protestant on a census form." Readers of this chapter will likely know peers who grew up Catholic (or Muslim, or Anglican) and who were faithful to that religious tradition until their social justice leanings could find no home there anymore; yet, they claim a spiritual identity for themselves and they live the vocation that was nurtured by the values and encouragement of their religion of birth.

THEORETICAL FRAMEWORK

We rely here on several bodies of theory that both inform and complicate the discussion. The first of these is the postcolonial writings of Bhabha (1994), particularly his insights into the interconnected ideas of third space, hybridity, translation, and negotiation. For Bhabha, third space is about identity politics, interrogating that most enigmatic space in our lives that makes us aware that identity is always in flux. We change our mind, we hold two opinions at once, we have love/hate relationships with ourselves and with others. In recognizing this third space, we are asked to acknowledge the ways we collude and collide with structures, essentialisms, and mixed notions of identity (see Baker, 2007; Hollinshead 1998). For Bhabha, third space is a fluid interstitial space that allows for the transitions and transnational nature of being in a global world. In engaging and developing these concepts and ideas related to postcolonialism, Bhabha has been able to advance some of the more complicated aspects of identity and to show that identity is neither stable nor fixed, that it allows actors to hold a variety of positions and views simultaneously, moving between and among competing notions of what one should be and do.

Born in India, and later moving to England and then to the United States, Bhabha (1994) has been affected by colonialism in a real and tangible way, experiencing geographic and identity dislocation through his moves from culture to culture. His scholarship reflects his interest in the ways in which the colonial subject begins his or her "presencing" or becoming in the world, after generations of oppression. The colonial subject recreates and constantly rewrites the narrative of being, and in the process complicates simplistic notions of a unitary subject position. Yet, Bhabha's work is not limited to those from "colonies" or imperial contexts like his own in

India. Insights from postcolonialism extend to those in the West who experience similar displacement and unsettled notions of belonging and identity, which often involve religion (see Khan, 2000). Bhabha has been interested in how the displaced person shifts and shapes between countries and identities, with the displacement affecting identity and creating ambivalence in one's relationship to nations and cultures. He has argued that the once stable subject position becomes unmoored and challenges essentialist readings of what it means to be Indian or Muslim or female. Leona English (see English & Mayo, 2012) and others have been drawn to third space because of the need for new conceptualizations of the in-between and inexplicable spaces and occasions that are part of our conversations. Whether one is Indian or Canadian, insights from postcolonial literature can help us understand our relationships to the other and ourselves.

Third space is not about shying away from challenge, nor is it about a wishy-washy middle, even if it is a radical middle. In fact, a consequence of third space negotiating may involve "taking sides," dependent on the situation. Third space is about possibility and choice, not about consensus and coming to agreement forcefully or about reinforcing mediocrity. Rather than being focused on development problems or issues, third space sees life, identity, race, and religion as simultaneously complicated and contradictory. The instability of the third space is seen as opportunity for changing to fit the situation and the challenges at hand. For instance, a Canadian working in Egypt in nonformal education with an international nongovernmental agency may have difficulty in knowing which country is home and which is the host country; indeed, neither may be home any more.

The in between third space allows for hybridity and indeed it is where hybridity is enacted and begins. Hybridity is both "epistemologically unstable and politically enigmatic, not open to dissection by the Enlightenment inheritance and its rationalism" (Baker, 2007, p. 24). Its characteristic is interrogative, asking questions and opening up new spaces. Hybridity is a complementary term that works against the ways in which we have been coded or reduced to our functions or tasks in society. It literally connotes the ways in which we slide seamlessly between and among places, depending on context, players, and issues. As an indeterminate space of being, it is a descriptor of the lives of some female educators who move between countries and practices and who must negotiate religious challenges and benefits. An American-born development worker in India may find points of connection with Hinduism that Christianity no longer provides in her life; yet, she may continue to self-identify as Christian.

Little has been written about the lives of women in adult education or development work. There has been a greater interest in exploring issues of dealing with organized (especially fundamentalist) religion (e.g., Deneulin & Bano, 2009; Khan & Basha, 2008; Mejiuni, 2012). A review of the past 10 years of development journals such as *Community Development, Community Development Journal* and the *Canadian Journal of Development Studies* yields little in the way of life history, personal narrative, or identity discussions of development workers in any sphere, let alone women. Yet, there is an emergent interest in the role of faith in development. Institutes such as the Berkley Center at Georgetown University have created the "Practitioners and Faith-Inspired Development" program (Berkley Center, 2011; see also Marshall & Van Saanen, 2007) to document the role of faith in the lives of activists and policy specialists working with issues such as HIV/AIDS, malaria, education, governance, and gender. Yet, even this project is limited in that it is mainly focused on personal belief and includes little in the way of complicated religious relationships, either personal or professional. Women in these narratives are often presented as bold, unflinching opponents of religious leaders, such as Marguerite Barankitse from Burundi who demanded that her bishop give the people their land (Berkley Center). There is no room for self-doubt, wavering, indecision; in short, they are much like male heroes and male leaders. What they hold in common, along with their prowess, is their deep commitment to their faith.

The same is true of narratives of women religious, such as those assembled by Maureen Fiedler (2010): they are brave, undaunted, and monolithic. Lost in the telling are the moments of indecision, broken identity, and resistance that are usual parts of human development. The intricacies of the person are forgone, and the literature is replete with tales of heroism, strength incalculable, and acts of defiance. There is no internal dialogue noted. Bhabha (1995), conversely, in talking about women's problems with religious fundamentalism, celebrates those who open up political spaces "reconjugating, recontextualising, translating the event into the politics of communities and public institutions" (as cited in Mitchell, 1995, p. 88). Another helpful approach is by Ched Myers and Matthew Colwell (2012), who ask us to begin breaking down boundaries of state, place, and religion in order to embrace all people, especially immigrants. The place of complication and friction needs to be unearthed and storied so that the reader has points of connection and identification.

This chapter is informed by an interpretative study of three women from Africa and North America who work in international adult education. The participants had at least 5 years in development work, had worked internationally, and were interested in religion and spirituality and its relationship to their work. The women were involved in a range of occupations and employed by an NGO or INGO; all were working to improve social and economic conditions in the Global South. Two of the women were from Canada, a country that has had a key role in development work through agencies such as Cuso International and its many faith-based organizations (FBOs) such as Jesuit Volunteers Overseas. Each of them identified as being raised in a religious tradition, though they varied on whether they were still connected to religion or a more broad-based sense of spirituality. The data were analysed using the constant comparative method. Questions centred on the background factors that influenced their choice of international development work, the nature and extent of their international experiences, and the motivations and supports for their practice and their political and spiritual or religious commitments.

Women who work in adult education on a global scale inhabit a world that is in flux; their identities are being continuously constructed by the push and pull of countries, subject positions, religious customs, political alliances, all dependent upon the call of the situation and the players at hand. Their lives, even in casual conversation, are revealed to be in transit and between several worlds, real and imagined, their life challenge is to consciously and unconsciously negotiate the positions that are ascribed to them and through which they become agents in their own lives. The categories of third space, translation and negotiation, and subaltern speech are used to describe their experience of working in and through religion.

Third Space Educators

International adult educators are neither colonizers nor saviours of yesteryear; they are aware of the way in which they are positioned and held by the viewer and the context. If their passport country is in the West, they may find themselves working in INGOs and community-based spheres in the Global South, negotiating where they belong and where home is. If their home countries are in the Global South, they may find themselves in NGOs and INGOs on the ground in their home, or in UN-type missions in other nations. To be a female development worker is to be a resister of labels and codes such as the good/evil American, the good/bad Hindu or Muslim mother, and the good woman, all of which are attempts at regulation and control. Theirs is a push and pull of signifiers, including religious labels and constraints that have shifting meaning depending on context and players. To be effective, they need to engage critically with the religious and cultural rules, politics, geography, and the people, whether they are in Sudan, Southeast Asia, or South Africa. In no arena is this more relevant than in their relationship with religion or the regulating discourses of fundamentalist religious groups that they may have imbibed in youth or in the environment in which they presently operate. They have resisted the "rules of recognition" through which they have been signified and effected into being (Bhabha, 1994, p. 100).

It is not uncommon for those who work as development specialists to have started as volunteers who went overseas to the so-called Third World for 1- or 2-year commitments. Some taught English as a second language (ESL), others worked in agriculture, and others were assistants in offices and community centres. Typical among them is a background in religious organizations, sometimes from birth, that fostered a sense of responsibility and a thrust to do good in the world. It is this background and the belief structure that accompanies it that sometimes positions them for later ambivalence and contradiction.

Typical are those who grow up in a religious home but as young adults became involved with religious groups that nurtured their spirituality and commitment to development. For example, one participant in the research, Mary Jean, spent most of her adult life working for justice and education in either Canada, India, or in South America, Her life story evidences her challenge to live out her convictions and negotiate a tension with religious commitment. In our interview, she talked of her present role in coordinating Canadian youth in their human rights work in Asia. She has been affiliated with a Christian justice group for more than 20 years. Although her commitment to the justice mandate of her organization has strengthened, as has her own understanding of gospel justice, her affiliation with Christian churches has wavered because she has had "trouble relating it to her faith." Her personal commitment to activism is deep, and she is not "interested in activism for activism's sake." Part of her mandate is to coordinate the departure and the repatriation education and support for the youth who have been overseas. She herself has an ambivalent relationship to the organization and to the larger institutional frameworks of religion.

This margin in the lives of the young adult educators becomes a third space in which they are trying to find a home, yet are unsettled because home is no longer identifiable. They want to be overseas and home at once, but do not quite fit in either the home or the host country. They are in a place that is "imbued with intent, that attempts to challenge, change, or retain particular circumstances, relating to societal relations, processes, and/or institutions" (p. 16). In their shifting geographic and cultural spaces, they become politicized and strategic in order to understand their religious environment or to negotiate their own spirituality, even though they may or may not be religious or affiliated with an institution or mainline religion. In some of the cases of young adults who are part of Mary Jean's network, the home Christian church is no longer a fully nurturing place—they have been sponsored by it but it does not allow for return as a hybrid being. The lives of these women disrupt notions of stable religious affiliations in that neither she nor they reject organized religion fully; rather, they continue to negotiate the points of connection and complication.

In contrast, when they are overseas in development placements they find what they have not found at home: deep spiritual experience in the signs and symbols of the South. In these encounters with the other, they realize the myth of their being there to help others. Mary Jean spoke of her own work in South America:

> I would say I missed a lot by not understanding their symbols and what is really important to them and how they see the world. …Our history was to take [religion] to them. Well we don't have to take it to them. We can listen to them and find out what gives them joy and meaning to their lives; what things in life and what symbols and what faith traditions.

It is this awakening that unsettles Mary Jean's notions of North and South and of how religion can work in another culture. She finds herself in a new liminal space in which religious divisions no longer apply (or help). The binary of us/them is no longer applicable nor desirable (Ingleby, 2006), and she struggles to find a way to nurture her justice-oriented spirituality in a way that makes good sense to her and the youth she is leading and directing. In coordinating her program, Mary Jean comes daily into contact with the stories of young development workers and in hearing their stories of conflict with religion, she recognizes her own. Each of them is finding an authentic way to live out her/his spirituality, sometimes in concert with a religious tradition and sometimes not. Similarly, in the AWID (Gokal et al., 2011) exploration of how to deal with religious fundamentalism, the insights are somewhat cloudy; women make complicated choices and hold complicated alliances with systems they simultaneously resist and embrace. As readers of their situation and of our own, we need to allow for complication and honour it. We also need to work against homogenous and unified readings of women of faith, such as some of those represented in the Georgetown University project (Berkley Center, 2011). We need to realize that to live one's faith may involve complication, public challenge, and multiple positioning.

Translators and Negotiators

For many years, the work of faith based organizations here and elsewhere was conceptualized as missionary work, and indeed an entire field of theology, *missiology*, focused on volunteering in the missions. The more secular organizations operated with a different language, though arguably a similar purpose. Strong in these sacred and secular conceptualizations were the notions of giving and service, and of the development worker as the one who acted on the colonial subject (subaltern) to save him or her from disaster. The women in this study, though influenced by their families of origin and often a religious upbringing, are confronted daily with what it means to have a faith commitment and be development workers (English, 2005b).

Similar themes came up in an interview with Selma, a thirty-something Ghanaian woman who has worked since her early 20s in development projects. She has been trained as a development worker in Ghana and is a practicing Muslim who struggles with the strictures of Islam. She knows that she wants to continue her home-based work of development, yet finds the local and cultural interpretation of Islam very limiting. When pressure mounts for her to stay at home to care for her family, rather than go out to work in a development project and actually "use" her training and education she is forced to form a strategic alliance with her husband to subvert the oppressors. The situation becomes more problematic when the oppressors include extended family members. As she describes it, they have very strong rules about what she should be doing: "I have seen and heard that through religion Muslim women are not supposed to be with men. They are not supposed to sit where men are. They are not supposed to talk when men are talking. They are only supposed to be in the kitchen, bearing their children and taking care of the house." These rules contradict how she was raised in her home with a father who believed in and supported education for Muslim men and women,

> Apart from that there is no value for a woman to go to school. …Since I love my work I just forget about whatever the man's [my husband] family says because of the religion. …Because I am working, I do not want to have many children and they even told the man that he should let me have many children.

She knows that in approaching her husband, the extended family have put him in a compromising position as well, but she is adamant: "I told them that he cannot force me to have many children. …I love to do my work. I cannot be carrying a child on my back to go to a community. …My husband agreed to me." In forming an alliance, she has fortified her case and resisted the pressure to conform to stereotypes.

Selma understands who the primary actors are and she games the system by working with the most important member of the system, her husband. In knowing how Islam has been misconstrued by family and community members, she is able to move with finesse around the situation, presenting herself in a "feminine" way to the world, while also working outside the home and travelling away from her home for educational opportunities. She is insightful in how she understands the local version of Islam and women: As she explained, there "is a big conflict …more with the way we have taken Islam than with the way it actually is. They [religious leaders] say that if a woman is being educated at some standard, I will not have time for religion. But that is not true." Selma has become adept at shifting and shaping herself in order to be political and subversive.

In Selma's case, third space is not about expert knowledge about Islam, Ghana, or development. She has entered a "third space, …a space in which local knowledge traditions can be reframed, decentred, and the social organization of trust can be negotiated" (Turnbull, 1997, p. 560). For Selma, third space is about recognizing the value of working from the local situation, that is, the conflict in her family and community, to build an understanding of development work and the development worker who at times resists expectations and at times adheres to them. In Selma's Ghana, there is a social, historical, and political context that she must negotiate, especially in terms of religion and her reading of Islam. Her context in the South reminds us of Pui-lan's (2005, 2010) observation that a pure, homogenous religion— whether it be Christianity, Islam or Hinduism—is a myth, as many world religions absorb indigenous practices and rituals.

Yet, we continue to insist on absolute affinity to this monolithic structure, without any recognition that we can operate in an in-between third space, where our ideas, affinities, and connections change to fit the demands of the system, situation, and the participants. Selma resists in a very strategic way what it means to be Muslim in her home town. Her enactment of alliances and her continued affiliation with Islam creates tensions that she is well able to hold as she moves forward to enact change and to participate in development issues. Unlike many of the women involved in the Georgetown University project (Berkley Center, 2011), she has had to deal with her religion and her beliefs in a public way. Whereas many of the women in that project spoke of how their faith sustained them, Selma must also defend in a public way her interpretation of what it means to be Muslim, female, and a development worker.

Many adult educators working in the global South find themselves having to use strategic language to negotiate difficult spaces in their life and work. Their own understanding of religion often shifts as they come to see their work as less of a missionary endeavour and more of a radical justice commitment. As a consequence, they are forced to monitor their speech and shift their language to fit difficult spaces. Where religion is taboo, they need to shift identity according to listener's needs and limits and to shift identity and language readily between situations. They are the ultimate third space actors who can negotiate and translate for effectiveness. No doubt this is challenging and complicated for them, but it also allows them to begin their "presencing," as Bhabha (1994) says. They work to resist labels.

From a postcolonial lens, these women adult educators are enacting a hybridity that could be problematic for them. Their position(s) and actions are a combination of political acumen, commitment, and strategy. Hybridity, for them, is a place of political activism and effectiveness; the point at which they realize that the use of "translation" is essentially a form of negotiation was a moment that Bhabha (1994) calls "The hybrid moment of political change" (p. 28), a point when they can be neither compliant nor defiant. Their stories of negotiating religion and nurturing their own spirituality is one which shows the engaging and contradictory ways in which these practitioners deal with crises, dualisms, and other challenges in their development practice.

The result is not a revision of the old way but a new, evocative, and creative way of being in relation to personal religious beliefs and development practices (see Fahlander, 2007). Indeed, the old way of representation or reproduction of major world religion and religious adherence as monolith is no longer possible in this third space theory of encounter (De Kadt, 2009). Being a global citizen and a development professional necessarily entails a constant shifting of identity, affiliation, and speech. In terms of spirituality, it may mean a tenuous connection to a religious faith and to a widening notion of what it means to be part of a world spirit that knows few limits when it comes to issues of justice.

Pushing the Envelope in Development

Women in the Global South who work in development education are also challenged. For instance, in India there are women who are challenged both by their religious commitments and development expectations who become adept at reading religious messages and codes, entwined as they are in culture and language, and in using them to subvert the oppressor and the oppressive development system and lifeworld. As a subaltern, they do have a voice, but it may be an unexpected one. They resist the essentialist coding of their families and peers who may see them as White, Western do-gooders or as equally homogenous African or Indian Southern subalterns. Rather than be regulated by these essentialist discourses, they daily negotiate their identity as fluid, or as operating in a third space (Bhabha, 1994, 1998). The women reject being reduced to their development services they provide and to the ways they are expected to act.

For instance, Reena is a Roman Catholic nun in late middle age who has been leading a development project in her home in India for many years. In the interview, she talked about how she lives out her vows in a very traditional religious community, ever walking between her own free spirit, and the narrow conformist expectations around her. Here is how she describes how she resists the limited coding of her life and actions:

And there are days I don't get to say my prayers but I live it. …but I do follow the laws and there are sisters and if it will upset them, forget about it. I don't stand up like a revolutionist. I have elders and sisters that have just come and they would be upset. I make sure I am with them and say all the traditional things so they are comfortable. But as a person that is not going to define me.

Reena realizes she must live her truth in a very complicated way, negotiating identities and practices to make herself effective. When she must conform, she will, and when she can defy these conventions, she will. There is a workable tension and hybridity in her life that allows her to shift between cultures, religious expectations, and in the in-between space of our world. She operates in a context (i.e., India) in which religion is a more visible element of public life than in most parts of North America, so she must walk carefully within her religious home and within the public sphere. To be effective as a development professional, she must both honour the religious rules and regulations and simultaneously resist them. In many ways, her stories of hybridity are what Rushdie (1991) calls, "a love song to our mongrel selves" (p. 394). Yet, a caution is in order. These postcolonial readings of identity do not erase Reena's issues with essentialised ways of performing Catholicity; she is not attacking them but rather subverting them. Hers is a hybrid space of possibility in which she can enact her resistance. We see here shades of subversion and possibility that do not distance her from her religious ties, but rather entangle her in a web of her own making, a web that allows her to shift positions and to embrace those aspects of Catholicity that support and nurture her, as well as enable her to work to justice in her home territory. Her spirituality is interlaced with her attention to race, class and gender.

Third space, in this instance, becomes intricately connected to social change, identity, and religion in Reena's life. Her identity as a development worker, a nun, and a person of integrity is very complex and diverse, as it is for many in development practice. She has to interpret the varied signs and symbols of her context in order to achieve what to her are gospel values of development practice. Although the toll can be great, she has found a flexible and hybrid way of being a nun and a resister; she is also a *local* resident of India who has a conflicted relationship to a *global* religious system. As Bhabha observes, "So much for the global village—it has its natives too" (as cited in Mitchell, 1995, p. 81). Reena's particularity is at times local and at times global. For those who work in development circles, these complicated religious affinities are familiar and an everyday part of being a development practitioner. While from the outside, these resistances may appear minor, they are in fact colossal and successful attempts to be authentic and effective. It is these everyday actions that make the global village possible, as Bhabha notes.

IMPLICATIONS

As we observe an increase in conservatism in a number of nations in the West with the influence of right wing thinking in government, expectations of development and of its workers become simultaneously more rigid. Islamic scholar Amina Wadud (2008) notes, for instance, that the dividing of male and female Muslims for prayer and other activities is becoming more pronounced in the United States. Women who work internationally in adult education and encounter religious and development systems suggest that rigidity and conservatism, whether in the North or South, can have the potential to destroy effectiveness and agency in development work. Yet, how these women have chosen to live their lives counteracts attempts at control and stricture.

Women have complicated relationships with religious traditions; Reena, in particular, has played a role in shaping and supporting her development work. Yet, as grown women and workers, their relationship to a rigid notion of religious adherence is increasingly one of ambivalence. Apparent in each woman's text is complication and tension (a third space), though each negotiates it differently. Reena is silent, Mary Jean finds new collaborative spaces, and Selma strategizes a solution to religious conflict. They each have found ways to retrieve and negotiate the ambivalence and the contradictory spaces within their religions. Viewed in this critical way, their international work appears to be quite complicated. Yet for them, the place of complication is a place of fluidity and freedom that they are strategic in managing. This managing would appear to be an intuitive flow from one space to another, a flow that is in sync with their own spirituality. Clearly, how they experience and live spirituality is not limited to religion and, in some of their cases, still includes it. It is a spirituality that embraces culture, justice, race and gender, a spirituality lived out in their own terms. One could say that much of what passes for discussion of spirituality in the West is a mire of feeling and self-absorption that ignores larger questions of oppression. Seen here in each of these stories is a spirituality that surpasses this and which deals in the nitty gritty of a life lived on the cusp.

Although Christianity and Islam are often not seen as allowing for great diversity and interpretation, these women embody the right to live out and to enact their religious beliefs in multiple ways. We see here that the colonization of the mind and of women's lives is a real and persistent force, both in the North and in the South. The once clear division in world religions between the colonizer (e.g., Christianity) and the colonized (e.g., Hindus, Buddhists, Muslims) is more blurred and indistinct as national and religious identities become more fluid and indeterminate. They are also more blurred as the conflictual spaces appear from within, be it in Islam (think Selma) or Roman Catholicism (think Reena). The once readily identifiable opponents —Christianity versus indigenous religions—is less relevant as workers name their internal struggles and hybrid solutions. The one-dimensional identification of colonizers and religious leaders as enemies has been replaced by the shifting and diverse notion of third space. Considering the global village and the interlocking relationship between local and global, it becomes more apparent that the third space can hold the differences and the tensions, hence its attraction for those who move between countries and religious structures.

When adult education, development, social justice, and religion/spirituality intersect in the lives of women, we can benefit from resisting the urge to essentialise them. More appealing is a problematizing of the connections, and a probing of the contradictions and the conflicts (see, for example, Bhabha, 1994, 1998; Khan, 2000). Multiplicity and third space provide analytic tools for exploring similarities and differences and for allowing women to be rendered as they see themselves. Categories of gender, Christianity, Islam, and development limit women development workers' active resistance and agency. Their daily negotiation of identity disturbs these categories and opens new possibilities for understanding them. Given that much attention in the West has gone to limiting women to one type, one form, and one idea, third space opens up possibilities for difference and change. We are reminded that, as in the AWID forum on religion and fundamentalism (Gokal et al., 2011), not all women reject religion, embrace spirituality, and reject their familial influences. Women are complicated and their relationship to one another and to themselves is necessarily complicated and changing. The stories told in this chapter witness to a life that is lived in fluidity and possibility.

DISCUSSION

Development organizations need to be increasingly open to how practitioners story their lives and the place of religion or spirituality in them. Though AWID's focus, named at the beginning of this chapter, is on the challenges of religious fundamentalism, religion may also need to be seen from a third-space perspective which moves beyond the equation of religion with oppression, illiteracy, and female inequity. Religious groups, or certainly members of them, may be closer sponsors, motivators, and collaborators than might first appear. This chapter destabilizes the notion of religion as enemy and shows the tenuous nature of women's relationship with women. Religion may indeed hold both liberating and oppressive agendas, depending on the context and the players.

There is an irony of sorts in Bhabha's (1994) use of third space, since it suggests the "third world" where much development work occurs. His provocative usage challenges us to think of how this imagined third space is really a place of possibility for women from the "third world" to resist continued colonialism by Western nations, development organizations, and essentialist readings by scholars from the minority world. This imagined space is a place of challenge and constant emergence; it challenges us to do development in new and hopeful ways.

CHAPTER 7

RESEARCHING FOR AND
WITH THE COMMUNITY OF WOMEN[1]

Collaborative research has the potential to support the work of feminist social and political activism, providing an opportunity for grassroots organizations to come together and to gather the evidence they need to advocate for change. Networks of women's organizations in Africa, for instance, demonstrate this documentation and mobilizing potential. Over the past few decades, FEMNET (African Women's Development and Communication Network) based in Nairobi, Kenya has played a central role in documenting and sharing information that has been fed into rights campaigns and gatherings such as the UN World Conferences on Women (Wainaina, 2012). They demonstrate the importance of the ongoing exchange between grassroots organizations and other partners to gather knowledge and share it—to do research—across sectors.

One FEMNET partner, the African Association of Women for Research and Development (AAWORD), compiled, for UN Women, a 10-country study gathering evidence on violence against women throughout West Africa (Fayé, 2013). As many women's organizations know, this report's authors reassert to governments that policy alone is not enough, that: "Today it is imperative to go beyond the texts and take action, in particular through prevention, but also through full legal, medical, psychological and economic support to victims of gender-based violence" (Fayé, p. 11). It is the research on the ground that documents the effect of the policies and also identifies the need for stronger support services for women.

In particular, the potential of collaborative research involving multisector partnerships has been noticed and is a point of focus for funders of research including international bodies and national governments. Such collaborations ensure greater representation and demonstrate impact at the community level. Researchers, in turn, frame their interests and actions to include partners with whom they may not otherwise normally collaborate. At the community level too, research in some form is seen as integral to practice, providing an opportunity to gather much needed evidence and for practitioners to have a voice in research. It is a rarity to encounter a literacy organization, for instance that is not involved with some form of action research to either improve teaching or results with students. The need to understand a situation is already well known to community groups. Responding to external demands to demonstrate program effectiveness or to lobby for policy change increasingly requires community workers to align themselves with supportive researchers. Similarly, there are cries of support when evidence based decision making is invoked, though a closer look shows that not all aspects of women's lives that are deemed valuable can be weighed, counted, and measured.

Yet, research collaboration is not always a straightforward process. In this chapter, we unpack assumptions lurking in the partnership discourse and provide a critical commentary on it. An admonition once attributed to bell hooks states that if women really wanted to solve women's problems, they would cut out conferences for a year and give the money to women's groups and causes. While there is no clear record of this often-quoted idea, it reflects a growing unease about whose interests are served in the research sector. That cynicism aside, women's groups themselves realize the importance of research to have the evidence on hand they need to advocate for policy change. Finding money for research outside of the academic realm takes an increasing amount of time and energy by community groups as they try to craft their proposals to meet funders' specifications, which often do not even consider research as a fundable endeavour (see English & Irving, 2008). For all the talk of this being a knowledge society, few are willing to support the work that enables grassroots actors to participate in this area.

Research funding, usually considered a good, can cause great complications for the community research picture. When the United States or the European Union or a major foundation such as the Ford Foundation gives money for research in communities, they likely assume that the funds will be used to demonstrate a measureable improvement in functioning of a community group in terms of jobs and other outcomes, in other words, the creation of efficiencies. Governments may assume that they can transfer responsibility to nonprofits the work of providing housing, education, and social services. We are reminded of the danger of beneficence, not unlike the idea of Big Society: under the guise of helping, responsibility has been shifted to the community (Bunyan, 2013). While the funding provides temporary relief and support for the community organization, the relief is short-lived and the organization's problems increased.

Around the world, especially in Europe and countries like the United States that are grappling with budget shortfalls, there is constant discussion of terms such as *deficit, debt, budgetary constraint, accountability, restricted funding, pressure, insecurity, competition,* and *fundable research.* The word accountability is heard across all government departments and funding agencies, and their priorities are constantly being negotiated. Faced with multiple commitments and requests—namely pressure to promote regional development and help communities, support higher education, and the need to increase the gross domestic product (GDP) and promote global competitiveness—government and other funders have to prioritize funding mechanisms. In response, women's groups in the community need to respond to calls for collaborative work that will maximize funding dollars and make them more efficient and accountable (Swift, 1999). Universities and paid researchers are drawn into the discourse and respond with the promise that their collaboration efforts will make measurable improvements in efficient use of research funds (Association of Universities and Colleges in Canada, 2005).

Governments in Western democracies are willing to give money for research as a way of building partnerships and decreasing government contributions to civil society aspects such as peace-building in Northern Ireland. And this conservatism brings with it the implication that research is more likely to be funded if it involves a partnership of community, academia, and sometimes government.

When there is a partnership or a cooperative agreement that involves academics with community partners, conflicts and complicities can arise that make it difficult for communities to be able to name their needs and goals, their contributions, and their interpretation of results. An example would be a community women's resource centre that is being studied in terms of its contributions to ending violence against women. The centre's primary need may be an assessment of available networks to support their work, when in fact the research plan prioritizes effectiveness and accountability to a funder as the primary goal. There is also the reality that any given research project can only focus on one or two issues and will have discrete results, making it likely that the broader and more complex issues will be sidelined.

When a feminist organization has the opportunity to work with a funder such as a government agency or development organization, the organization usually is disposed positively to the opportunity, that is, willing to partner, to "create really useful knowledge" (Johnson, 1988, pp. 21–22) about gender and learning. At the same time, the members may be resistant to perceived attempts to co-opt their labour. More often than not, the government or the funder is trying to find ways to make the community group more efficient or more productive, rather than listening to them. We are reminded of resisters such as Janice Gross Stein (2003) who critiques *The Cult of Efficiency* and calls upon us to ask, "Efficient at what?" (p. 12). Does efficiency become an end in itself? Stein uses the example of hospitals boasting of savings from staff layoffs without acknowledging loss of service. Sadly, layoffs often occur at the bottom level where the most vulnerable workers are employed. The discursive effect of the efficiencies and the partnering is cynicism.

We need to recognize, however, that there is a certain attraction to being involved in research. After all, it is a commonplace to defer to research results as a support for our arguments and actions in the community; the government uses phrases such as "studies show" and the "research proves," when in fact, it may be one study (or none, since it is not named often) and also such phrases promote an unfettered belief in studies that (a) may or may not have been done, (b) may have been done poorly, or (c) cannot be replicated. This use of language like this has an uncanny ability to help control public discourse. Along with this is the discourse of *newness*, the idea that things have to be created anew when, in fact, the old may indeed work. It is also true that women's groups may be lured by the promise that their research partnership may help them become influential in setting public policy or helping determine their funding. We only have to think of how often the government makes announcements that are prefaced with "the focus groups we conducted show that this new policy is a good one" to realize how seductive it is to be involved in those focus groups or in that research.

The international development sphere has had long experience with partnerships. Especially problematic for this sphere is the unquestioned emphasis on partnerships, and assumptions around participation (Hickey & Mohan, 2004). Adult educators who work with women's groups will be familiar mostly with the participatory research dimension, though perhaps less so with the extended critiques. Debate over the utility, politics, and practice of participatory frameworks came to the forefront with the "tyranny of participation" discussions that challenge received wisdom on participation (Cooke & Kothari, 2001). These writers have subsequently worked toward a new conceptual framework that underscores the need for criticality, reflexivity, and renewed politicization of the term *participation*. Follow-up research in this field employs poststructuralist analyses (Cornwall, 2004) to the power imbalances and resistances, analyses that are particularly instructive to our understanding of the situation both development practitioners and adult educators face.

What a feminist group brings to a partnership, and which is most attractive to a funder is their indigenous or local knowledge. They bring the legitimacy of grassroots organizations; this must be protected, but it is difficult to do so. If we truly believed that the community had the knowledge, we might do our research differently. Linda Tuhiwai Smith (2012), in her *Decolonizing Methodologies*, notes that even the word *indigenous* is not from the communities, but from researchers. The notion of research is also a Western concept that is not known in this way to indigenous peoples, and in which power issues are always embedded. Of course, Smith is not saying that indigenous groups not do research but that we are careful of how we do it and that we bring a critical eye to it.

One of the questions that arises or should arise for women's groups is the worth or newness of the study. That is, how likely is this study to contribute to new knowledge for the community? We need to ask ourselves how many more studies are needed to determine if poor people exist in our communities? If children have enough to eat? If women are being abused? At what point can we and the public at large come to consensus on public issues and move forward to create solutions. Can we not believe what we already know and hold to be true or do we have to keep researching topics and interviewing participants to find out what we already know about poverty, literacy and childcare? (see Quigley & Kraglund-Gauthier, 2008). While women's groups would do well to insist that the research have a solid basis and rationale, they are often afraid to say no because funding will be affected. A strong alternative would be to have the women themselves develop the participatory research stemming from their own needs (Titterton & Smart, 2008). Karen Dullea (2006) argues that they need to be the ones who name what they need more work or study of. Those who do the research with them need to be guided by their needs and wants.

Fay Blaney (2003) writes of her work with the Aboriginal Women's Action Network (AWAN), who do participatory research to address issues such as violence and legislated discrimination through public policy. She notes, "The oppression that Aboriginal women in Canada face on a daily basis, has until fairly recently, resulted in their lack of access to both formal and informal education, and therefore, to their very limited production of knowledge" (p. 156). AWAN works to uncover discrimination and the influence of patriarchal practices within their own cultures.

Community based groups need, at times, to reclaim their rights to their own knowledge.

There are good proactive organizations among communities that protect their rights and freedoms in research. We commend these and hope that more communities can organize in this way. The Mi'kmaq Nation in Canada, for instance, has set up its own organization to determine who can do research on them. Their organization, Mi'kmaq Ethics Watch, is an example of a group of community members united by race and culture who have claimed the right to review and approve any research on themselves (see www.cbu.ca/unamaki/research).

Competition for research funds is very important, not only for community groups who can use the funds for unstated purposes like retaining staff, but also for academics who use the funds and research to create new knowledge and to sustain academic careers. This competition can result in a creative partnership, but the power relationships and agendas must be unpacked so that its intricacies are clearly seen. Also, what openings exist for community members to become full research partners in the process is key, as these discussions still seem to assume researcher as outsider. The Australian Research Council (2012) has worked to strengthen the network of researchers among the Aboriginal and Torres Strait Islanders through a funded Network. Their funding is intended to help to facilitate collaborative and innovative approaches to planning and undertaking research, and to enrich research training and to build capacity for Aboriginal and Torres Strait Islander researchers. Such a network helps to build capacity and to allow them to "develop and lead research, research training and career development programs" (Australian Research Council). A goal is to increase participation by Aboriginal researchers. It will be interesting to see what lessons are learned in this process to find ways to allow people in these communities to become authors of their own research and to develop their own rules of engagement about research matters that concern them.

From our perspective, the discourse of partnership and cooperation/collaboration may constitute and sustain unequal power relations (Fairclough & Wodak, 1997). Though social scientists have shown increasing interest in partnerships (see Baum, 2000; Cobb & Rubin, 2006) few if any have analysed it critically. This partnering-for-research phenomenon not only shapes interactions in and among the partners, the community and university for example, but also the knowledge produced and the nature of inquiry itself. Researchers who have an interest in gender will be especially interested insofar as partnering or collaborating is a regime of truth within gender and feminist studies. Our view is that research with community groups is not an unproblematic event and nor is partnering. Following Foucault (English, 2006a), we want to pay attention to micropractices in which resistance is embedded in partnering. Resistance can be quietly refusing to participate, talking back to power, or taking part in the more visible form of public protest. We are most interested in the subtle resistance that is enacted by women in nonprofit organizations who must distinguish the potential benefits and losses in any constructed partnership.

Community and university groups alike have been affected by the partnership discourse. In a global fiscal climate where adult education programming and research are not given priority, academics face increasing pressure to find external funding. The sought-after publicly funded research grants are increasingly allocated to collaborative efforts and to prize-winning topics such as interdisciplinary health and environment projects. Community organizations face a similar situation with government cutbacks; for example, the shift from stable core funding to tightly regulated, short-term project grants. They are increasingly driven to participate in community–university funded projects. In the hallways of conferences and across email, the discontent mounts and yet few have taken on the discourse of partnership. Below we use a poststructuralist lens to examine the seemingly benign partnering phenomenon, highlighting the ways that women as researchers are affected and affect the research process.

ANALYSING THE PARTNERSHIP CONUNDRUM

We build on conversations with colleagues, participation in women's organizations, publicly available documents, and our own research experiences to explore the social and historical context, the competing discourses, and the power – knowledge nexus of universities, government, community, and feminism. Within this context of coerced partnership, we pay particular attention to the social relations of power that operate in the knowledge generation process, especially as it affects feminist researchers. Finally, we look at how the partnership phenomenon might benefit from repeated engagement with poststructuralism and critical discourse analysis.

Foucauldian poststructuralism (Foucault, 1980, 2003) helps us to delve into how power is exercised (used) and embedded in the complex web of relationships and discourses (languages and practices) that surround the partnership process. Power can have negative and positive effects. Attention to the flow of power helps us, as feminists, to understand more about how government funding agencies operate and helps to complicate the organizational charts used to map the hierarchies of government and universities (see Brookfield, 2005; Chapman, 2003; English, 2005a).

Poststructuralism, and especially critical discourse analysis (CDA), attends not only to what is produced (the research project), but also to how it is produced (in partnership) and to the history and contexts that surround its production (mandatory partners, streamlining of funding). This allows us to focus on the use of power to discursively create the players in funded research—the university, the academics, the administration, and the community as well as the feminist researchers. And this power is productive—its use produces knowledge, researchers, and practices, as well as diversity and competing discourses. This diversity is needed in political discourse as a way of "avoiding a language of consensus which disguises differences"

(Fairclough, 2000, p. 161). As well, we explore the discourse of research partnerships when community groups are coerced into joining funding applications and research projects.

This critical discourse lens (Fairclough, 1992; Mills, 1997) allows us to pay attention to the social relations of power operating in knowledge generation processes, especially as they affect feminist researchers in adult education. We propose an alternative vision of partnerships which values politicization of the term *partnership*, attention to civil society, mapping of resistances, and valuing of the process by all partners. This analysis seeks to understand the effects of power and the discourse within the larger research culture that operates internationally. This culture encourages collaboration and partnerships with the public and private sector and especially with the community. The range of stakeholders (government, community, higher education administration, academics and feminist academics) and competing discourses are typical of research partnerships worldwide. These discourses include, but are not limited to finances, social agendas, and academic ideals. Not only are there competing discourses among the stakeholders (e.g., feminist versus government) but also within groups of stakeholders such as between academics who uphold social ideals and academics who insist on following the bottom line, no matter the cost. These data are illustrative not exhaustive.

To make the discourse more visible we have followed Leslie Treleaven (2004) who constructed a CDA of Australia's university restructuring process. We pay attention to competing discourses among government, university administration, feminist academics, and community activists. Building on Treleaven's methods, we discuss the various issues arising.

DELVING INTO THE DISCOURSE

Informed by the use of CDA by Treleaven (2004), Fairclough (1992) and Mills (1997), we looked at the everyday background, as well as the historical, economic, cultural, and political setting in which the data (language and practices) were contextualized. Since each partner—feminist, academic, government, community and higher education administration—is positioned with different agendas and mandates, each responds to and co-creates the dominant discourses of partnerships and efficiency uniquely. Several discourses stand out and we analyse them here, allowing the theory to intersect with the data when relevant.

Government and Other Funders

The discourse of *partnership* has become dominant in the realm of government funding agencies such as the Social Sciences and Humanities Research Council of Canada (SSHRC) and likewise the EU's focus on *cooperation,* as a way to create efficiencies. Although collaboration and alliances are also popular, we note that partnership is the preferred term; it is not lost on us that business and legal institutions favour this word to designate economic ties. Such partnering brings with it unreal expectations and assumptions within universities or communities. In reality, there is no uniform identity—within each there are competing discourses (see Baum, 2000). Nowhere is this partnership discourse more apparent than in research publications from various government bodies. Partnership terminology is not new in government discourse; it is highlighted in Human Resources and Development Canada's own manual on partnership building that "partnerships are an important vehicle for building community capacity and undertaking community development activities" (Frank & Smith, 2000, p. 1).

Higher Education Officials

Researchers often depend on government funds. Higher education administrators (think deans, academic vice-presidents, provosts, boards of governors) are attentive to the *partnership* and efficiencies chatter and have created a discourse of their own, sometimes in sync with the government (think a collaborative partnership to produce first rate research, worthy sites of fundable research activity) and at times at odds with it (think academic standards and research integrity, autonomy). The discourses exist simultaneously, each producing a separate and parallel regime of truth. Faced with global competition, higher education administrators reward funded research and *entrepreneurial* activity by academics to diversify revenue streams. Government wants assurances that the knowledge creation activity it funds has impact and practical utility (*results-driven, usability, strategic*). It is not uncommon to see the promotion of successful private sector collaborations that demonstrate the transfer of knowledge to the marketplace; similarly, universities highlight entrepreneurial achievements in annual reports and websites.

Academics

Academics also use the discourse of cooperating, partnering, collaborating, and sharing (e.g., Butterwick & Harper, 2006). The enlightened (and successful) researcher has responded favourably to the discourse and begun to use it, becoming *team* members, *collaborators,* and *co-investigators* if the funding regulations and specifications call for it. Researchers resist to some degree with a discourse of *independence* and *research integrity*, embodying it in Research Ethics Boards and Academic Integrity committees, and campaigning to have research untainted by funders such as pharmaceutical companies (see Owram, 2004). Yet, the quest for funding continues and the academic subject position that is produced is made up of multiple and contradictory identities (Ford, 2006). Many adult education and development practitioners who have a commitment to the community have partnered for funding and produced texts from these collaborations, yet there have been few critiques of the process (e.g., Butterwick & Harper; English, McAulay, & Mahaffey, 2012).

Community Organizations

In the quest for research and funding, community and grassroots organizations also embrace the *partnering* discourse. Literacy coalitions and feminist collectives often arise out of the need to apply collaboratively for funding. More recent examples are even larger consortia such as the National Collaborating Centre for Aboriginal Health in Canada. An increasingly common question is who actually is involved and can the actors be identified apart from these conglomerations. Although partnering among and between community-based organizations is integral to grassroots activity, partnering with universities and government to survive has taken on a new form. Whereas once universities looked to communities as sources of data, now communities look to universities for funding to operate. Without the research community organizations cannot justify to funders that they are credible.

At issue in all these discourses is a concern for *civil society*, admittedly a term used as vaguely as community and partnership. Civil society, often comprised of grassroots groups and *bona fide* partnerships, is understood at the community level as people outside of government mobilizing to address shared goals. As a movement, civil society has become a popular focus for academics, and has been courted by government because of its "productive" capacity. The mandate of neoliberal governments to offload public services has been given new life through the promotion of partnerships with civil society organizations. This has forced the organizations to compete for funding and to adopt the discourses and practices of business rather than those of community development (Swift, 1999). Collaborating academics can find themselves caught in partnerships that undermine the very community strength they want to support. Adult educators such as Welton (1997) also critique this cooptation of civil society.

Community groups resist with the discourse of indigenous knowledge, grassroots organizing, and at times, authenticity, integrity, voice and legitimacy. This knowledge *for* the people *by* the people discourse, however, is parallel to the partnering and survival discourse. Now the community has to write proposals for funding, participate in university research projects, and use the *marketspeak* of executive directors in order to do community work. Their skill set is often not strong on research language, so they become minor players in the alliance (Cottrell & Parpart, 2006). They worry that their knowledge will be appropriated and co-opted (Cooke, 2004). As well, their goal is community impact whereas the university prioritizes publishable work.

Partnership is a troubled discourse that magnifies distrust and resentment that the university has stolen from the grassroots. While community groups seek subsistence funding, theirs is not an unquestioned gratitude. Rhonda Braithwaite, Sarah Cockwill, Martin O'Neill, and Deanne Rebane (2007) document their extensive efforts to overcome "the profound research initiative fatigue" (p. 68) within communities before embarking on new collaborative projects. As community-based action researchers, they detail the challenges they faced throughout this process. Negotiating the insider-outsider dynamic, for instance, was time consuming and ultimately not rewarded in the traditional research sense. Furthermore, the partnering discourse assumes a monolithic community group as partner (see Baum, 2000). The troubling reality is that no entity can be clearly marked community—there are differences and competing agendas even within single community groups (Cornwall, 2004).

Feminist researchers within the academy negotiate the competing discourses of *collaboration* and *scholarly integrity*. Allied with university and community, they struggle for their share of research funds while trying to honour participatory, collaborative processes inherent in feminism. Often, they see the opportunity to work with community as a way to enrich "both academic theorizing and community activism" (Cottrell & Parpart, 2006, p. 16). Feminist research has the potential to draw attention to the ways in which women are unequally and differently positioned, yet funds for this work are shrinking (Manicom, Rhymes, Armour, & Parsons, 2005). Ideally, the research question drives the research method, but increasingly government efficiencies are in control. Feminists face challenges when their participatory and time-consuming methods are questioned by the funders who promoted the partnerships in the first place (Butterwick & Harper, 2006). As well, feminist researchers often bear an unequal share of the labour in community-based partnerships, regardless of who handles the money. Irene Malcolm (2012) points out that in listening and walking with women participants in the community, the feminist researcher may carry much of the emotional labour of stories of trouble and problems. This labour must not be overlooked when the value of and cost of the partnerships is assessed.

Paradoxes in Partnership

In an examination of how partnerships tend to work, several paradoxes emerged. The first paradox is that most *partnership* discourse is dictated downward creating a discursive effect of surveillance and resistance from the so-called partners—feminists in the community, academics, government and other funders, administrators, community researchers. There is an expectation of collaboration between teams, and the terminology implies equity where it may not exist. Effective community workers resist by working independently of *partners* as much as possible. They are averse to false collaboration when convinced that such partnerships and meetings would not be helpful to the process or the product. At the community level, as Andrea Cornwall (2004) notes, the very presence of partnering external agencies can reinforce inequalities when they remain as "simply pseudo-democratic instruments through which authorities legitimize already-taken policy decisions" (p. 80).

Another paradox is that the fund-driven partnering relationships are often devoid of productive relationships. Utilitarian and short-lived, these relationships often do not contribute to lifelong learning or to an authentic knowledge culture. With much project-driven research, time to reflect and respond to the various research processes involved is not encouraged or supported. These paradoxes raise questions about project and organizational longevity and its effects. On the one hand, partnering creates a research culture and on the other hand, it militates against relationship. A revisioning process is needed.

TOWARDS AN ALTERNATIVE

In the spirit of the partnerships that we value, we avoid giving a list of prescriptions or lessons (see Prins, 2005) to use to "do" partnerships right. Rather, we propose that feminists in the community consider the following elements of a participatory and reflexive paradigm.

Further Politicization of the Term Partnership

In the cooptation of partnership by higher education officials, funding bodies, government, and other groups, the term has lost meaning and purpose. We borrow here from Hickey and Mohan (2004) who have suggested a more political perspective on participatory discourse. Any discussions of collaboration of partnership need to acknowledge the effects of the power, the direction of the power, and the ways in which we are "disciplined" by participation. In interrogating the compliance to rules, the stringent policies and procedures of applications, and the imposed control of language we politicize the term partnership to challenge the ways it is described and practiced. We are encouraged by studies that are trying to critique partnership and propose alternatives (Hollander, 2011; Titterton & Smart, 2008). New Zealand-based researchers Walker and Shannon (2011), for instance, critique research partnerships and suggest that developing case study research on communities is a way to build strong, mutually beneficial partnerships. Notable in their discussion is that case studies are not merely descriptive accounts of the community activity but they can be critiqued in terms of power relationships and inequality.

Partnering for Civil Society

With the stress on partnerships for efficiency that we have highlighted above, partnering for civil society has been lost. We suggest that renewed attention be given to civil society and the long-term good of stressing it. When partnerships of economy and efficiency are given pride of place, the community is lost. Ironically, there is an efficiency built into partnering for civil society: a strong citizenry is tied to having a strong economy. The future health of a community and its index of productive citizenship can be attended to by strengthening relationships, prioritizing community needs, and resisting government co-optation. Caroline Moser, a key feminist critic of international development, reminds us of the "need to shift focus from emphasis on participation as a means (efficiency, effectiveness and cost sharing) to participation as an end (empowerment and capacity building)" (as cited in Elabor-Idemudia, 2002, p. 229). This helps us to shift focus from donor-driven goals to meaningful building of capacity at the local level.

Identifying Resistances in the Partnerships

Part and parcel of any productive partnership is attention to the resistances. As Foucault (1980) reminds us, resistances reside in all relationships, and they are especially important in partnerships such as we have been discussing here in higher education and community. Attending to the flow of power as it courses through the partnerships brings our gaze to the resistances that are always there. Glyn Williams (2004) notes that "Any configuration of power/knowledge opens up its own particular spaces and moments for resistance" (p. 94). Community resistances to being taken over by the academy, for instance, may show in poor attendance at meetings, back-talk about proposals, and lack of willingness to lend a voice to the process. Resistances can shed light on suppressed power imbalances that affect partnering.

Valuing the Process by All Partners

As Braithwaite et al. (2007) remind us, there is a need at the outset to build relationships, overcome distrust and negotiate the insider-outsider dilemmas that are inherent in community-university research teams. They observe the community incredulity that the time spent writing up the research was valuable or beneficial for them. In uncovering this troubled dimension of partnering Braithwaite and her colleagues disclose the unmentionable challenges of partnering within the community. Nina Wallerstein and Bonnie Duran (2006) advise, "Partnerships need to have opportunities to reflect on the issues that surface related to participation, privilege, power, and race and/or ethnicity and to help identify structural changes that can support mutuality instead of dominance by one stakeholder" (p. 320). We encourage the researchers to publish findings and analysis of the process.

We are not naïve enough to assume that all partnerships can become co-equal nor are we desirous of a return to the lone scholar phenomenon or top-down policy development. Yet, to overcome the quest for the "mythic participatory ideal" (Williams, 2004, p. 98), we encourage sensitivity to the research dynamic and continuous interrogation of the motives, processes and procedures. As Barbara Cottrell and Jane Parpart (2006) acknowledge, open communication involves persistence as community and academic partners identify issues of power and control. Yet, the effort can result in more effective collaborations. Andrea Cornwall (2004) encourages us to bring this practical challenge to the institutional level. Unfortunately, there is also the very real dilemma that a call for renewed action to overcome power imbalances, while apparently reasonable, can seem impossible to achieve (Cooke, 2004) in a managerial context. Maintaining the energy to work for improved collaborations in the face of deep welling cynicism is difficult.

The funding environment that is produced and reproduced in the collaborative discourse is one that sometimes creates resentment and is the fabrication of unity. Yet, it also allows, albeit in a circuitous way, all the stakeholders to function. We wonder aloud if the discourse of partnership could be open to more examination and critique and if the "partners" might be able to suggest meaningful alternatives. For instance, the international aid agency, ActionAid (David & Mancini, 2004), as a donor agency is turning the tables on accountability by allowing the recipients of funds to define and evaluate impact, so that the funds do achieve what is in the best interests of the community, rather than the supposed interests of the funders.

As part of the restorying process of creating healthier partnerships, a stronger emphasis on relationships is needed in the early stages of the research. We are heartened by the example of Margaret Lombe, Chrisann Newransky, Tom Crea, and Anna Stout (2012) who describe an international collaboration in social work research in Ghana from which they develop guidelines to follow in "planning and conducting international research collaborations." They put an emphasis on the initial process of starting and fostering the collaboration and in planning the various parts of the research process. The authors emphasise the importance of respect and cooperation.

Mutuality in doing these kinds of research projects is needed in international settings with limited resources. Francisco Ibáñez-Carrasco and Pilar Riaño-Alcalá (2011) describe a strong working partnership between university students and community organizations, in which the students undertake community-based research and do so in a way that honours all participants. Of course, since funding is not directly involved, this partnership is decidedly less political, but at least it offers a model for how respect might be developed and maintained, possibly a first step in developing research partnerships between universities and community groups.

Alternative Relationships and Methods

There are resistances to the perceived issues in research in the community. For instance, there is growing acceptance of non-traditional methods, long supported by feminist researchers, need to be promoted even more. A prime example is the use of popular theatre as a means of illuminating and exploring research issues in the community. Canadian adult educator Shauna Butterwick has spent many years in participatory projects in which she does research on learning in feminist community organizations. In 2003, she and co-researcher Jan Selman (Butterwick & Selman, 2003) used popular theatre as the methodology to understand issues of conflict, feminist politics, theatre processes, and the creation of democratic sites of learning. They used popular theatre to generate a storytelling process called Transforming Dangerous Spaces. Along with 10 participants and 2 research assistants, Butterwick and Selman were able to go much deeper into the organizational and communication dimensions of feminist organizing than any traditional research process might allow. While not all projects lend themselves to lengthy and participatory means and representations, Butterwick and Selman show that these are possible sometimes.

Integral to all of these discussions is the capacity of women's organizations themselves to take leadership roles in gathering and disseminating research. Many community collaborations still primarily start from the assumption that community partners inherently lack the skills to produce credible knowledge. Feminist research organizations such as AAWORD and FEMNET have a great deal to teach us about developing expertise within organizations to engage at all levels of the research process.

DISCUSSION

From a cursory feminist point of view, the partnership discourse is to be emulated and lauded, suggesting as it does both relationship and strength. Yet, when CDA is employed, we see that partnering can run counter to relationship and authentic community discourse. It raises questions of the use of partnering to create efficiencies. The community-based women's organization asks questions about how these partnerships will strengthen their identity and their work. The feminist academic wants to know if partnering is a discourse that has a long shelf life and if it contributes to sustained partnerships and knowledge creation. Higher education administrators negotiate the competing discourses of partnering and efficiencies, forever questioning the effects and the need to create a discourse that is sustainable. In fact, the potential for partnering is disrupted by the competing and somewhat contradictory discourses and the relative distributions of authority in the research process. Uncovering the power dynamics lurking within the discourses help us to figure out how and where to engage in the process to ensure research partnerships do actually contribute to understanding and the social change that feminists are seeking.

NOTE

[1] This chapter draws on: C.J. Irving & L.M. English. (2008). Partnering for research: A critical discourse analysis. *Studies in Continuing Education, 30*(2), 107–118. Adapted with permission from Taylor and Francis, 2013.

CHAPTER 8

CRITICAL FEMINIST PEDAGOGY

Learning about women's oppression and the path towards social justice leads to new ways of understanding the issues, as well as new ways of understanding and enacting the learning process itself. Feminist pedagogy draws strength from its engagement with feminism and vice versa.

A case of creative and critical pedagogy concerns the women of Arica, northern Chile, who were among the initial resisters, the change agents, and the informal leaders who opposed and demonstrated against the violent Pinochet regime that murdered 3000 people from 1973–1990 (Chovanec, 2009; see also Chovanec, Cooley, & Smith Díaz, 2010). The women of Arica came together to struggle for basics like food, shelter, and safety, and to oppose Pinochet and the human rights abuses that occurred under his dictatorship. In 1983, far from the capital of Santiago, the women met and formed two organizations devoted to overthrowing Pinochet (or Pinocchio as they called him disparagingly): MODEMU (Movement for Women's Rights) and CEDEMU (Women's Study Centre), the latter being the more feminist of the two. With the strength of the organizations behind them, these mothers created a vibrant social movement that protested Pinochet, celebrated International Women's Day, and made themselves heard in the streets of Arica. In writing about these brave women, social movement theorist Donna Chovanec emphasises the learning that occurred through social movements such as this one. Chovanec calls for the deliberate educational and critical thinking component in all social movements. In her words, "Everyone thinks, but we may need help to learn to think critically" (p. 113). It is this strategic, critical teaching and learning component that is at the heart of this chapter on feminist pedagogy.

Only one of the organizations in Arica—CEDEMU—was overtly feminist though both were populated by women. Both had emancipatory goals, but only one looked explicitly at women's issues and took a political feminist stance. Similarly, women's learning and feminist pedagogy are both practiced with women (and often with men) but they exist on a continuum, concerned as they are with women, but in slightly different ways. Whereas some adult educators emphasise the categories of voice, subjectivity, and connection in terms of teaching women, others such as Shauna Butterwick (2005) and Elizabeth Tisdell (2005) want to move well beyond inclusion to address issues of power, politics, and practice in their teaching. However, they share an emphasis on women's experience: a belief that many women have been silenced in learning environments, and that it is desirable to create safe and open environments to support women in their learning journey. Critical feminist pedagogues are often radical in practice and intent (Tisdell, 2000). They are guided by concern for examining beliefs about women and teaching (e.g., our assumptions), as well as examination of the content of our teaching, the ways we teach (e.g., our pedagogical practice).

We use the term *critical feminist pedagogy* as it puts a deliberate stress on women and resistance to power in learning situations, whether they are in social movements, higher education, NGOs, or community based groups. Ours is a decidedly political agenda that helps continue the conversations begun in *Women's Ways of Knowing* (Belenky et al., 1986) and *Women as Learners* (Hayes et al., 2000) and adds the connections to community, resistance, and change, that is, a decidedly feminist pedagogical approach.

BACKGROUND

Of course, we recognize that feminist teaching practices, especially an emphasis on holistic learning, have become somewhat mainstream and basically considered good pedagogy for all (see Brookfield, 2010). So, setting up classrooms in circles and allowing alternate ways of knowing, which initially were considered to be focused on women, are now a variety of settings with women and men, often with the political edge dulled. However, the intent and the theoretical foundations of feminism that undergirds good teaching have not become mainstream. We would like to push the envelope a bit by increasing the stress on the intersectionality of power, ability, politics, culture and race in our teaching, that is making our pedagogy deliberately feminist (Crenshaw, 1991). While critical and feminist pedagogy may hold pride of place in nonprofit organizations like Kairos and AWID, it is often not a given in adult education and certainly not in higher and continuing education. Planning and participating in this form of knowing is challenging and it has its own risks, yet it is important for women's concerns.

Goals of Critical Feminist Pedagogy

Critical feminist pedagogy stretches beyond personal development and inclusion, as worthwhile as these are, and moves toward social transformation (see English, 2006b). What starts small needs to move outward and have a deliberate and focused agenda. Here are some basic tenets of feminist pedagogy, as we see it:

1. Fostering social analysis. Not only are we recommending women's learning and supporting women's voice, both literally and figuratively, but we are recommending that our teaching move beyond creating safe, supportive spaces, to a more critically engaged pedagogy that routinely practices social analysis and critique.
2. Supporting women's leadership. According to Batliwala (2011), one of the goals of feminist approaches to learning and teaching is to foster leadership that is *by* women, *for* women. A capacity-building approach to women's leadership

recognizes that it is not enough for women to feel included in a learning situation. In order for the change that one person encounters to become more widespread, women's leadership needs to be increased so that more women are positioned to make decisions and to lead change.

3. Building organizations. We need to work towards having this individual and group leadership of women transform the organizations in which they work. These organizations in which they work ought to be places where social analysis and critical pedagogical approaches are engaged, places where participants are learning together, not alone, as they are in most institutions of higher education.

4. Creating social change. Beyond the individual and the group level, and even beyond organizational change, feminist pedagogy needs to work toward societal change, beginning at the civil society level so that the world is transformed in some way by the learning that occurs. This sense of learning as a collective to change the world is reflected in the increasingly popular term, *transnational feminism*, which unites women in common cause, learning in initiatives for change (Manicom & Walters, 2012). The term *women's learning* simply does not do this.

Proponents of feminist pedagogy include bell hooks, Darlene Clover, Patricia Hill Collins, Shauna Butterwick, Libby Tisdell, and Patti Lather, among others. They are inspired by years of research, and by the teaching and practice of women in the arenas of education, civil society, politics, and social movements. They draw creatively from the writing of Mary Wollstonecraft, Harriet Beecher Stowe or Audre Lorde, and they are enriched by their own personal stories and biographical influences, that is their own stories and experiences which they bring to bear on their theory and practice. Whilst it has become au courant in critical pedagogy circles to name Paulo Freire and Myles Horton as the signature figures in practice (e.g., Manicom & Walters, 2012, p. 3), and there may be good reason for this, we argue that these leaders were not the only inspiration for women. Freire, as powerful as he has become in discourses of criticality in adult education, was one in a line of critical thinkers, more a bearer than a creator of that tradition (Schugurensky, 2011). If we look closely at the field of adult education, we see that many of those who are given seminal status – Malcolm Knowles, Cyril Houle, Roby Kidd—were in fact carriers of our field and not the original practitioners or thinkers, though they did indeed publish many important works that helped establish adult education as a field of study. We need to be critical of how males' positionality as the promoters of ideas such as self-directed learning are responsible for individualistic and masculinist tendencies in our theories and our field (Eichler, 2005; Stalker, 2011).

If we were to story our field from the perspective of both ideas and practice, and not seminal writers, we might tell a story of more cooperation. Our narrative might include the life of Mary Arnold and Mabel Reed, organizers of cooperative housing projects in the Antigonish Movement (Neal, 1998), or the women of Highlander (McDermott, 2007, 2008) or the emancipatory action work of Jane Addams, the founder of Hull House for immigrants in Chicago (Bauch, 2007), or of the important work done on conceptualising power by Mary Parker Follett (Smith, 2002). How we have chosen to tell our stories has affected our notions of ourselves, our field, and our possibilities for action. It has also affected how we have taught, what we have taught, and how we have viewed education—mainly as a traditional passing on of knowledge.

Feminist pedagogy is about how education and learning may be enacted in higher education or the community, through informal, nonformal, and formal means. It is not limited to discussions of physical place, though *place* as socio-political context has a bearing on the learning that occurs. Feminist pedagogy may refer to community based activity such as pedagogy that teaches women to agitate for rights as in Zambia or Chile. Within higher education, feminist pedagogy may refer to an approach to learning feminist theory, or processes that are used to stimulate thinking around issues that affect women such as in adult education or women's and gender studies, but it might also refer to processes used to teach economics or politics or history. What feminist pedagogy brings to the table is the power of questions, the use of inclusive teaching styles that challenge, and the stretch to have teaching reach to societal impact and change. In all cases, there is overt attention to the ways in which women as a group are affected by policies, principles, and practices. For instance, in economics, attention might be given to how changes in the national budget categories affect the wellbeing of women in rural areas, or how World Bank decisions affect women in the Global South. How this analysis is done is often participatory, highly dependent on dialogue, and through mutual political engagement of players.

Feminist pedagogy also brings the notion of grassroots knowledge, of the citizen as knowing (Gramsci's organic intellectual), and of the place for traditional intellectuals (Chovanec, 2009). It is not surprising then that the term *popular education* has become closely allied with feminist pedagogy. Popular education has been associated with Freire in the South in the 1960s and 1970s (see Allman, 2001) and has formed the basis for community worker manuals engaged in grassroots social change (Archer & Cottingham, 1996; Hope & Timmel, 1984/1999). Though it is a term closely associated with the South, it can refer to education anywhere. It refers to informal or grassroots types of education that are planned and participated in by people in their immediate environment as a way of enacting change. It can be for males, females, and families, etc. Like Freire's work with literacy, popular education begins in people's experience and involves intensive engagement and identification of the issues that concern people. For instance, popular education might involve theatre (as noted in Chapter 4) where people create and enact scenes that represent issues in their own lives. Together, they strategize solutions and they act on them. Popular education techniques can be brought into formal classrooms, but it is more usual for them to be site-based and grassroots, and located in the informal and nonformal spheres. Applied to feminist issues, popular education would include many of the same activities and processes, but would focus primarily on women's experiences as a starting point. In their collection on feminist popular education, Linzi Manicom and Shirley Walters (2012) provide examples of feminist pedagogy such as providing space for women to write. One of the contributors to their collection, Tobi Jacobi (2012), profiles the use of writing workshops in a women's correctional facility as a means of protesting the lack of agency and self-worth that are characteristic to prison settings. Jacobi notes that women's experiences of prison are different than men's, so a particular kind of educational model is needed to address their sense of alienation.

The importance of a feminist pedagogy and the need to be educated in this pedagogy is underscored by Maeve O'Brien (2011). In her discussion of feminist research on care which she overlays with Freirean conscientization, as a way to address rational, masculinist thinking. In her words: "To realize Freire's vision for transformation through dialogical education, the education of teachers themselves needs to reflect the call to the vocation of becoming human, not a call to increase technical skills for a knowledge economy (Ball, 2003b)" (p. 32). O'Brien is clear that we have to do more than talk about transformation, care, and "emotional relationality" we have to formally integrate transformation and care into programs, so that these concepts do not remain on the fringes. Of course, it is a challenge in times of "rational performativity" to do this integration, especially in formal education settings. Yet, work such as O'Brien's forms part of the growing resistance to the neoliberal infiltration of learning with social justice goals. Lyn Tett, Mary Hamilton, and Jim Crowther's (2012) research on literacy in the UK is a case in point. Analysis is needed as much as ever to push back against a dominant system that still privileges the wealthy, individualizes blame for inequalities, and suppresses dissent.

ENACTING FEMINIST PEDAGOGY

The techniques of feminist pedagogy are common to good pedagogy, regardless of the participants. The perspective and assumptions that undergird feminist pedagogy, however, are *sui generis*. Clearly, no one technique is feminist but it may carry with it the intent to enable a political mobilisation of women, to engage in projects in their own freedom. It likely begins with unpacking what Peggy McIntosh (1998) referred to as our own knapsack of privilege or, more precisely, considering our positionality which unlike privilege shifts with the situation and the actors. This unpacking or consideration of all our forms of capital and the resources at our disposal, is important in that it forces us to think about the advantages we all have be it connections, skin colour, money, education, or other. Yet, as Timothy Lensmire et al. (2013) remind us, confessing our privilege or being contained by oppression is a complicated process and is clearly not sufficient. We need not only to recognize our advantages and barriers, but also to move forward with action to create equity in society. Similarly, feminist pedagogy does not stop with awareness but rather moves to active engagement with issues such as race, dis/ability, and sexual identity. Here we look at some aspects of feminist pedagogy.

Aspects of Learning, the Body and Intuition

A critical theory of pedagogy ought to look at how the body is brought to life; it also ought to look at how the body is part and parcel of our lives and how we integrate it. For feminist writers, the body is a source of knowledge and of support, though it cannot be easily known, and for some of us, it may take a lifetime to figure out. Randee Lawrence (2012) draws attention to somatic knowing or embodied learning in her writing on this topic. She points to how we bring in this knowledge to our awareness—senses, perceptions, and the connection of the mind to the body (p. 29). Though we know rationally that we need to listen to our bodies, we often are not really sure what listening means (Clark & Dirkx, 2008).

Some authors have looked at women and learning and honoured the use of intuition. We are thinking here of Elizabeth Hayes and Daniele Flannery (2000) and others. They have noticed, as have women writers such as Lisa Ruth-Sahd and Elizabeth Tisdell (2007), that intuition is important for women. When Ruth-Sahd and Tisdell studied the working lives of nurses, they saw that most of what the nurses did was connected to the use of their intuition in the care of patients they were responsible for. Yolanda Nieves (2012) also highlights the role of intuition when she discusses the case of the Puerto Rican women she worked with in a community development project who were learning intuition from their lives and especially their bodies. Examples such as these enrich our conversation about what it means to listen to our bodies. In Nieves' words: "What we call 'gut feelings'—the intuitive or sixth sense—is a type of energy that shifts and grows like the fluidity of an embryonic membrane. Acknowledging this energy can be the force that drives social action" (p. 34). Nieves views intuition functioning like a skill or resource in the learning situation, and she suggests that we need to capture and nurture this intuition as a critical aspect of feminist pedagogy. Similarly, Carolyn Clark (2001) called our attention to the ways in which honouring intuition is part and parcel of honouring the whole body in learning. According to Clark, our bodies speak to us and we can hear what they say, if only we listen. She encourages teachers to help students reflect "on their somatic and emotional response to the experiences" (p. 87). Clearly, intuition can be nurtured through actually learning and teaching in the body.

Voice and Silence

It bears repeating that how women come to know is as varied as women's being. For some women, silence may mean exclusion and for others it may literally be preference, taking time to think and process ideas. As well, *voice*, another popular feminist term—certainly from *Women's Ways of Knowing* (Belenky et al., 1986)—can mean literally speaking in a group or it may mean being heard in print, in small conversations, through dance. Voice and silence are different for all women. One of the products of the Western education system is the valorizing of speech above all, be it in conversation, the all-hallowed dialogue, and the use of debate. Less helpful is the constant use of words and the neglect of any action. Feminist pedagogy, to be effective, needs to have some resolution in action, whether inside or outside the learning situation. Theory and action are entwined in the critically reflective practice. There is no one way of all women learning any more than there are ways of all men learning.

Teaching Format and Structure Vary

A given in feminist pedagogy is that learners sit side by side, in circles so they can see each other and so each person can feel free to contribute equally to the dialogue. In many ways, the circle is seen as a way to resist patriarchy and hierarchy. Yet, many writers have made it clear that the circle can cause problems and exert undue pressure on the next in the circle, for example, who has to come up with a brighter, more acute answer than the previous person (Foertsch, 2000). Circles, the *sine qua non* of feminist groups, might be varied with other teaching configurations and our ways of exchanging and enacting ideas shifted along with it. In some ways, circles and sharing limit our conversation and ignore the variety of ways in which people learn and the ways in which they are challenged to learn, to analyse, to critique. From a poststructuralist perspective, even circles can embody power relations—they can be coercive and force compliance or a refusal to speak to avoid the perception of being out of sync with the group. Power is an integral part of every classroom, and how we structure and organize the learning is an exercise in power relations. Pedagogues might try alternate modes of evaluation, encourage discussion, and allow for new ways of being; they may also pay attention to who resists and why, who does not participate, who is not engaged, and who needs a bit of space. Education strategies developed to help people learn the various forms and expression of power in their lives and work (e.g., Pettit, 2010; VeneKlasen & Miller, 2002) can help at the microlevel of understanding and addressing power within the classroom. This analysis looks at people's own situation to examine power in terms both of challenges of resistance and opportunities for empowerment.

Indeed, in the 21st century, adult educators ought to challenge the notions that we have to look at each other, face to face, and share our deepest feeling and thoughts in order to be feminist pedagogues. Learning can occur online in virtual classes, asynchronously, or self-directed, as well as through the usual venues of classrooms and nonprofit organizations. Ultimately, our task is to create the spaces where students, colleagues and participants can have open and critical discussion of power, class, gender and how these intersect. Our benign practices such as creating a warm and friendly teaching arena ultimately may not be honest unless everyone is included, has the right to be silent or vocal, has a variety of means of expressing his or her learning (art, text, journals, for example), and has the capacity and support to handle difficult issues.

Complicating the Pedagogical Role

There is great variety in motivation for learning and motivation can never be assumed. Some participate for occupation reasons and others for social or intellectual reasons; indeed, the reasons for participation have remained consistent over time (Ginsberg & Wlodkowski, 2010). Despite our acknowledgement of variety of motivations for participation, when the topic of feminist pedagogy comes up, we are inclined to think everyone is there to share a feeling, be transformed and start a revolution. Educators do not need to be reminded that learning occurs differently for different people and any given learning encounter might attract a variety of learners.

There may be an assumption, for instance, that all women want to engage in critical self-reflection. Australian writer Mike Newman (2008) has uncovered for us the challenges with many of self-focused practices and ideas—many people are not interested. Andreas Fejes (2011) reminds educators that self-reflection may involve a form of confession that makes people uncomfortable because it is surveillance. A colleague jokingly says she would never take her own classes because she uses group work, dialogue, and reflection, teaching and learning strategies that she "knows" work for her students but not for her. It bears repeating that we have to take learners where they are, and we would do well to realize that there may be a critical distance between our educational intent or motivation and the participants' perception of it. Elizabeth Ellsworth's (1989) stirring essay of the challenges of liberatory teaching in higher education comes immediately to mind. The title alone of her essay "Why doesn't this feel empowering?" hints at Ellsworth's constant struggle to motivate college students, overcome divisions, and create emancipatory learning experiences for each person in her classroom. The fact that this article is still cited regularly 25 years later is telling. Quite simply, a feminist pedagogue will need to experiment with a variety of approaches, be ready to meet resistance, and come to terms with the variety of learners and motivations.

Owning the Role of Pedagogue

For many, the role and position of critical pedagogue has been honed from years of experience and from educational achievements and credentials. Educators often come to a feminist teaching situation with this experience and knowledge, and learners are mostly aware of it; yet, their role as learner cannot be diminished or eroded in the quest for equality. Paulo Freire (1994/2004) had a good point when he wrote that "Dialogue between teachers and students does not place them on the same footing professionally; but it does mark the democratic position between them" (pp. 116–117). In a community setting, educators need to be mindful of those who came to hear a lecture and those who came to share in intellectual curiosity. For all our ideals and our beliefs, each teaching situation is different and each learner is too.

Feminist pedagogues have the responsibility of teaching learners from where they are and yet encouraging them to think a bit deeper, a bit longer, and a bit more clearly about issues that affect them and the world around them. The pedagogue's task is to take the learners' points of connection and to link them with larger social issues. We have the implicit mandate created from our political ideas to move deeper with the learner to crucial issues such as feminism, globalization, and world poverty. Staying with the personal will not do, as many disciplines and fields have found out; single issue politics and subjects such as "women" are mostly integrated into broader studies such as global issues, development studies, and more integrated programs that look at the interlocking issues of class, race, and ability. One of the fundamental educational challenges is to avoid becoming a ghettoized field that is removed from political, cultural, social conversations.

QUESTIONS WE MIGHT ASK

There is no doubt that the pedagogue—whether online, in the community, or in community college—has a responsibility to not only teach students, but also to prepare for the learning encounters, classes, or participatory processes in ways that challenge the choice of text, the choice of language, and the assumptions undergirding all pedagogical choices. As the second wave feminist educators criticized course syllabi comprised of the dead white European males (DWEM), we need to continue expanding our awareness of inclusion and exclusion and what this means in terms of content and action in addition to representation. Do our texts present life in its complexity or do they reinforce the status quo? Do we perpetuate myths such as that all women are the same, all teachers are women, all women are caring, and that all people can succeed and all it takes is determination?

Feminist pedagogical space is a space in which women challenge power, acquire gendered understandings, and collectively learn to create change. This organization provides a space for the ongoing critique that is necessary for the movements. Kalpana Wilson (2008) highlights the dangers of scaling back ongoing collective analysis and action. This scaling back occurs because of lack of resources to do it and also because of the conflicting priorities of donors. Yet, there is great need for this ongoing analysis. Wilson argues that neoliberal ideologies are persisting in gender and development (GAD) approaches that fail to challenge the patriarchal ideologies that lay at the foundation of processes that perpetuate inequalities. Without some collective activity or analysis (e.g., feminist pedagogical activity), this is hard to stop.

Wilson (2008) encourages a robust critique of how terms like *agency* have been coopted by government to suit their own purposes; they have overlaid it with neoliberal discourses to mask practices that fundamentally are not as empowering as they are made out to be. To point this out and to challenge the government's use of it is to subject oneself to the charge that agency is a good thing and that the government is in the business of promoting it. The government is using it to focus on what individuals might do to pull themselves up by their bootstraps. Using the terms in this way avoids the critical discussion of what factors oppress women and how the intricate interplay of social, economic, and other factors has inhibited agency. Similarly, agencies have befriended terms like *efficiency*, abstracting it from the global context of competing demands, and supporting programs to make women more efficient by some market-defined measurement.

When it comes to the actual pedagogical design, it is crucial to think of how to connect the educational encounter to the everyday lives of women: How is it that this discussion in this class, at this moment in time, connects to the needs and concerns of women globally? We might ask: Do we make deliberate attempts to make policies, ideas, practice related to women's lives? If the topic is literacy, do we connect this to underfunding for women's housing or violence prevention? If we are dealing with social movement learning, and if the learning and teaching are embedded in the social movement, as they often are, this is less complicated since shared interest brings us together as in the case of the Women in Arica, discussed at the opening of this chapter. If we are working in an NGO dedicated to pre-employment training for women, we might think about how workplaces are structured against family life and indeed privilege white males who may not have the "burden" of childcare. Or, if the training centres on ICTs, we might look at how women are usually only considered as end-users and not designers of the technology (Foroughi & English, 2013). Feminist pedagogues have a responsibility to provoke, to stir, and to challenge the status quo.

DISCUSSION

There are indeed tensions in our feminist pedagogical work and in our educational conversations that encourage us to walk the fine line between safety and edginess and to find a way to be creative and fruitful in our pedagogy. Often in discussions of women and learning, there is a stress on creating safety in the classroom. Humanists like Jane Vella (2002) who are sympathetic to women's ways of knowing, err on the side of having all people feel comfortable, engaged, and have their voices heard both literally and figuratively. At issue is the point at which the decision to be safe and nurturing is a limiting one, causing participants to seek harmony at all costs, to avoid contentious subjects. The teacher or facilitators may privilege peace above all and may avoid getting to the heart of the matter and of naming and probing problematic issues.

Susan Bracken (2008) notes that one of the most challenging aspects of her teaching is naming it as feminist and of having her students engage with the term. Feminism, at least in the United States, has a negative connotation for many. Bracken struggles with whether to call the work feminist and whether to insist with advancing her feminist theory and pedagogy. The luxury of being a higher education student may be that there is a disconnection from the issues of oppression in one's immediate environment which make the political seem foreign. It may also be true that the right-wing agenda of "learning for earning" pervades higher education or that critical perspectives involve emotional labour that students are unwilling to take on. Education becomes the commodity of the knowledge economy where the market dictates what learning is valuable or marketable. The issues are complex and seem to be more prevalent in the West, where speaking the language and practice of feminism can be avoided.

It is true that women bear the brunt of the world poverty, with statistics like those provided by the World Bank (2012) that tracks economic progress around the world. The Bank describes "sticky domains" where gender disparities stubbornly persist despite decades of development work. These include health status, economic participation, wage gaps, responsibilities for unpaid care work, ownership and control of assets, and agency, both private and political. These gaps remain in both low-income and high-income countries. It is also true that women are comprised of more than poverty and issues. The point at which all our conversations in feminist pedagogical practice are about problems is the point at which we need to revisit our goals and effects.

These issues of feminist transnational debates are much broader today than ever. While there may be a need for women-only spaces in some conversations as a starting place or as an incubator of ideas, the reality is that life issues are people issues. We need to make what Mechtild Hart (2002) call, "the poverty of life affirming work" or motherwork, everyone's work and issue. Feminist pedagogy is important if we are to continue to raise questions and to integrate local and global concerns into our teaching. It is important if we are to engage in change with learners and to both think and act, the dialogical relationship of practice and theory that is assumed in praxis. Perhaps, as Donna Chovanec (2009) has said in her reflection on the women in Arica, Chile and their social movement, we may need to move from looking at what our role is to thinking about how we are affected by the movement and how are we shaped by it. As those engaged in feminist pedagogy, we have a responsibility to think, not only of what we bring but also how we are affected. An effective feminist pedagogy involves, above all, an ongoing conversation with our colleagues, with our participants, and with ideas about what we need to achieve and how we might achieve it.

CHAPTER 9

SOCIAL TRANSFORMATIVE
LEARNING AND WOMEN[1]

The Activist Mothers of Xalapa is a group of women in the state of Veracruz, Mexico who provide support for each other in a political struggle with a patriarchal and corrupt government that has allowed their children to be taken from them in custody hearings where false charges are often trumped up against them (Facio, 2013b). This movement draws upon the strong devotion or respect for mothers in Latin cultures and provides a space for mothers to share grief and to take action as a united group. In banding together for a political cause, they subvert the notion of a mother as a quiet, docile woman who stays at home and accepts the various abuses of the patriarchal judicial system. The stereotypic power and celebration of motherhood is drawn upon to marshal strength for the movement in which these political mothers protest the male-oriented judicial system and demand that their children be returned. They are not a large group, but they are mighty in their commitment, shared outrage and determination.

Social transformative learning is a helpful lens through which to view the experience of these women and their learning. Transformative learning, at least in the tradition promoted by Darlene Clover (2006b) and Carole Roy (2012; see also Hansman & Wright, 2005; Jeanetta, 2005; McCaffery, 2005) has the potential to help us understand the ways in which women become engaged in learning in various venues: nonformal learning in the community, formal learning in higher education, incidental and informal learning in both the home and the workplace. Yet, insufficient attention has been paid to the gendered dimensions of transformative learning and of its social transformational possibilities.

WOMEN AND TRANSFORMATION

How women, social transformation, and learning have become disconnected is a curious matter when there seems to be a veritable explosion of literature on transformative learning including published handbooks (e.g., Taylor & Cranton, 2012; Mezirow & Taylor, 2009), journal articles (e.g., Hanson, 2013), and conference presentations (e.g., Mejiuni, 2009). Though there has been considerable interest in understanding the theory and much of it applies to women's personal experiences, what is unclear in the literature are the points of disjuncture and connection between transformative learning and social transformation learning. The former, transformative learning as it is often understood, is more closely allied with the annual American conference and *Journal of Transformative Education*, and follows in the largely individual-focused school developed from the work of Jack Mezirow (Mezirow & Taylor). Admittedly, as Edward Taylor and Patricia Cranton (2013) note, much of this scholarship misses the fact that Mezirow was originally influenced by feminist and critical concerns, namely the experience of his own wife returning to school in midlife.

Social transformation, in contrast, has been an integral part of the history of adult education, and is more tightly bound to the critical perspectives on education inspired by Freire (1970). Social transformation is well represented in collections from Linzi Manicom and Shirley Walters (2012), and Angela Miles (2013). The social transformation literature, which focuses on global concerns and international debates, could benefit from engaging the American literature on women's experience and personal transformation, as this is important to understanding transformative learning experiences for women. A case in point is the transformation that quantum physicist Vandana Shiva experienced when she decided to turn her attention to genetically modified crops and the environment in India. Her personal and family relationships, and her understanding of what was happening in agriculture in her country, encouraged her to focus her life work on genetic engineering and eco-diversity (Mies & Shiva, 1993; Shiva, 1994). This personal awakening led to her engagement with global issues and concerns, a link that is often obscured in the social transformation literature.

Feminist researcher Nancy Taber (2012) gives an autoethnographic account of her own life path beginning with her training as an air navigator in the military and then serving on a destroyer as a helicopter tactical coordinator. In later years, when she made the transition to academic life, she was able to turn a critical gaze at this militaristic and patriarchal world and see her own evolution as a researcher and feminist. Rather than leave the military behind in her academic work, she has taken up her experiences as data for examination and social critique. For Taber, "It is not enough to engage in an evocative representation of experiences and understandings; an analytic critical examination that focuses on power relations is key in order to work against systemic societal marginalization and oppression" (p. 82). Taber makes the point that rather than stop with relating experiences, we must move to analysis and examination as she herself has done in interrogating the isms of her life in the military.

Similarly, there are very real connections between local events that we experience on a daily basis and global movements or struggles. On the spectrum one can imagine a local group, say in India fighting for women's safety from rape and sexual violence, and on the other end of the spectrum, UN-sponsored global conferences. The issue is pushed from both ends to accomplish goals in women's freedom. Sometimes the push starts with the local area and it goes upward, as in the Indian rape case. Sometimes, the issue starts from the international venue and disperses through to workshops and advocacy campaigns. After the Fourth World Conference on Women in Beijing in 1995, from which many documents were issued, local groups of women internationally turned to these very documents to support their local work (Caglar,

Prügl, & Zwingel, 2013). Examples such as this call to mind the inanity of wanting to separate the personal and the social worlds—there is always overlap and indeed these experiences can yield rich information regarding the local–global nexus.

Healing the Divisions

Social transformation learning bears a close resemblance to the practice and efforts around popular education, ideas that are developed in the other chapters of this book, especially the chapter on health. Though efforts are often made to link the individual and social strands of transformative practice, they have become increasingly discrete. In this book, we are working to build alliances between these strands.

Women and their learning have not been a key feature of either of the schools of transformative learning, though it is clear that the social transformation proponents are more likely to consider women and certainly more likely to consider the gendered aspects of learning (e.g., Hanson, 2013; Manicom & Walters, 2012) than the mainstream understanding. Although there are two somewhat separate trajectories, there are traces or undercurrents in many discussions and programs of a particular transformative experience for women. Even Taylor (2008), who provides a major overview of transformative learning, avoids naming gender as a central element of transformation. When international organizations such as UNESCO, who do have a social transformation agenda, stop naming women (and gender) in their major pronouncements of priorities, as happened at Belém, Brazil (CONFINTEA VI) in 2009, it is very difficult for smaller groups and organizations to keep women's rights in focus (Stromquist, 2013). Indeed, a perusal of most mainline organizations and publications shows that gender and women's rights are subsumed under other categories, as if they had already been accomplished and could be easily accommodated in larger discussions of mainstreaming and inclusion. When we look around at the university to which we are both connected, it is clear that women continue to make up the majority of the student body and professoriate in adult education.

In the attempt to unite with other causes in the struggle for equality and to tone down feminist rhetoric, adult education scholars appear to have foregone special attention to women; de-politicization like this means that women's needs and causes are increasingly hidden. Experiences such as race, disability, and class are highlighted, without particular attention to women, though the reality is that women are disproportionately affected by the issues they raise (English & Irving, 2012). Naming women's transformative learning as a central concern puts the spotlight on these interlocking issues and on women specifically. Those who come into the adult education field from the worlds of health, nursing, and business, for instance, often have not had exposure to social science insights on women/ feminism/ gender. Gender and feminist insights help those in such areas of practice think about their work as having a critical and social transformational goal, not just a self-actualizing one, rooted in humanistic and constructivist assumptions.

Much of the discussion on women and learning presupposes positive transformation, dealing as it does with personal and institutional challenges that affect women's entry into educational programs and their active participation in them (see Filliponi-Berardinelli, 2013). It is also true that much of transformative learning theory is rooted in humanistic and constructivist theories, which are focused on positive growth and development. The reality and subsequent study of women's challenging location in the workplace, the community, the home, higher education, and the development sphere has lent itself to extended discussions of transformation and whether it can always be positive (Taylor & Cranton, 2013).

In adult education, there is less and less interest on research on women as a discrete category. This is surprising given the overall commitment of adult educators to women and learning and to feminism more specifically (e.g., Ryan, 2001). When it comes to transformative learning, the record is also not stellar. The *Journal of Transformative Education* has published few related articles (e.g., Clover, 2006b; Williams, 2006), and the accompanying annual conference on transformative learning also has few. Now, with the demise of *Convergence*, a likely publishing outlet for articles on social transformation, there are few scholarly places to develop these ideas; exceptions include the UK journal *Concept: Journal of Contemporary Community Education Practice Theory* (see http://concept.lib.ed.ac.uk/).

Part of the silence is around the vocabulary used for transformative learning, with practitioners likely to use terms such as *conscientization, empowerment,* and *transition* (e.g., Arnot, 2006; Stromquist, 2006) to name the experience of people's engagement in radical social change. Meanwhile, writers such as Nancy Fraser (2005, 2007) use the term *redistribution* to approximate what we mean by radical social change or the redistribution of structures and material wealth. The language matters and in our quest to find the right language to describe the experience and the learning, we sometimes veer in different directions and miscommunicate. Whether we can ever resolve this issue is unknown.

ENGAGEMENT OF THEORY WITH WOMEN'S LEARNING

One of the possible reasons that much of the discussion about women and transformation has been limited to individual concerns is that many writers and thinkers rely heavily on the humanist writing of Belenky et al. (1986), who have one of the first publications on women's learning. Most of the subsequent work on women's transformation pays homage to it, either directly or indirectly (e.g., Cranton & Wright, 2008). Writing more than a decade later, Mary Belenky and Ann Stanton (2000) were gently critical of Mezirow's (1978) linear and rational version of transformative learning, noting that "Critical discourse, the doubting game, can only be played well on a level playing field" (p. 89), suggesting that the field is rarely level for women. Belenky and Stanton's critique has not been not widely noted, though we could benefit from hearing it; our ability to see and understand women's transformations is affected by a reliance on a masculinist discourse and framework that privileges rationality. Belenky and Stanton acknowledge that such an approach devalues the experience of women. In looking back at Mezirow's attention to "reflective discourse, critical thinking, and evaluating one's basic assumptions" (Belenky & Stanton, p. 91), they see that he seems to celebrate separate knowing as opposed to the connected knowing that they celebrate. As a way forward, they offer practical strategies for integrating their theory in teaching and learning situations, stressing the metaphors of voice and midwifing and focusing on what adults need and want to know. Similarly, Claire Forest (2009) points to the value of enabling women to examine the underlying meaning in their life experience and to highlight their interests and needs. Critiques such as these bring our attention to the ways in which existing understandings of transformative learning do not make way for women's experiences or potential engagement in social action. Working from collective experience—their own and others—women learners can then move forward collectively to engage and enact change.

Clearly, Mezirow's (1978) separate and rational way of knowing may not occupy the central place that he asserted, especially for women's experience and collective action. While critical and rational thinking is important, especially for oppressed groups whose voices have not been heard, it is also important to work with emotion, experience, and relationships as a basis for further change (English & Irving, 2012). One of the ways to bring individual and social transformation together is by naming the benefits of transformation including those for social change and for personal transformation (Ferris & Walters, 2012). This calls for more direct attention to building on insights from practice and the community. When we discuss critical educators and activists such as Nellie Stromquist (2013), bell hooks (2001, 2013), and Nancy Fraser (2007), we might see them as exemplars of the social action and transformative struggle. In not deliberately naming these activists *social transformers*, we miss an opportunity to sharpen our lens of transformative learning. Similarly, we might look back at major adult education and literacy work such as the Cuban Literacy Campaign in the 1960s, or the Occupy Movement in the 2000s (that used learning strategies similar to the consciousness raising work of second wave feminism, see Rebick, 2013), and use these as a place for directly making our understanding of transformative learning more robust by incorporating or contributing concrete examples of activism and change.

FACILITATING WOMEN'S TRANSFORMATION

There are some areas that can be developed to make the transformative learning theory on women more robust and the practice in the field stronger. We recognize the importance of the core elements of transformative learning theory such as individual experience, critical reflection, dialogue, holistic orientation, context, and authentic relationships (Taylor, 2009), but argue that there are other elements important for women's transformation.

Importance of Relationships

Relationships are key in women's transformative experiences (Ferris & Walters, 2012; Hanson, 2013). In the words of Heather Ferris and Shirley Walters, we can encourage relationship building through a heartfelt pedagogy (p. 85), which engages both our compassion and our sense of solidarity with the other. This connects to Annie Brooks' (2000b) notion that the opportunity for women to share their life narratives is at the heart of their transformative experience. Repeated over and over again in discussions on women is the significance of an enclave or gathering for women, which can facilitate friendship, trust, and transformative learning (Cooley, 2007) or the value of collaboration and support (Cooley). Nigerian writer Olutoyin Mejiuni (2009) uses the term "transformative mentoring" (p. 277) to describe transformative learning among women in academe.

Although, arguably, relationships and mentors are an integral part of transformative learning for both men and women (Cranton, 2006; Taylor, 2009), they are especially important for women and even more for women in crisis. The collective aspect of women's experience in groups as the catalyst for transformation seem to be very important as well, perhaps more than any disorienting dilemma. Adult educators need to continue to build relationships and supportive conditions in which women's transformation might occur. This happens in all sectors of transformative learning—hence the need and emphasis for the collective. Indeed, Elizabeth Whitmore, Maureen Wilson, and Avery Calhoun's (2011) collection on activist movements, such as the Raging Grannies that "work" shows that relationships are their strength.

Importance of the Body

A decidedly female version of transformative learning is developed by several writers, including Linda Armacost (2005) who writes on menopause and its transformative dimensions, Alison Buck (2009) who looks at the use of photography to understand women's midlife spirituality, and Kimine Mayuzumi (2006) who examines the physical ritual of the tea ceremony for healing and transformation of women. The body is the impetus and the site of learning, creating change and enacting new possibilities, in some cases encouraging women to undertake physical activity as a means of challenging stereotypes of aging (Kluge, 2007). Through the body, it is possible for women to be transformed in self-perception, moving from stereotypes and negative self-image to "increased connection with and confidence in their bodies" (p. 187).

Adult educators have showcased the role of the body in women's learning and have focused specifically on embodied knowing and experiential learning (Michelson, 1998; Tobin & Tisdell, 2015), as a way to challenge the predominance of the mind in learning. Non-cognitive modes of knowing and engagement are, therefore, possible, and the mind-body disconnection is diminished (Barnacle, 2009). Insights about the body can be used to inform transformative learning theory and to move it beyond the metaphors of midwifing that are less relevant to many women. They also lend support to the teaching domain by encouraging us to give pride of place to the body in learning and to refuse to give rational, cognitive learning all the space in the teaching and learning encounter. If we took the body seriously in our discussions of social transformational learning, we in the West might better understand social movement learning, which involves the body in activism and protest as a literal barrier or shield (see Chapter 10).

Importance of Emotion

Along with the body, we can bring the role of emotion to our understanding of social transformation learning. Much of the transformative learning literature on women focuses on oppressive conditions that surround women's learning. These conditions directly and indirectly affect their transformation either by stymieing it or by serving as a catalyst. It seems women who became stirred up by their circumstances, who worked together with other women, had the ability to be transformed by the "drama and extreme emotional distress" (Hamp, 2007, p. 176) that is sometimes part of women's learning. This suggests that emotion plays a particular role in transformation for women, though it is not always named directly. For instance, Stephen Jeanetta (2005), Claire Forest (2009), and Shondrah Tarrezz Nash (2007) speak to the critical awareness fostered in women about their desperate life circumstances, but never directly name anger, resentment or even peace and love among the women. Curiously, emotion is virtually silent in many of these narratives. Yet, we know from bell hooks (2001) and Freire (1970), emotion plays a role in transforming one's life circumstances. Applied to social transformational learning, the identification and inclusion of emotion in our discussions allows us to appreciate it at a deeper level. Naming and working with emotion can be key to facilitating the transformative learning of women.

Importance of Understanding Race, Class and Oppression

As we move from a focus on individual women as learners through relationships, emotion, and the body, we come to the social, cultural, and economic factors that affect transformative learning and women. Race, class, gender, and ability are dealt with a little in the literature, yet collectively we see that they are major factors to be considered in understanding the intersection of women and transformative learning. For instance, in her work, Johnson-Bailey (2006, 2012) highlights the role of race and suggests that struggle is part of the transformative learning process; few other writers take on these issues directly. Her race-centric perspective holds much in common with certain strands of feminism and is reminiscent of Hill Collins' (1998) work, which suggests definite links for those interested in pursuing the transformative dimensions of women's learning. Although there may be an uneasy alliance between some aspects of feminism and some of the theory of transformative learning, given occasional competing claims between transformative learning and social change adherents, the benefits of a critical lens would be useful. From our Canadian perspective, we realize that attention to the First Nations communities is especially needed. There little written in this area and our practice is correspondingly weak. Barbara Walberg (2008) notes the potential transformative learning has for First Nations students working to understand the implications of colonialism on their lives and ways of thinking, as well as contributing to their healing.

It is significant that much of what we know about transformative learning and women is derived from studies of women's experiences in oppressive conditions. For instance, Susan Meyer (2009) studied lower class women in East Harlem, Nash (2007) examined the impact of intimate partner violence and social dynamics on African American women, and Laurel Jeris and Jaya Gajanayake (2005) worked with Mezirow and Taylor's (2009) theory to examine perspective transformation among women in Sri Lanka. Implicit in these research topics is an understanding that tragedy, violence, or other social factors can be instigators of a disorienting dilemma (the traditional precursor of transformation). The issue is that it can limit discussions of women's experience to disasters and problems, and focuses on personal problems as opposed to group experience, and the possibility of moving to the next stage of social transformation, which engages our capacity to hope for a better life.

Similarly, Deborah Kilgore and Leslie Bloom (2002) draw from their work with women in crisis to point out the challenges of facilitating transformative learning with people struggling. They suggest that educators need to work to really hear the voices and experiences of these women and to reinterpret the transformative learning in light of their insights. Theirs is a challenge to the rational and linear expectations of Mezirow and Taylor's (2009) theory in that it offers a roadmap to facilitating change; this is a roadmap of a circuitous journey that involves a stress on voice, story, and listening.

Underlying all these approaches is the need for the centrality of the collective experience for women, as a starting (but not ending) place. Juanita Johnson-Bailey and Mary Alfred (2006), for instance, bring in the experience of black women educators, noting the relevance of their own experiences of race and transformative learning. They stress that educators need to understand their own process of transformation as a precursor to their own teaching. They also need to understand the culture in which transformative learning arises, the cultural story that ought to be named and understood. Speaking from the perspective of feminist poststructuralism, Annie Brooks (2000a) highlights the importance of valuing the cultural stories of the learners as well, and of allowing multiple narratives to emerge in the teaching and learning encounter.

As Juanita Johnson-Bailey (2012) observes, the positionality of racialized women is a complex one since they deal with race, sexual orientation, culture, gender, age, ability, and so on to overcome challenges or exclusion. They have been classified and included or excluded on the basis of a variety of factors. We slot people in and out in terms of who they are; knowing and incorporating the experience of the body and of race is crucial to our understanding of social transformation for women. Whose culture? How is it encountered? Why does it matter?

A number of adult educators have pursued the links among women, class, and learning. These links have been developed primarily in the UK by researchers including Sue Jackson (2003, 2010; Jackson, Malcolm, & Thomas, 2011) at Birkbeck College and Jane Thompson (2007) of the National Institute of Adult Continuing Education, among others. They are interested in the interlocking nature of the multiple systems of oppression—race, class, gender, and sexual orientation—and with how these have affected or facilitated learning. It would be a logical leap to conjoin these insights with transformative learning and to make deliberate attempts in practice to be aware of how race, class, gender, and power affect learning for women. We cannot avoid discussing these interdependent social factors with our participants, even if the dialogue is charged and challenging.

Negotiating Tensions

We would encourage those interested in women and learning to work further on healing the divisions between individually-oriented and social justice-oriented transformative learning, the two basic directions of the theory (Johnson-Bailey, 2006). It would seem that the writing in transformative learning and women has been predominantly influenced by Mezirow (1978) and Belenky et al. (1986; see also Belenky & Stanton, 2000; Brooks, 2000b). The latter group might learn from the more global and social justice strain of transformative learning pursued at the Institute for Development Studies at Sussex in the United Kingdom and at OISE/University of Toronto, in Canada. These perspectives are decidedly revolutionary, change-oriented, and rooted in the conscientization process envisaged by Freire (1970), Nellie Stromquist (2013), and Heather Ferris and Shirley Walters (2012). The same recommendation to diversify might be made of the Freire group and their seeming division from personally oriented transformation. The inability to see change on a continuum from personal to global has halted our understanding of transformative learning for women. Being able to see the theory as existing on a continuum will enable transformative learning theory to become more robust and to further strengthen its claims to both social and personal transformation. We need to keep asking: Are we building bridges between varying perspectives, or are we further bifurcating the field? Are we reaching out to build alliances with other disciplines and their theories? For instance, Blunt's (2007) work serves as an exemplar of how theoretical perspectives on social work might inform and strengthen transformative learning. Other likely areas for investigation include nursing and health promotion theory, where little work has been done. We need to keep looking for ways that transformative learning theory might inform our work, and to lessen the ways in which we suppress it.

DISCUSSION

We recognize here that many of the historic contributions from studies of feminist theory and pedagogy have become mainstream in adult education. For instance, Brookfield (2010) observes that we have now come to consensus that "learning is holistic" (p. 76), an insight that was once applied only to women's learning. Therefore, we encourage researchers in transformative learning to examine whether some of the gendered dimensions of learning that we have identified for women such as emotion and the body might be applied to all of transformative learning. In part, we see this focus on women's transformative learning as a possible incubator of ideas and practices for adult education generally. We would suggest that researchers ask questions such as: Is the body as important to men's learning as it is for women's? Does emotion play a key role in men's transformation?

As seen above, there is little research that substantially builds on the theory connecting gender and transformative learning, though the synergies are implied. Since women's learning is central to adult education, given the gendered nature of our field, there are many reasons why we need to pursue this line of inquiry. The feminist movement was founded on women's experiences of naming and understanding their experiences. Educators in women's centres and support groups often witness transformations of women's understanding of themselves and of the systems that oppose them. Transformative learning offers a strong theoretical framework from which to understand learning and the particular challenges that women face in gaining access; consequently, we encourage research in this area. Yet, we want to be careful not to further essentialise women and their experiences or contribute to their further marginalization in society. This is a tension that we will need to be mindful of in this important area of inquiry.

NOTE

[1] This chapter draws on L.M. English & C.J. Irving. (2012). Women and transformative learning. In E.W. Taylor & P. Cranton (Eds.), *Handbook of transformative learning: Theory, research and practice* (pp. 245–259). San Francisco, CA: Jossey-Bass. Adapted with permission from Jossey-Bass.

POWER, RESISTANCE AND INFORMAL LEARNING[1]

In 1977, 14 women met to form the Mothers of the Plaza de Mayo to find out what had happened to their children who were disappearing in government raids and abductions during Argentina's Dirty War. The women started marching peacefully in front of the presidential palace to draw attention to the disappeared and to demand the government answer for its crimes and its part in killing their youth. The Mothers grew to be a force to be reckoned with, gaining scores of participants, and eventually factioning into two groups, one oriented to legal reform and the other to overt political action in protesting the secrecy, illegality, and murder of their children. These mothers were by and large nonpoliticized women who became well versed in legal matters, protests, and strategies for change. As a movement, the Mothers of the Plaza de Mayo helped Argentinians to name their oppression and to become skilled in the political ways and means to bring the government to account (Bouvard, 1994). Their marching peacefully in front of the presidential palace is what Parviainen (2010) calls a "resisting choreography" (p. 311); not a dance but rather a performance of resistance that uses the body as a political tool to enable and facilitate relationships between actors and with those who witness. In describing these performances, Parvianinen draws attention to other choreographies of resistance such as the group-crawling performance for striking nurses in Helsinki in 2007, the protest by Greenpeace at a nuclear construction site in 2007, and a protest in the 1989 Chinese student movement. Like the Mothers of the Plaza de Mayo, these social movement actors are using their bodies to teach and perform resistance in a way that challenges violent means and assaults.

LEARNING AND THE COMMUNITY

Despite the evidence in examples such as these that community groups and organizations can be the site of major learning and strategic action, the bulk of state education funds still go to schools, colleges, and universities; moreover, citizens, by and large, support this distribution of funds, though they might protest inadequate funding for particular community groups and nonprofit organizations. While the government may spout rhetoric valuing community-based education and use the language of lifelong learning, they counter this stance by privileging formal institutions over people's movements, and prioritizing learning for earning over learning for living. The informal learning sphere has been both underfunded and neglected, despite the fact that most adults are continuously learning in their everyday lives, though usually not for credentials and diplomas (Livingstone, 2012). Meanwhile, Margrit Eichler (2005) and Eichler et al. (2010) have documented that women, in particular, do considerable learning in their work in the home.

Perhaps as important for women in organizations as what they are learning is the lack of recognition for this learning, though it has implications for how we look at skills for employment and credentialling. In his comprehensive studies of informal learning, Livingstone (2012), with his team of researchers at Ontario Institute for Studies in Education (OISE)/University of Toronto, has documented much of women's learning across time. Livingstone points to the ways that women are unqualified on paper and lack the recognition that their work has brought them. His colleague, Margrit Eichler (2005), has worked with him in the Work and Lifelong Learning (WALL) research network to highlight just how much women have learned that has been undocumented and unacknowledged. Her analysis contributes to a broader understanding of women's motivations for learning and the various ways they are involved in learning. Eichler et al. (2010) created a better understanding of the learning involved in women's housework when they examined the ways in which women's tasks in the home are a site of continuous and often beneficial learning and complicated learning. Areas of learning include: home maintenance, cooking, home renovation, and budgeting. Based on data collected in three different surveys – 1998, 2004, 2010 – by the WALL network, Eichler et al. explore how women learned specific and complicated tasks in carework and housework, and how this learning is undervalued and unrecognized by the workplace. Learning in the home has been undervalued for reasons such as a stress on androcentric research and the androcentric voice, not to mention our alliance with capitalist systems that privileges education for professionalization, credentialing, and the workplace (a basic human capital argument).

The transformative elements of women's everyday learning are not as yet fully explored, when this might be a site of considerable transformation. Clearly, market values are not care values. Despite the value of such motherwork (Hart, 2002), which has already been named, they look specifically at what women learned (see categories above) and made an argument to connect with the marketplace.

We would add that it is very much part of the history of women to have them learning through participation in folk arts activities and in community centres craft guilds as well in movements such as the Women's Christian Temperance Union (WCTU) where they learned public protesting, strategizing, and acting in the name of temperance. In many ways, women are drawn to the informal sphere where they experience mentoring and coaching, supportive relationships, and learning through dialogues—in short, all the facilitators of informal learning. In recent times, feminist nonprofit organizations such as community centres and services for victims of abuse, not to mention the YWCA and Women's Institutes, have become popular public learning spaces for women. In order to document some of this informal learning, this chapter focuses directly on female employees and board members of such nonprofit organizations to explore how they have learned about feminist pedagogical practices, funding opportunities, grassroots organizing, and leadership, and how to actively pursue a social change agenda.

This chapter draws on a study of 16 women connected with feminist nonprofit organizations (English, 2005a, 2006a). Increasingly, such feminist organizations are alternatives to the traditionally male and gendered institutions of higher learning; yet, they are often ignored by government, adult educators, and gender researchers who have been more interested in how women enter or are excluded from the halls of academe (see Benseman, 2005; Filliponi-Berardinelli, 2013). For working class, low literate, and vulnerable populations of women, feminist nonprofit centres may provide a sustainable and safe lifelong learning pathway. In this chapter, we propose a closer look at such informal venues which often help women make the transition to schools, enter the workforce, or become more active citizens. Here, we explore these sites of learning as both complex and contradictory, yet highly effective in facilitating informal learning at the community level.

Some cautions are in order. To begin with, it would be simplistic to read all feminist organizations as holding similar views and practices of feminism, given that feminism has many forms (see Miles, 2013). What these feminist organizations do share is a concern to improve the lives of women through political and social change, though how they do this varies with the institution and its members. It would be simplistic, too, to do a reading of nonprofit organizations as good and caring and higher education as bad and rigid, or to paint informal learning as good and formal learning as awful. Instead, a Foucauldian poststructural lens (Fejes, 2011; Fejes & Dahlstedt, 2013) is used to shine light on the intersection of power, knowledge, and discourse within feminist nonprofit organizations to further understand how women learn and lead, as well as work for and against government, within these organizations (see also Brookfield, 2005; Chapman, 2003; Dreyfus & Rabinow, 1982; English, 2006a). Through Michel Foucault's (1977, 1980) poststructural lens, we can look at women's so-called preferences and choices more critically and view them for the complex and multilayered events they really are (see Hakim, 2003 for support of women's free choices). As Foucault's theory suggests, even benevolent organizations such as feminist nonprofit organizations are sites of power, knowledge, and resistance. It is precisely within this context that significant learning occurs, often because of the complexity.

Theoretical Underpinning

Several bodies of theory are helpful to this discussion. The first is Michel Foucault's (1977, 1978, 2003) poststructural theory of power and knowledge, which is used to analyse the learning content, strategies, and resistances (Burke & Jackson, 2007; Fejes, 2011; Hughes, 2000; Kopecky, 2012) that are part and parcel of this informal learning. Poststructuralism, or at least the Foucauldian approach to it, allows us to look at the intersection of power and knowledge in women's learning, especially as it relates to their interpersonal relationships with colleagues and board members, as well as to their external dealings with the bureaucracies of government and the community. Foucault draws attention to the ubiquity of power and its refusal to be located only in recognized and hierarchical structures such as government, the divinity, or the presidency. In particular, he acknowledges the pathways of power that flow capillary-like through all our relationships and through our bodies, as well as the resistances that always seem to accompany that power. He wants us to attend to the particularities of the familiar and how this minutiae is imbricated in each moment and interaction. It is within this minutiae that learning occurs.

Foucault's (1980) interest is in the less overt and more political ways that power is exercised (used, not owned); in this case it would apply to how women are created as learners, activists and feminist subjects in the process. According to Foucault, power is not a commodity we possess; it is relational and exercised between us at all times. Power is effected through practices, techniques, and procedures—what he calls *technologies* or *practices of power*—all of which we use constantly. According to Foucault, every time power is effected, there is a resistance; when closely examined, this site of resistance reveals the intricacies of power and its effects. Part of the learning and the creation of knowledge within feminist organizations is bound in this network of using power and resisting.

Foucault (1980) proposes a pastoral power, in lieu of sovereign power, to explain the seemingly benign exercises of power by groups such as government. Applied to government, pastoral power is exercised through the provision of money to care for women, such as providing housing and income support and introducing supportive policies around schooling and employment. The government becomes a socialist presence, ensuring care for everyone, even taking criticism for not caring enough. In so doing, governments oversee how women conduct themselves (see Dreyfus & Rabinow, 1982, pp. 208–226). Yet, the pastoral power is productive in that it avoids punishment and "encourages" individuals to choose or to desire conditions that lead to their improvement. Women on social assistance benefits, for instance, may take the training course in hair styling that is offered, in order to appear willing and able to work, even if they have no transportation and child care money. Yet, these same women may resist by finding creative ways to have expenses reimbursed, while earning their diplomas and becoming self-reliant.

Pastoral power is also confessional (see Fejes, 2011). In turn for the care, women must confess or bear their souls by filling out means tests, which require them to reveal the most intimate details of their lives. The hallmarks of this pastoral power, exercised by both the feminist organizers and the state, include intrusion into the private life of the individual through these various confessional practices, or micropractices and technologies of power. Through micropractices and techniques, feminist organizations and their members and directors are subjected—and subject themselves—to self-discipline (see Foucault, 1980), that is, in fear of who is watching them, they check their anger at government and poverty in order to appear docile and compliant, that is, deserving of funds. The strength in this theory is that it allows for some degree of choice and pushing back on the part of women.

A related body of theory here is on women and learning, which has been developing steadily since *In a Different Voice* (Gilligan, 1982) and *Women's Ways of Knowing* (Belenky et al., 1986), pointing to some of the unique aspects of women's learning in the last quarter of the 20th century. It became au courant to speak of women's learning as caring and connected and to separate this from men's ways of knowing, which are seen to be more logical and impartial. What ensued from these publications was a large body of responsive and supportive literature that addressed some of the dangers of a stereotypic and essentialist reading of women as unique and precious (e.g., Goldberger, Tarule, Clinchy, & Belenky, 1996). Yet, some stereotypes of women being relational (Fletcher, 1998), caring and connected (Belenky et al., 1986), and inclusive (MacKeracher, 2004) remain. Admittedly, within adult education itself, later literature tended to be somewhat critical, and to be open to multiple positions and actors within feminism (Hayes & Flannery, 2000; Malcolm, 2012). Slowly there is more being done to focus on women outside the official educational sphere, especially in the nonprofit sector where women are notably great in number (Jackson et al., 2011). There has been some attention to informal learning among women in technology (e.g., Butterwick & Jubas, 2006; Lin, Tang, & Kuo, 2012) and some attention to learning in nonprofit organizations generally (Sousa & Quarter, 2003) but none specifically on women's learning in nonprofit organizations. This chapter helps fill the gap.

Given that there are multiple forms of feminism—radical, liberal, critical, to name a few (see Miles, 2013)—it makes sense that not all feminists or feminist writers have welcomed poststructural/postmodern theoretical frameworks. Marxist feminists such as Shahrzad Mojab and her student Sara Carpenter (Carpenter & Mojab, 2011; Carpenter, 2012) protest that in focusing on non-unitary subjectivity and fluidity, postfoundational theories undo the achievements of modernity for women in addressing patriarchal systems that oppress them. Other critics charge postfoundational feminists of stripping away notions of agency and unitary subjectivity, of playing with women's lives, and negating material bodies—all of which have been important to feminists' struggles to unite against patriarchal institutions (see also Butler, 1994, 1999). Poststructural feminists such as Bronwyn Davies and Susan Gannon (2005) take on the detractors, pointing out that feminist poststructuralism is not about taking away agency for women or denying that institutions exist:

> The *agency* that feminist poststructuralism opens up does not presume freedom from discursive constitution and regulation of self (Davies, 2000a). Rather it is the capacity to recognize that constitution as historically specific and socially regulated, and thus as able to be called into question. (Davies & Gannon, 2005, p. 318)

It is precisely in the attention to the ways that women are regulated and discursively produced that Davies and Gannon (2005) have thought women and feminism can be reconstituted. In this chapter, we draw heavily on Davies' substantive work of negotiating the tensions of feminism and Foucault. Like Davies, we are concerned with acknowledging the ways in which women are produced as subjects and how they can effect change of that production, so that they are not determined as subjects. We are concerned with how they can create their own identity(ies) as knowing subjects who are, indeed, agentic.

A third body of theory that is of use here is informal and incidental learning theory. A prime example is Livingstone's (1999, 2012) study and analysis of informal learning in Canada. Building in part on the scholarship of Malcolm Knowles who studied informal learning in the 1950s, and Alan Tough who quantified informal learning in the 1970s, Livingstone's research indicates that 90% of adults are involved in informal learning for work or for general interest, and that the average amount of time they spend on such learning is 15 hours per week. This is an increase from Tough's (1979) finding that 70% of the 66 adults studied had been involved in a learning project that they had developed themselves. According to Livingstone, such untapped learning is problematic for those who lack credentials or who have perceived barriers to learning. In particular, he found that "those with self-rated poor reading skills tend to spend considerably more time in informal learning activities than those with greater reading facility" (p. 69). For Livingstone, and for all with an interest in lifelong learning, inattention to this group of informal learners is very problematic. He notes that "the collective recognition of this informal learning and its occurrence across the life course can lead to people more fully valuing both their own learning capacities and those of other social groups" (Livingstone, 1999, p. 68). It can also provide higher education and government with more accurate information with which to design learning programs, as well as to meet the needs of those who already possess considerable skills and knowledge. Livingstone's findings have particular relevance for women who have low literacy and are socially disadvantaged, individuals the organizations in this study typically serve.

One of the foremost writers on informal learning in social action is Griff Foley (1999) who writes about how people learn in and through the community. Yet, as some argue (see Gorman, 2007), Foley writes about individuals being learners and of them learning by themselves. Rachel Gorman brings a feminist perspective to bear on informal learning, pointing out that learning by women in social action is more often done collectively. She critiques Foley for focusing on men's experience and for narrowing women's experience for learning in the home. Significantly, Livingstone (1999) looks at women in the home too. For Gorman:

home may be a place of isolation and deprivation. The second problematic assumption is that informal learning is an individual process. This implicit notion of the "individual learner" is part of larger shift from education to learning (Ramdas, 1999), which depoliticizes learning. Applying theories of informal learning to social movements makes the theorization of political consciousness almost impossible. In his book on informal learning in social movements, Foley (1999) does not sufficiently deal with the power relations of race, class, and gender in the cases he provides. (p. 192)

This is a strong critique, but it bears repeating, as our focus is women in the social sphere, in the nonprofit organization. Similarly, Linzi Manicom and Shirley Walters (2012) point to the tension between recognizing individual differences and the collective dimensions of learning.

Gorman (2007) sees learning as about more than learning to improve oneself. She, in fact, sees it as very much about learning about oppression, exploitation, and political consciousness (p. 183). In this sense, research related to credentialing unskilled workers (Livingstone, 2012) is not a good basis for understanding women's learning in nonprofit organization. Rather we need a different theory of learning, one that embraces the political intent that is at the heart of women's nonprofit activity. Gorman notes that in any discussion of informal learning, there is a tension between an individual learning to survive and individuals and groups learning to resist and struggle against the oppressor. Gorman is clear that informal learning is deeply related to women working together to create change.

Methodology and Data Collection

In earlier work, English (2005a, 2006a) studied the learning of 16 women who were involved in nonprofit organizations as clients, employees or staff, directors, occasional visitors, and board members. Some of them may have held various identities over time (e.g., clients who became board members or directors, or board members who became directors). This research used a purposeful sample (Merriam, 2009) comprised of board members and directors to explore their learning within the organization. These participants were chosen because they were accessible for research given their regularized contact with the organization for work and meetings. As well, they were most likely to be knowledgeable about the inner workings and offerings of the organization, and to provide the most meaningful data. Of the 16 women interviewed using a semi-structured protocol, 8 were directors and assistant directors (minimally paid) and 8 were board members (volunteers). The participants ranged in age from 25–60 and had been involved from a minimum of 1 year to a maximum of 25 years (the median length of involvement was 5 years). Four of the board members were no longer serving on the board but were still attached to the organization. Of the 16 interviews, 4 were done by email, 4 done in person, and 8 done by telephone. The data were analysed with particular attention to strategies around relationships, dealing with conflict, and feminist practice. Questions centred on how these women learned about feminism, how they worked with/against government and each other to negotiate power in the organization, and how they learned from each other.

Typical of the nonprofit centres discussed here were local women's centres, transition or safe houses for women who are victims of abuse, and counseling centres for women. In addition to the nonprofit organizations that offered shelter were those that offer programming including pre-employment training, literacy instruction, and personal development courses. Located in rural and economically disadvantaged areas of Canada, they also offered psychosocial support for women through a drop-in centre, while others had lending libraries. The organizational structure and particular feminist orientation varied from organization to organization, yet they were all for women by women, and they had a political agenda to forward: the cause of women. The general structure consisted of a paid director, one or two paid staff members, and a volunteer board of about 10 members. In almost all cases, the organization relied on government funding as well as contributions from the community.

Context of the Study

The interview data highlight the participants' increasing knowledge of how they are affected by geography, economic conditions, and social class. And, as Foucault (1980) and Marshall (1990) note, it is the differentiation of the legal, traditional, and economic conditions which enable or bring power relations into play. In becoming part of a community unit, that is, the feminist nonprofit organization, these women learned informally how a collective voice could be more effective in achieving justice. Whereas individually some faced unemployment, or were underpaid and underemployed, coming together in this local collection was a learning experience. The organization was a place for them to take stock of their own circumstances and their shared plight. The nonhierarchical environment, participation in board decision-making, and engagement in feminist activism often provided the impetus for learning skills that might not have been otherwise available given their social and economic location. Factors such as illiteracy, lack of employment, class difference and access to higher education played into their narratives. They also affected their key areas of learning: learning to use resistance, silence, subversion, and strategy to create themselves as feminist actors and knowers.

Technologies of Power and Resistances

Although half of the 16 women interviewed had university degrees, and most indicated that their learning about feminism and feminist organizations occurred informally and incidentally through participation in the local organization. They learned by observing the daily operations, talking to more experienced members, participating in board meetings, and organizing commemorations and events for women. They learned about feminist participatory practices such as sharing in circles during board meetings, using consensus to come to decisions, and participating in committees. The regime of truth in these organizations was that these feminist practices are best practices, helping to further the notion of women as collaborative.

Feminist procedures such as circles and talking things through are technologies of power that produce effects; they produce power that is not negative—it is in effect, very creative (Foucault, 1977, p. 194).

Learning through Participation

One of the key areas here is with regard to the ways in which women's organizations operate. For instance, on the surface, they function in ways that are democratic and participatory. For instance, the directors encouraged a participatory structure where routine meetings are informal, often involving food and chat, and where leadership is shared. Common is the use of a living room type setting where participants sit in a circle intended to encourage conversation and sharing. Intentional learning activities are structured into these meetings and in the overall operations of the board. Attempting to practice or enact equality, the directors want to help board members learn about or be introduced to the ways of the organization: how to chair a meeting, how to apply for funding, how to organize a women's event (e.g., an anti-violence protest or International Women's Day celebrations). Given the particular structure of endorsing informal learning and inclusion, talking about issues of power and conflict in this research was difficult for both board members and directors/leaders.

For many of the board members feminist practices were new. There is indeed sharing and cooperation in traditional community groups, but what was new was the intentional effort to increase skills in self-reflection and organization. Some had never chaired a meeting or taken minutes before. An experienced director pointed out the span of her learning: "I have been involved since '84, kind of working on projects...the learning experience is everything from learning how to engage with government to understanding women's oppression." As one director noted, "we come to decisions though collaboration and negotiation." Another pointed out they were able to work through the issues because "it was all women on the board; women are less inclined to grandstand or to engage in impression management."

Yet, for some of board members, these feminist participatory practices were not without their effects. While directors were inclined to use the discourse of negotiation and consensual decision making, some of the board members experienced this discourse as a technology of power that suggested top down and patriarchal ways of being. One woman explained why she left after 5 years serving on the board, noting she just gave up since "We had become like a men's organization." The woman who left felt the power of seniority and position of the designated leader's voice and the undue influence of more senior board members (in some cases founders of the organization).

The feminist pedagogical practices of group sharing and consensus, not to mention collegiality, furthered and helped to reproduce the regime of truth that women work together well. It also produced a parallel, albeit minor, discourse of resistance among the leavers. As Foucault (1980) notes, "Each society has its regime of truth ... that is, the types of discourse which it accepts and makes function as true" (p. 133).

This regime of truth enables the nonprofit organization to run smoothly and produce educational and other opportunities for women. It also produces resistances when women who do not feel they have been heard leave. Feminism is a contradictory and complicated frame, and only in being involved do the women learn this. Women who are active in the organizations learn to negotiate the contradictions, allowing care and conflict to operate as parallel regimes of truth.

For rural and socially disadvantaged women, one key aspect of learning is about effective ways to be an advocate for oneself and others through lobbying government (i.e., activism). The "effective ways" constitute a different kind of activism than the public activism of feminism's 20th century first and second waves, which often involved marches and protests. For 21st century women in a grassroots nonprofit organization, the activism often consists of silent, subversive, and strategic approaches, reminiscent of James Joyce's (1968) "silence, exile and cunning" (p. 251). That said, taking to the streets has not been abandoned entirely.

The nonprofit organizations studied here were tasked to care for, advance, and defend the rights of women, especially through promoting education and literacy training. To support this work, the organizations needed to engage creatively with government funders. The women were learning that a simplistic view of activism as only visible protest, and of voice as only talking, is naïve: Like Alecia Jackson (2004), they "rely more on [their] actions and daily practices to disrupt the category of...woman" (p. 688, note 6). And, many feminists are like Jackson; they are less concerned with making their voices heard in traditional ways and more focused on accomplishing the work of the Movement in strategic and subversive ways through their actions and their daily practices. They also work to enable women to learn and exercise voice. Yet, this does not negate the fact that some women do visible protest; the point here is that the women in this study learned that these are not the only forms of resistance.

Resistance through Silence

Much of the time in board meeting and in the regular running of these feminist organizations is taken up with funding: learning how to access it and learning how to retain it. When viewed through the lens of Foucauldian poststructuralism (Foucault, 1980), silence becomes a micropractice of resistance to the funder's (government) exercises of power. The government exercises power by holding and controlling the funds and dictating public policy around how the funds can, or will, be shared with feminist organizations. The first specific technology of government power is in its categories of funding. Government typically allocates funding to women's organizations through two main envelopes: core funding for the regular running of the organizations and project funding for specific activities that must be applied for, like preventing date rape and reducing teenage pregnancy. Government keeps core funding to a minimum, which produces the effect of the organization constantly having to devise ways to get more, or even to keep what it has. If it really wants to provide education to women for literacy purposes, it may have to strategize to attain a long-term or sustained program.

The opportunity to apply for project funding for special causes such as AIDS and crime awareness, or LBGTQ safety training is made available to nonprofit organizations by government (Marple & Latchmore, 2006). Feminist organizations apply for these funds, complying with the rules of full disclosure of funds on hand and needs in their organization. In bearing all in this confessional practice, they appear to be meeting the government's demands. Their written proposals mirror the government discourse of management comprised of executive directors and boards of directors, a hierarchical discourse that they claim not to use in the routine running of the feminist organization. The power of government seeps into the feminist's proposal prose, yet they get the money and are, as one board member said, "creative with how they use it." Women learn to subvert these infralaws of the state (e.g., not actual legislation but policies determined by efficiency-seeking bureaucrats) by using the money for other purposes. As one director explained, "We have no choice but to apply for what's on the go. We spend a lot of time filling out forms for projects but at least they keep us afloat." In learning to keep quiet, feminist organizers can become effective challengers of government, using project funds to cover core costs or to engage in projects they believe worthwhile for women. They learn through networking that this strategy of silent resistance is utilized by feminists in other jurisdictions (see Fuller & Meiners, 2005, p. 170) and, through their actions, expand the definition of what counts as resistance (Thomas & Davies, 2005, p. 718). Silence, however, is one of many strategies they learn to use.

Using Strategy to Resist

Another technology of power exercised in feminist nonprofit organizations is strategizing. Women directors and board members learn quickly and often incidentally that they need to be strategic in what they ask for and how.

In response to the government discourse of inquiries, hearings, and other bureaucracies, the women in this study strategically and routinely complied with their own discourse that at times mocked that of the government. The women in this study noted that they did the expected public protests before government inquiries and supplemented it with their own strategies. They resisted the government structures with the use of "hidden transcripts" (Scott, 1990, p. 4), private discussion and decision-making, as opposed to public expositions. They resisted by fostering their commitment to egalitarianism through the use of consensus, circles, and shared decision-making. In essence, they were learning how to be strategically democratic and active in their own future. One experienced board member in her mid-40s explained what she had learned: "In terms of practical skills I have had both formal and informal learning. I have learned to lobby government, to be diplomatic, as well as to find strategies to try to work with government. It is no easier these days than yesteryear to do that and to secure funding."

Such exercises of power rendered the feminist organizers post-activist and post-heroic (see Ford, 2006, p. 84). They were learning to be activists of a new era, who sometimes used public displays of protest (for example, one woman in the study talked about Take Back the Night marches) and sometimes a subversive and quiet form. They learned to use a "subtle, routine, low level form of struggle and challenge" (Thomas & Davies, 2005, p. 720) that may not take down a government but will produce effects. Their resistance was built from within the system to some degree, which is not without its effects on the feminist organization. More importantly, though, these women were learning to be 21st century agents of change and were doing so from within the grassroots. These post-activists still use the visual rhetoric of posters and marches, but have learned that they can be even more effective by adding to their repertoire the sophisticated strategies of silence, subversion, and strategy. Their power has been exercised collectively and individually through each of these technologies.

The 16 women in this study were learning to be an integral part of the feminist movement, which, in its very existence, is a resistance to bureaucracy, a way of disrupting smooth readings of organizations and those who work in them. The nonprofit feminist organization exists as a public resistance to state control over women's bodies: their wellbeing, economic security, and self-image. The organization pushes into the public sphere the discourse of woman, sexuality, and feminism. In studying these feminists through power theory, we see how they lend a gendered and contextualized view to Foucault's theories of power (see English, 2006a). They not only perform resistance in observable acts and behaviours, but also in their multiple subject positions. And through participation and informal learning, the women in this study became seasoned actors and protestors.

Using Subversion to Resist Government Discourse

Government-speak is managerial and businesslike, as represented in the discourse of agendas, proposals, deliverables, funding envelopes, directors and boards of directors, and fiscal restraint. This official discourse can have the effect of deflecting attention from the actual intent of government actions, pronouncements, or policies. Some of these participants reported being "initially overwhelmed by the sheer volume of the paperwork and the bureaucracy" which, arguably, is government's intent. Women in this study reported performing resistance to this totalizing bio-power (i.e., control over women's bodies) by the use of their own technologies of power. One subversive way was forming alliances with other groups (see Butler, 1999). Here is how one organizational director, who described herself as very political, talked about the response to funding cuts in her province. "It's been very convenient for politicians, and media and some bureaucrats to foster that. To paint us all as being a bunch of whacko, militant, man hating, blah, blah, blah, to dismiss us." This reverse discourse is post-heroic and post-activist, in that it uses quiet, forceful and non-public means to effect change (see Ford, 2006, p. 84). And, at times it is non-cozy, subversive and creative or as one woman described it, "sometimes we pretend to be agreeable and ladylike." What is interesting here is that groups of women within these organizations learn to work together to effect change, publicly or privately. The importance of women's collective action has not changed, though these women are learning to use it for their advantage.

The creation of the resistant and subversive subject is one of the effects of this government exercise of power. Yet, it is also true that governments' and feminists' objectives are very different. Foucault's attention to the "types of objectives pursued intentionally by those who act upon the actions of others" (Marshall, 1990, p. 24) is helpful. The feminists within the nonprofit organizations had learned to subvert government technologies of power by collaborating with other similar organizations and working with them to lobby government. Their resistance is a unified voice, which has the effect of making government listen. One director described an instance of how she did this: "All the women's centres, all the transition houses and all the men's programs, we all got together and formed a loose coalition to address these funding cuts which at this point they have, they've stopped." Subversion becomes a technology of power that is an alternative to public protest. Feminists learn informally and incidentally how to be most effective in dealing with funders.

As feminists, they resisted the identity that has been ascribed to them (e.g., militant, crazy activist) and they engaged in a project of identity re-construction. The narrative of subservience ran through the feminist organizations. For example one board member admitted "We take what we can get from government;" and another said "we spend all our time trying to find out where the money is". Yet, there was a counter narrative also at work; these feminists had created yet another subject position: that of effective and caring worker, subversive feminist, and community development practitioner. One director described her leadership as "trying to do what she can for and with the women in the community" and helping "women on social assistance get the most they can from this system." The latter is in sharp contrast to the government labeling of women's organizations as deviant social organizations. Traced all through the interviews with these feminists was a reflexive construction of themselves as leaders and resistance fighters, who, as one executive director put it, really "showed government bureaucrats a thing or two." And, for most of these women, learning a new way of being had occurred gradually through active participation and not through courses or direct instruction.

The visual rhetoric of marches and banners, which characterized early versions of feminism, have been supplemented by a post-heroic and post-activist stance which is sometimes less visible, operating beneath the surface and coursing through the veins of these feminist organizations. This is a feminist activism that resists the government expectation of constant confrontation or simplistic compliance with the policies of the state. In taking the masculinist government technologies of power (inquiries, grants, competitions, etc.) and subverting them, these women have become post-heroic and post-activist. They do not conform to the essentialist expectations of heroes (often military, male, and macho) or of activists (often loud, abrasive and confrontational). Theirs is an activism and heroism of cooperation, linkages, and support (see also Thomas & Davies, 2005), which are longstanding dimensions of feminist activities. One only has to think of Rosa Parks who quietly refused to give up her seat. The learning and collaborating she experienced at Highlander that nurtured her confidence to resist (Horton, 1989) is often overlooked in the popular retellings of this supposedly spontaneous act. Women's groups such as the suffragists and temperance activists who knew the importance of forming alliances long before it was considered heroic (McCammon & Campbell, 2002). This contemporary enactment of feminism has been learned through trial and error and everyday struggle.

And, working in silence, as with most of these analyses of power, there is the resultant spate of overlapping and competing discourses that these women have learned to negotiate (see also Ford, 2006). This study revealed a number of them: inventors, creators, victims, militant warriors, subversives, and shrewd negotiators. Here is how one veteran director described herself:

> You learn...all on your feet. There was no manual to pick up. I mean even with our re-entry program here, which we started about two and a half years ago, maybe three years ago. When we started we had bits and pieces of information.... We had to invent that ourselves. We learned together.

These discourses work simultaneously, sometimes pitted against each other, to create subjects who are at times divided about the worth and integrity of dealing with government in these ways. Yet, these discourses also work to create subjects who are post-activist, who carefully negotiate a fluid identity to support their beliefs, their organizations, and their causes. They have developed the capacity to entwine discursive knowledge with financial resources, and the ability to decide how these resources can be apportioned. Their ultimate technology of power is knowing— intuitively and otherwise—that the capillary power of government is embedded in the daily practices and decision making of their feminist organizations, yet they can and will resist alignment with the state. Their resistance does indeed count as a source of social change and becomes a useful life skill for them. The supportive structure of the organization allows them a safe place to sort out and live these contradictions.

ANALYSING THE ISSUES

It would seem that feminist nonprofit organizations not only have a role in keeping feminism as a movement alive (see Ferree & Martin, 1995), but they also have an important role in supporting and facilitating women's learning. Yet, this learning is largely undocumented and unacknowledged. Like the women in Gorman's (2007) study, the women in this study were learning both individually and collectively. Much of the learning was political and emancipatory in intent—it was about striking back and moving forward. It was conducted in the public sphere against entities such as the state and the funder.

One of the key areas of learning that surfaced in this study is in how to exercise power, whether in positive or negative ways. Borrowing from Lesley Treleaven (2004) and Burke and Jackson (2007), who have applied Foucault to organizational learning, we noted four particular ways that these 16 participants had learned to exercise power and, in so doing, become effective, knowledgeable, and skilled in practice. Power was exercised *productively* by them in the creation of circles, as well as democratic and inclusive spaces for women from all social economic strata. Power was exercised productively in creatively drawing on the available funding to increase access to employment, further their literacy levels, and develop personally. Power was exercised *relationally* in the way the directors and board members worked with each other to develop relationships and to create lifelong learning spaces. Power was exercised discursively through the organizing and dialoguing that made the lines of power with government visible. Yet, power was also exercised coercively by government in its troubling of funding guidelines and practices and within the nonprofit organizations by feminist practices such as coerced sharing.

These 16 participants were complicated multidimensional subjects, a view that a feminist-Foucauldian lens makes possible. Power, resistance, caring, and complicity were operating, possibly all at once because of the women's willingness to deal with contradictions and to learn on their feet. This all-at-once experience confirms Malcolm's (2012) study of emotional labour where women often do not have the luxury of bracketing parts of themselves; they were often at the lower end of the economic spectrum and worked in positions that called them to give their full person—their emotional energy/labour—to the situation they were in. They may be both resistant and caring all at once, as the situation demands, and they cannot hive off that part of themselves that is problematic. As adult learning theorists such as Dorothy MacKeracher (2004) note, they learn through experience and from the everyday. Consistent with the early learning literature which characterized women's learning as caring, people centred, and connected, these women did and did seem to learn in relationship. And they learned from that relationship that not all women are caring and connected. In these sites of learning, they negotiated the politics of their situation, not only with respect to government but among themselves—a dimension of learning not well developed in much of the women's learning literature such as Hayes and Flannery (2000). The capillary power of feminism affected them as did the operational power of senior members and of colleagues. The women had learned to push back, resisting control and enacting agency, in short they exercised power and resistance, which are at the heart of Foucauldian analysis. In a challenge to detractors of poststructuralism (e.g., Carpenter & Mojab, 2011), these feminists were actually able to see how they have been constituted by social and political factors, and to reconstitute themselves as knowing subjects.

Yet, like the individuals in Livingstone's (1999) study, as well as those in Marsick, Watkins, Callahan, and Volpe's (2009) study, these women's learning was largely undocumented. Through technologies of power—silence, strategy, subversion—they had resisted the regime of truth produced by government and perpetuated by higher education officials and faculty that only higher education can educate. Through their collective resistances, and as named by Gorman (2007), they produced the truth effect that learning can indeed occur in the community and that it can be valuable. Their varied micropractice draws attention to the many women in the community who do not have access to credentials and yet who have experienced lifelong learning in a very real and effective way. Learning can indeed happen within a nonprofit organization: Studies such as this one open the possibility that this informal learning can be documented and recognized in some way.

These participants have a great deal to teach higher education about what counts as learning. Not only are women learning in these nonprofit organizations, but their very presence and influence in them also serves to change traditional notions of *bona fide* learning communities as well as government policies on fundable learning providers. Some of the women who are active in women's centres, for instance, have been excluded from traditional places of learning because of illiteracy, financial exigency and social class, factors that Benseman (2005) and McGivney (1993) have highlighted. Community-based nonprofit centres for women provide an alternative education as well as a rallying point for activism around funding policies for areas such as literacy and pre-employment training. In lobbying for change, women in these centres provide social and political support for other women. They gain confidence and skills that help them can potentially help them cross the class divide into higher education (McGivney, 1990, 2001). For those who already have a postsecondary education, their new learning can help them assist other women, increase their own job opportunities, and advance the cause of women generally.

Given the uniquely feminist orientation of each of the nonprofit organizations from which these women came, they were forced to deal with issues of power and resistance. By their very mandate of addressing political issues that affect women, these nonprofit organizations were in a unique position to foster learning in challenging areas that other community-based organizations such as the Red Cross, faith based initiatives, or craft associations might not have to grapple with in a direct way. A stated feminist perspective means that their learning has indeed been challenging and has forced introspection and critique, and increased the participants' ability to be active participants in civil society. This is a unique contribution that these organizations make to learning.

In some cases, these women will pursue higher education, and if not them, the clients that they are serving through the nonprofit organization. Women in their literacy programs for instance, might register for community college or employment training. Even with a prior learning assessment and recognition (PLAR) process in place, though, much of their experiential learning about power, bureaucracy and feminism will not be valued, further enforcing the patriarchal nature of higher education and the discourse of government which sanctions only formal learning.

Studies such as this one challenge such a narrow view. Educators can look to what happened here to see how these women have defied stereotypes of female learners, how they have challenged the norms of caring and connected knowers, yet at the same time, have valued a generally non-competitive space to work out their differences. This study suggests that it is precisely because they are female knowers who value community and emotionally supportive environments, lauded by feminist learning theorists, such as MacKeracher (2004) and Belenky et al. (1986), that they have managed to learn all they do. In the absence of the bottom-line agenda that drives commercial organizations, they have safe spaces within which to practice strategies of resistance and to try out new ideas.

The data here may also be helpful in changing how government funders view feminist nonprofit organizations. The feminist nonprofit organizations can indeed be useful conversational partners in the funding and education drama and can be sites for more training programs and pre-employment initiatives. Government and higher education can become more open to recognize women's informal acquisition of skills and knowledge such as community building, organizational skills, activist skills, funding strategies, feminism, conflict, power, and negotiation. Perhaps more threatening for government is the women's learned expertise in resistance to funder pressures, their strategic forms of protest, and their abilities to negotiate conflict and to exercise their own power.

The women in this study have moved outside the homeplace, unlike those in the work by Foley (1999) and Livingstone (2012), and have chosen the inbetween informal venue of women's organizations as their learning space. Nowhere is this activism more apparent than in attempts to garner and protect educational and training funding for women's education programs, whether oriented to literacy, anti-violence education, or positive space (anti-homophobia) training. Yet, for all the heroic celebration of these women's lives and learning, we hasten to add a caution. Although they resist, these women are not always in a place of full choice or control. As Davies and Gannon (2005) point out, their agency is not in protesting evil institutions or standing outside them. Their strength and agency are in recognizing how they are affected and effected as subjects through their encounters. They exist somewhere on the continuum from oppressed to emancipated. So Catherine Hakim's (2003) notion of the independent women making clearcut decisions on careers or employment (*preferences*, in her terms), apart from their "discursive regimes and regulatory frameworks" (Davies & Gannon, p. 318) does not necessarily apply here. This study shows that women's choices are affected by the interplay of power, discourse, and resistance among the various actors in the nonprofit sphere. It is within the nonprofit organization with multiple competing discourses that they are constituted as knowing subjects capable of being and acting. The lines of power make choices and resistances far more complex and difficult to trace than merely saying yes or no to an array of options. Yet, within this situation they engage in multiple forms of learning that contribute to feminist activism and agency. The women in this study are exemplars of the informal learning that Gorman (2007) highlights: learning that is about "oppression, exploitation, and political consciousness" (p.183). They have used resistance of various sorts to learn their way into empancipatory and freeing positions. They have done this through a combination of individual and collective learning.

It is also useful to note that the study participants have found possibilities—they are able to imagine a different future for themselves and for their organizations. Their learning has been generative and has, despite the challenges, offered them hope and creative alternatives. We believe it is important to tell these kinds of stories in a book on feminism and the community, especially in a time when we are besieged by the negativity and disempowerment.

Given the data gathering technique of semi-structured interviews, it is difficult to quantify participants' informal learning, much less to assess it directly for credit or PLAR recognition. That, however, was not the intent, especially since the purpose of the learning was political in a social movement sense. In many ways this study works, as did Margrit Eichler's (2005) study of housework, in the spirit of the lifeworld—learning that is about participatory democracy, "where people's character and citizenship are shaped" (p. 1024). Rather that answering the call of a capitalist demand for measuring discrete moments of learning for prior learning and assessment, this study offers an initial insight into how learning occurs in the feminist nonprofit sector. As with most qualitative work, this study provides the groundwork from which other studies may be generated.

DISCUSSION

In this chapter, we have looked at some of the ways in which feminist nonprofit organizations serve to nurture informal learning for women. They appear to provide spaces where women can be initiated into funding and negotiating strategies, learn from each other, and become more aware of and active in the political dimensions of caring for women. These nonprofit centres function as incubators of new ways of being feminist and of actively creating one's own subject position(s).

Our goal with this chapter was to further the development of a more critical body of literature on women and informal learning, by using the insights of poststructuralism and gender and learning. By focusing on specific informal sites and instances in which women gather to learn, we can uncover women's everyday learning practices, and critically reflect on them. This enables us to know better how we can support women and encourage their learning processes inside and outside official institutions. In the spirit of Alecia Jackson (2004), we have disrupted categories of totalitarian government bureaucracy and powerless and victimized women, and have shown how feminists' daily practices work to interrupt labels and essentialist views of learning as occurring only in formal post-compulsory education.

NOTE

[1] This chapter is based on L.M. English. (2011). Power, resistance and informal pathways: Lifelong learning in feminist nonprofit organizations. In S. Jackson, I. Malcolm, & K. Thomas (Eds.), *Gendered choices: Learning, work, identities in lifelong learning* (pp. 209–225). Dordrecht, Holland: Springer. Permission to use and adapt this chapter was granted by Springer in 2013.

THE NEXUS OF POLICY, PRACTICE, AND PAYMENT[1]

The *Charter of Feminist Principles for African Feminists* provides a new model of leadership for African women. Rather than promote the single, independent, charismatic leader, it proposes in this *Charter* to promote collective leadership that inspires hope, builds on group strengths, and which works counter to patriarchy. The *Charter* provides a blueprint for women to follow, and encourages them to work to encourage participation and to inspire younger women, to promote love, to cultivate time for thinking and reading, and to share ideas and strategies. This model is a challenging one in that it calls women to work together and to resist creating hierarchies, single leaders, and more patriarchal structures (Chigudu, 2014).

RELEVANCE OF POLICIES

Policies like the *Charter* serve as clarion calls and provide a direction for women in development areas. Though they are not rules, *per se*, they set the tone—in this case, collaboration—for feminists' ongoing conversation about how they will act and interact in achieving goals to improve the lives of girls and women. In a similar vein, this chapter examines the international policy context for adult education and women, practice, and issues of payment, asking the question of implications for feminist adult educators in an increasingly neoliberal context.

There is a general sense of optimism with regard to feminism's relevance in the 21st century, though this is tempered by some setbacks and obvious opponents and drawbacks. At the policy level, feminism is struggling to regain the visibility it once had in the mainstream press and public discourse, such as the role the National Action Committee on the Status of Women (NAC) once played in Canada's constitutional process (Rebick, 2009). As Sylvia Bashevkin (2009) laments, no other feminist organization in Canada has filled the gap left by NAC in terms of national political presence, as funding and policy spaces have shrunk. She calls for greater alliance building to advocate for change.

Indeed, feminists have worked across sectors identifying the common sources of injustice; they have made common cause with many grassroots social movements, both old and new, campaigning for rights and protection in the areas of labour, First Nations, gender identity, anti-violence, anti-racism, and environmental protection (Miles, 2013). In many of these areas, there has been a strong learning and community development component. Sylvia Walby (2011) notes how feminism and its emancipatory goals have been integrated into many sectors of civil society. Yet, this mainstreaming and integration have also led to the undermining of feminism's distinctive visibility and contributions to social justice both domestically and internationally.

Over the years, adult educators have also observed the ebb and flow of feminist contributions to learning, such as transformative learning theory (English & Irving, 2012). Recent literature on feminism, community development, and education (Manicom & Walters, 2012; Miles, 2013) in the international realm contrasts with much of the North American literature that appears stalled in earlier research focusing on classroom-based women's learning (Hayes & Flannery, 2000). Focus on classroom experience is valid, but it does not encompass feminist learning in the community where much political learning occurs. The influences of feminist theory and pedagogy have informed broader adult education practice (Brookfield, 2010), but one must ask: To what extent have these practices lost the original political intent? The causes of feminism such as just labour laws, gender equality policies, and anti-violence legislation have long been the content and subject of this politicized learning and policy making, yet feminism's distinct and continuing role was too often absorbed into other aspects of the social democratic tradition of radical adult education. The effort of reviving political energy of feminism and radical adult education, in the tradition of Jane Thompson (2007) and Paula Allman (2010), is a vital source of political learning for policy change. So, the glimmers of hope evidenced in Miles' collection (2013) cannot be overstated. Sustained analyses of the intersectionality of oppression (Crenshaw, 1991) can help identify the opportunities for alliance building that Bashevkin (2009) promotes.

Yet, the practical challenges to a resurgence of interest in feminism and adult learning in Canada are great, given that the infrastructure to mobilize women and to engage them in political causes in this country is in tatters. In the heady days of the repatriation of the Constitution in Canada in the early 1980s, it was possible to have major efforts and grassroots involvement in making sure that women's rights were enshrined. The subsequent shackling of Status of Women Canada, the disappearance of funding for the National Action Committee on the Status of Women (Bashevkin, 2009), and the paltry funding for women's centres in Canada makes it hard to think of who would be influential today in enacting policy or creating a meaningful voice for women in this country. Indeed, it is difficult to name a feminist champion in our government or on a national stage. Of great concern is the growing neoliberal trend to silence women's voices. Witness the cancelling of the Thérèse Casgrain Volunteer Award, established in honour of Casgrain's work to secure women's suffrage in Quebec and for being the first woman to lead a federal party (Stoddart, 2014). With this neoliberal federal agenda as a backdrop, it is hopeful to see Linzi Manicom and Shirley Walters (2012), Angela Miles (2013), Sara Carpenter (2012), Nancy Taber (2015), and Darlene Clover (personal communication, October 5, 2014) raising the feminist flag.

The Education and Learning Dimension

Recent international feminist voices in adult education bring a decidedly political learning agenda to the table, and reach toward the kinds of political action and learning that is necessary for social transformation. For some, such as Sara Carpenter (2012), the vision for adult education involves reaching back to Marx to see how his theories can advance an equitable feminist agenda. Similarly, Margaret Ledwith (2009) in the UK draws on Gramsci's insights on hegemony, the organic intellectual and everyday material life to find the arenas in which women's voices and agendas can be heard. Ledwith suggests that Gramsci provides a way forward to think about feminism and its struggles and dreams. Along with Carpenter, she intends to renew community practice by revisiting the older theoretical frameworks and concepts and adapting them in an imaginative way to deepen critiques of neoliberalism.

As adult educators, we share with feminism not only a goal of political, economic, and social equality for women, but also the belief that in achieving equality, both the learning process and the movement matter. For adult educators, including Manicom and Walters (2012) and Carpenter (2012), feminism always involves a learning and education component.

Many women who work at the policy and practice level learned feminism in community-based contexts, and need that continued linkage for credibility and effectiveness (Manuh, Anyidoho, & Pobee-Hayford, 2013). A strength of the women's movement in the 1970s was the deliberate effort to make links collectively among learning, practice, activism, and policy change. Given that people need to connect to their own experiences in order to learn, critical adult educators work to link experience to the larger social structures. Critical adult educators are mindful of the critiques of the individual focus of some areas of feminism and education, such as the recent observation that unpacking Peggy McIntosh's Knapsack of Privilege (see Lensmire et al., 2013) can sometimes lead to participants becoming satisfied with identifying their own privilege, rather than moving on to further action and involvement. In some ways, the West has privileged the personal and has not been strong on moving to policy or political feats.

Vis-à-vis Margaret Ledwith (2009), effective feminist-infused adult education needs to move beyond the narrow focus on personal experience and the individual. She proposes:

> potential sites of liberation. These three dimensions are: i) *difference*: age, 'race', class, gender, sexual identity, 'dis'ability, ethnicity; ii) *contexts*: economic, cultural, intellectual, physical, environmental, historical, emotional, spiritual on another, and iii) *levels*: local, national, regional and global which form a complex set of interrelationships which not only interweave between axes, but which also intertwine on any one axis. (p. 694; emphasis in the original)

In bringing these three areas to the fore, Ledwith challenges adult educators to move onwards from discussion of difference and experience. The level that is of most concerning, and which adult education in North America has not been strong on, is the third, the multiple levels that involve policy, practice, and most of all decisions about who pays. As women's centres close due to funding cuts, feminists need to trace the money trail back to where policy and funding decisions are made. With the backdrop of new publications on feminism and adult education, and with the evident need for more groundwork, policy, and practical action to infuse these theories and writings, as hopeful as they are, we look now to the global sphere to see what is being *done* on the ground and in the corridors of power to reinvigorate and forward the cause of women internationally. We argue here that the interrelationship between grassroots/local activism and international policymaking and practice (Caglar et al., 2013) are at the heart of feminist visibility in countries, mostly in the Global South, where feminism and gender have not been forgotten largely due to stunning inequities and challenges for women. In moving beyond our classrooms and our continent, we observe what is happening globally to enact policy, engage political actors, and involve women in funding decisions to see what is possible.

Looking Globally for Insight and Inspiration

In some ways, women in the West have privileged critical analysis and identification of issues in particular organizations and local arenas, or as identified by Ledwith (2009), the old way of identifying patriarchy and oppression. A second option has been most evident in the larger global sphere: Finding new strategic ways to resist patriarchy. For example, international agencies and nation states have chosen to tackle head-on the material issues confronting women by focusing on international agreements and declarations. Over the past two decades, there has been substantial evidence of both progress and regress in the advancement of women's rights in the field of adult education and in broader contexts of human development. Many at the UN level recognize this concern for women, learning, and feminism and continue to keep feminist and critical adult education issues central to policy discussions. For example, when the 58th Session of the Commission on the Status of Women met in March, 2014 at the United Nations in New York City (UN Women, 2014), participants explored the many stalled or disappearing commitments on women's empowerment globally. In the words from the *Agreed Conclusions from the 58th Session*, progress has been "slow and uneven" (UN Women, #18). As the MDGs, which did stress education but only at the primary level, expire in 2015, this world gathering took stock of the situation and the funding that had been streamed for many years into primary education only, and called for new strategic directions in which women, "quality" education, and development were given centre stage. They reiterated that there are many existing declarations, agreements, and instruments that need to be revived and acted upon.

Global Agreements

Progressive policies and statements, especially from the United Nations, have acknowledged the intricate connection between feminism and adult education, and their integral role in promoting social democracy and other development goals. The MDGs and other global efforts such as CONFINTEA do not exist alone and are not raising new themes about feminism, education, or development, as they follow in a long line of critical policy efforts that cannot be ignored. As the current round of negotiations continues, there is a sense of déjà vu; we ask ourselves, "Haven't we been here before?" The crux of the issue is how to achieve the hoped-for change. What role does critical adult education (possibly social movement learning) have in this situation? Here we revisit some of the key agreements to take stock.

CONFINTEA.   UNESCO's fifth conference on adult education, CONFINTEA V in Hamburg, Germany, in 1997, was notable for the recognition of the importance of both gender and knowledge, and the advancement of women through education. Alejandra Scampini (2003) notes the importance of coordinated efforts of women's organizations in promoting these issues at CONFINTEA. A strong adult education presence and the leadership of Canadian adult educator Paul Bélanger were forces to be reckoned with at this conference.

There was great hope and enthusiasm for learning generated in Hamburg (CONFINTEA V) for women, adult education, and global change, and this hope was clearly evident in the resulting *Hamburg Declaration on Adult Learning* (UNESCO, 1997). Alas, much of the promise and commitment of this Declaration has yet to be realized. Nellie Stromquist (2013) reflects on the woeful lack of evidence of substantive progress, noting that part of the problem lies in implementation: "Their discourse (and that expressed in the various other official documents of international conferences) underwent minimal translation into operational levels" (p. 34).

More recently, the goals linked to feminism and adult education have slipped off the UN agenda, and, consequently, off funding priority lists of national and regional governments. As Stromquist (2013) reminds us, CONFINTEA VI in Belém, Brazil in 2009 did not even mention challenges facing women or identify empowerment as a goal (see also UNESCO, 2009). This silence threatens gains that have been made and thwarts further progress. Although the Belém conference had other strengths, namely an emphasis on nonformal learning, women or women's concerns were not strongly articulated. We wonder if this situation came from a lack of women's participation or the absence of strong feminist voices at the conference. Stromquist laments the "predictable path" (p. 34) whereby goals are articulated repeatedly over the years with little evidence of progress, or where the goals are watered down, or are voiced with no plan for action. Like Scampini (2003) she sees the role of local women's organizing as the realm where the issues are most clearly understood and where creative solutions are developed, but, sadly these contributions tend not to be noticed at the formalized levels of research and policy. And as been seen in Canada, when grassroots activist organizations struggle for funding, their ability to act is compromised, undermining the accomplishment of any meaningful goals.

MDGs and the post-2015 agenda. To put education within the larger context of human development goals, we turn to the MDGs, which have defined funding and action priorities for human development and poverty reduction around the world for the past decade. Commissioned by the United Nations' Secretary General, the eight MDGs were developed by UN agencies, the international non-governmental sector, researchers, policymakers, and government representatives (Sachs, 2005). Almost immediately, a groundswell of criticism arose from women's organizations who were particularly concerned with the MDG's narrow definition of women's issues and the apparent ignorance of existing declarations that had been implemented since the 1980s promoting women's empowerment (Barton, 2005). The third goal—*Promote gender equality and empower women* (MDG3)—is often referred to as the "women in education MDG." Despite its broad sweeping title, this goal promotes equality in primary and secondary education for women, although in practice the emphasis has been predominantly on access to primary education for girls, to the detriment of other stages of learning. There is another MDG on maternal health (i.e., care of mothers and babies), but it is narrowly focused and does not extend to broader issues of equality and education.

By and large, the MDGs focus on access and service provision and not on a broad understanding of empowerment and rights, thereby ignoring underlying inequalities. Attention needs to be given to the basic issue—not the services, *per se*, as important as they are, but to the underlying causes. To accomplish MDG3, considerable work must be done on issues of power, patriarchy, and policies, yet it was set without a strong analytical framework or plan to achieve it. It is not enough to say there must be an end to oppression of women; feminists have taken a long time to get to this point, thus demonstrating it cannot be addressed quickly. In some ways, the MDGs are part of the Western mindset that we can reach these goals quickly if only they are identified and named. The work that goes with undoing patriarchy is long and complicated, and it involves not only action but analysis.

By the time this book comes to press, the MDGs will be at their expiry date, given that they were mandated to be achieved by 2015. With accomplishments falling far short of aspirations, attention is now shifting to the "Post-2015 agenda," now being discussed. Women's rights advocates who felt marginalized by the MDG process are determined not to be sidelined in this new agenda and are working to get the core declarations and conventions and commitments of decades ago back to the centre of policy and funding. Who is at the table to advocate for this more fundamental change is yet another matter, as are questions of priorities and motivation within the feminist movement. Srilatha Batliwala (2012) gives a frank critique of mainstream feminist organizations which have shown signs of being co-opted, in what she sees as a shift from movement building to organization building. In her view, emphasis on service delivery through feminist organizations thwarts the efforts to continue pushing for more radical change that addresses root causes of persistent inequality. Batliwala points out that groups at the margins have been much more innovative in their practice. While her critiques sting, they are a reminder that needs on the ground are substantial and the voices of critics can be hard to hear over the outcry over mounting poverty, gender inequity, and global violence that directly affects women and children. International nongovernmental organizations (INGOs), it must be said, are at the frontlines and make hard choices every day.

CEDAW: A policy of one's own. One of the most important guiding documents for women globally is the Convention on the Elimination of Discrimination Against Women (CEDAW; United Nations, 1981) which was adopted in 1979 and ratified in 1981. CEDAW has a concern that "in situations of poverty women have the least access to food, health, education, training and opportunities for employment and other needs" (para. 8). Despite the fact that it is decades old, CEDAW is one of the cornerstones of the feminist movement internationally. It is held up as the document that obliges nations to take issues of gender inequality seriously and to develop concrete actions to combat it. In the wake of the losses for women in CONFINTEA VI and in the MDGs, women globally harken back to the promises of that document and draw on its insights and promises for current debates and challenges (Terry, 2007).

CEDAW serves as a reminder that women need the same opportunities for access to programs of continuing education, including adult and functional literacy programs, particularly those aimed at reducing, at the earliest possible time, any gap in education existing between men and women. While feminists might look askance at many public policies, and question the need for global bodies like UNESCO, there is a strength in drawing on them to enhance women's roles and education. They serve as a reminder of world commitments and understanding of the complex global problems women face. The ongoing challenges are not due to a lack of awareness or evidence, but of chronic lack of understanding and political will for implementation to deal with the issues once and for all.

On Policies and Laws, and Education

Once these policies and documents are being considered or even implemented, it is imperative that the grassroots, many of whom helped these come to fruition, be able to read, comprehend, and work with these politically-charged and power-laden documents. As Rosalind Eyben (2012) remind us, "Policies are instruments of power that classify and organize ideas and social relations to sustain or change the current social order" (p. 17). She then explains how this power is contested and challenged, and proposes ways for activists to be more effective in their advocacy work. Indeed, they can work for women and in their favour—they are political tools to be strengthened and used.

To understand and work with global pronouncements, legal documents, government policies, and to work with the political system globally and locally requires what Jim Crowther and Lyn Tett (2012) describe as *political literacy*: knowledge that enables people to interrogate the experts. In explaining this type of literacy, Crowther and Tett draw out the distinction between learning for conformity and learning for dissent. They define the purpose "literacy for citizenship and democracy has to address making power visible and accountable" (p. 123), but note the variety in starting points. "If people are to gain a voice—to question and speak back to power—they will need the confidence and authority that comes out of experience, reinforced and tempered by study" (p. 125). Being politically savvy around policy and policy-making is challenging and speaks to a role for adult educators. If adult educators are to be effective at the most basic of levels, then they have to be involved in educating women about rights, policies, and laws.

At the heart of much education and law/policy work is the analysis of power, as Eyben (2012) highlighted in her study of women's unpaid care work. She described the effects of the assumptions around "evidence-based" policymaking, which begins with the assumption that policy is created through the analysis of sound evidence. In this type of policymaking, it is understood that if an issue is absent from policy, then the evidence highlighting the issue is flawed or it has been poorly communicated. But what is really going on is "strategic ignorance" – to acknowledge the issue would take too much work and too much money to resolve. If it is a systemic problem then the system needs to be changed for it to be resolved (pp. 12–13). Like Eyben's issue of trying to make unpaid care work quantifiable in economic terms, it is near impossible to make all women's issues count. Playing by the policymakers' rules can sometimes undermine the possibility for change.

LEARNING FROM PRACTICE IN THE GLOBAL SOUTH

Global agreements, policies, and initiatives are being carried out in a very strategic way in the South, far removed from Western discourse analysis and identity politics. The material world and needs of education, food, shelter, and safety for women come starkly to the fore, in global contexts. While much is spoken of the praxis cycle of reflection, consciousness raising, and action, too often it is repeated as a mantra without renewed scrutiny of what it looks like in practice, and how adult education practice renews and adapts to changing circumstances and new theoretical insights. In the feminist literature within social sciences, there is considerable attention paid to the importance of policy-level change, and of the importance to ground this work continually in grassroots experience for validity and for efficacy. While many North American conversations about women remain limited to conceptual analyses and at times to personal and classroom levels (e.g., Hayes & Flannery, 2000), it seems wise to look to the South where many creative and effective movements are being played out. This section looks at one process of participatory democracy that is growing in popularity—participatory budgeting (PB). Attention is then given to specific international women's organizations that are creating spaces for democratic participation.

Participatory Budgeting

A rising trend in engaging grassroots citizen participation in public processes, participatory budgeting, is garnering attention among adult educators (Foroughi, 2013; Lerner, 2010; Pinnington & Schugurensky, 2010). Participatory budgeting processes like the model developed in Porto Alegre, Brazil, and now elsewhere, are intended to involve citizens in the allocation of public funds for projects and programs, presenting myriad opportunities for learning among citizens and bureaucrats alike. Lerner describes how people's activities in this process typically follow five steps: "diagnosis, discussion, decision-making, implementation and monitoring" (p. 243), and summarizes some of the learning that has been identified from participating in the steps from identifying projects to ensuring successful completion. Knowledge and skill development in participatory budgeting is diverse, ranging from practical technical and political know-how to confidence-building and awareness-raising of the situation of others. Lerner also emphasises the learning by staff and politicians to raise their consciousness of community issues and perspectives, and more effective and authentic collaboration with community participants.

Feminists caught in the ongoing struggle of trying to secure funding might welcome such an opening for participation in the allocation of public funds. Looking to the evolution of the process in Recife, Brazil, some key lessons have been identified for including gender in the participatory budgeting process. Removing barriers to access such as providing child care and raising awareness of the need to invite women specifically have helped increase involvement (Zarzar, Meneses, & Azavedo, 2002). Setting up the model alone is not enough. A further trend within participatory budgeting is to focus directly on women's issues as part of this budgeting. Through gender based budgeting, citizens are able to address the issues that confront women globally (Eyben, 2012). Beyond opening the space for women's participation, an example from Cotacachi in Ecuador tracks the progress of traditionally marginalized Indigenous women whose actions in the participatory budgeting process led to specific programs to ensure rural inclusion and to reduce illiteracy (López & Adanali, 2007). The literacy strategy was so effective that the UN has declared Cotacachi the "first illiteracy-free canton in Ecuador" (p. 12).

Gender-based participatory budgeting allows women to have a voice in issues that confront them daily when caring for their families. Leaders in Cotacachi have shown remarkable leadership in acknowledging this fact and in putting women in strategic locations to decide on their future. Practices like participatory budgeting allow citizens to become more economically literate and to make decisions about the welfare of their families and communities. This collective decision making helps everyone participate, learn, and build healthy public policy, and maintain public accountability for community investment. Beyond having a voice in how tax money is spent, the learning that occurs through the process itself is vitally important. By being involved in decision-making processes traditionally reserved for experts, bureaucrats, and politicians, participatory budgeting has the potential to empower citizens.

One problem, however, is that participatory budgeting is an "invited space" (Miller, VeneKlasen, Reilly, & Clark, 2006) for participation, with limits imposed from those in charge. The budget is typically small, focused on deciding upon local projects and allocating limited funds to the successful applicants. This does not look much different from the vicious circle of project funding that has plagued women's centres for years. That said, the concept is useful, and as long as educators remain aware and critical of its potential, they can carve spaces for learning that can be transferred for bigger goals elsewhere. The solutions for complex issues are a mixture of large-scale and small-scale efforts such as this one. Given the repeated calls for alliance building, this democratic space, despite its limitations, has the potential to be a rich learning venue for the inclusion of feminist analysis to issues of mutual concern and to be a space to find allies to collaborate in social action.

Women's INGOs

Along with specific strategies like participatory budgeting at the ground level, women's INGOs are key sites for change and development for women. Despite critiques that see large organizations losing touch with the grassroots, INGOs have a vital role due to their wide reach, networking abilities, and financial stability which can help open the spaces for smaller activist organizations. In particular, we highlight a few unabashedly feminist organizations that place learning and activism for policy change at the centre of their work. Their creative work is not often recognized in the mainstream of adult education literature, a lamentable omission, as these three illustrate exemplary practices of organizational leadership (CREA), analysis of political power (JASS), and funding (AWID).

CREA. CREA (originally called Creating Resources for Empowerment in Action) based in New Delhi, India, has an international reach in its programs to educate and train women at the local levels in South Asia, Africa, and the Middle East (CREA, 2014). The organization has several areas of interest, but it is their feminist leadership training focus that is most informative. CREA describes their work this way:

> By building on the theory and practice of feminist leadership, and developing understandings about the intersections of sexuality, gender, rights, and development, CREA seeks to support feminist leaders who can further the transformative goals of the feminist movement. (para. 2)

The use of the term "developing understandings" is CREA's modest way of representing its many informal and nonformal educational activities for helping organizations develop leadership that is truly feminist and transformative in thought and action. As Batliwala (2011) emphasises, "Feminist leadership means the ability to influence agendas even without the formal power or authority to do so, and the capacity to leverage larger-scale changes (in policy, legal rights, social attitudes, and power relations) with very marginal resources" (p. 66). CREA has remade the feminist movement in its own way by focusing on the intersection of real life issues—not just identity issues but the issues of rights and development, along with gender and sexuality. Just looking at what is happening for women in organizations such as this in the Global South makes it clear that feminists in the West have a long way to go to catch up in terms of sustaining interest and explicitly connecting education to rights and policies. It is this broad-based approach that characterizes INGOs like CREA and sets them apart.

JASS. An example of the effectiveness of an umbrella INGOs for women's popular education and empowerment is JASS (Just Associates, Washington, US) which has a global reach bringing together many funders and donors to support education and development work in South Asia, Southern Africa, and Latin America. Their focus is on movement building and on developing the skills to strengthen movements through research, education, alliance building, and political mobilization (JASS, 2014). They have been actively involved in bringing a feminist lens to analyses of power (see Miller et al., 2006). For example, a program in Malawi helps women describe themselves and their experiences in terms of power and ways to challenge power on multiple levels. For these women, the "personal is political" in a very active way that and they have taken their activism from the home and brought it to brokering with local chiefs and government representatives, and into organizing their own networks and organizations in constructing budgets and plans that address their needs. The empowerment programs link up with issues in a range of sectors such as ensuring public health funding commitments in Malawi are enacted (JASS, 2013).

AWID. Feminist INGOs are the bridge between policy and funding. Once the policy has been created, as with the JASS case noted above, sustained efforts at implementation are required. The Association of Women in Development (AWID), makes this point clearly in one of its three-part series on women and funding— *Women Moving Mountains: The Collective Impact of the Dutch MDG3 Fund* (Batliwala et al., 2013). The report offers valuable evidence to support what women's organizations have been claiming for a long time about aid effectiveness. They provide research evidence to support what women's organizations have said for years—how short-term funding cycles cannot hope to have the same impact as secure, flexible funding over the long-term. Long-term support resulted in organizations "increasing their legitimacy and credibility as an organization (74%), strengthening their organizational systems (71%), building their human resource base (71%), enhancing the role of young women activists in their organizations and movements, and strengthening a range of other capacities" (p. 69). Just as participatory budgeting offers an opportunity for activists to develop local-level public budgeting skills, AWID's research makes an important contribution to helping women demystify funding mechanisms and bring forward evidence to advocate for changes in budgeting processes at a broader level.

In order to be successful, organizations such as CREA, JASS, and AWID usually start in the local community and build up using social and economic capital in the process. Alison Gilchrist (2009) draws attention to the social capital that is involved in organizations and movements, noting that linkages and networks are more important than ever. Yet, in contexts of community work, she observes that this capital is being fragmented through short-run project funding cycles, making it harder than ever to accomplish strategic goals. The benefits of the networking are "slow burning," so it is hard to demonstrate measurable results in standard evaluation frameworks. Using complexity theory to embrace this chaos, which brings vibrancy and diversity to networks, Gilchrist describes how community development has a role to provide spaces for networks to grow and flourish.

Against this backdrop of Southern efforts and exemplars of feminist adult education for change, we turn now to some of the implications for adult education locally and internationally.

IMPLICATIONS FOR ADULT EDUCATION AND FEMINISM

International direction and policies to forward the cause of feminism and education for women have sometimes fallen short, especially in terms of global policy and efforts to make change possible. Yet, there are glimmers of hope in specific practices such as gender-based participatory budgeting and organizations. In looking to the Global South, there are ways for Canadian women to put ideas, hopes, and aspirations for feminism into effect.

The cases from the South show that an engaged, participatory democracy can strategically employ adult education practices. Given the immediate material needs as of the Indigenous peoples in the Cotacachi, Equador, for example, immersion was needed (López & Adanali, 2007). Time out for schooling in budgeting was not available, so the participants learned through nonformal and informal means. In engaging in safe and engaged spaces like the thematic stream for women's budgeting in Porto Alegre, women enhanced capacity and economic literacy and created a community space imbued with immediate learning intents, an adult education initiative for women. Yet, it is important to note that participatory practices at the community level do not exist in isolation. They are supported and abetted by international policies such as the CONFINTEA's *Hamburg Declaration* (UNESCO, 1997) and other UN level goal statements. While it can sometimes be dispiriting to think of what is lost in some of these policies and at that global level, the global community of practice can provide inspiration.

From the perspectives of community and international development, feminist writers including Miles (2013) and Ledwith (2009) are creating a resurgence of hope for a feminist oriented and inspired adult education sphere. They remind us that feminism's unique contributions to adult education in addressing social and economic issues are important. Theirs is a caution that in blending feminism with social democratic or other social movements—indeed, the infusion or mainstreaming of feminism with any and all partners uncritically—is problematic in that it risks the clear and articulate ground that feminism gained. We must prevent the disappearance of our feminist agenda and the misattribution of feminism's achievements with the state. In order to have a critically-oriented adult education field that is truly about inclusion and protection of worker education and higher education, not to mention literacy programming, we need to keep putting feminism on the agenda and acting upon it through critical adult education policies and practices. One way to do this is think larger, to look outward to our sisters around the globe, and to cast our gaze beyond formal education to informal, nonformal policy and practice.

Indeed, it is increasingly clear that policy and practice, politics, and, more importantly, funding become the axis on which women's learning is promoted, defined, and enacted. Policy and practice dictate funding priorities, and funding dictates practice. It comes as no surprise to anyone experienced with AWID's findings (Batliwala et al., 2013) that the short-term project funding cycle for organizations is inefficient and drains potential for sustained activism and change. Adult education for social justice cannot thrive in these conditions. The international sphere sheds light on the vibrancy and networking needed to avoid the whims of politically-manipulated funding regimes.

At the global level, adult education involves community development and organizing, social movements, policy making, and political literacy. Similarly, feminism is more than women's individual empowerment—it is about communities working to change inequitable structures. As a joint force, feminism and adult education are collaborators working with people, for people, for change. The particular strength of collective voices for feminism and learning on the international stage is that they honour the primacy of the critical.

Though some have focused on feminism and the community (e.g., Ledwith, 2011), feminist organizations internationally have included a decided educational focus that embraces both social movement learning and feminist pedagogy, which have been a rich part of feminism's practice. There is a learning nexus here of critical adult education and feminism, one that poses provocative questions about what it means to infuse and sponsor social transformation learning at the community (social movement, nonformal, and informal learning) level as well as in more formal educational arenas. This nexus may also be a way to put intersectionality into practice, not just a theory but a way for people to see the worth of a whole range of theoretical/practical perspectives.

DISCUSSION

In many ways, the voices and practices of groups such as AWID, and writers including Miles (2013) are reminders of adult education's historical commitment to process, content, and lifelong learning traditions in the struggle for a progressive feminism to effect policy change. Adult education has a long history of recognizing the links and common goals of feminism, radical adult education, and social democracy. Stories of Canadian suffragettes such as Thérèse Casgrain (Tremblay, 2010) illustrate that feminists have often been educators and promoters of progressive policy, using the tools at their disposal, especially educational and learning tools. Feminist adult educators bring critical voices that push beyond formal classroom learning and individual experience, divorced from our larger social and economic structure. They cast their gaze to the international sphere to see where policies have been enacted and challenged and to see what partners in the Global South can teach about learning, policy and critical decision-making. Yet, they continue to work at the grassroots level to work with women to increase their practical and analytical skills to claim a place in policymaking.

There is cause for feminists to be optimistic. The articulation of rights through broad-based policy statements such as CEDAW, and more recently the discussions for the Post-2015 congresses on future priorities, make it clear that feminist adult education is alive and well, working with partners globally to change the world.

NOTE

[1]   This chapter was previously published as L.M. English & C.J. Irving. (2015). Feminism and adult education: The nexus of policy, practice, and payment. *Canadian Journal for the Study of Adult Education, 27*(2), 16–30. Permission to use it here was granted by the *Journal.*

CHAPTER 12

ADULT EDUCATION AND THE COMMUNITY

Making the Feminist Connections

The Raging Grannies defy all stereotypes of older women. Organized globally through local chapters, their members are feminists in "granny-like" costumes who sing protest songs about peace and environmental justice. Seemingly harmless "old women," they create parodies of traditional songs and sing them in public at rallies and protests. Their chronicler, Carole Roy (2004), sees them as subversive women who utilize both humour and music to communicate and teach citizens about the world they want for themselves and their children and grandchildren. The Grannies show up at random events in costume and sing songs that they have either composed for the occasion or ones they have rewritten to suit the cause. Their clothing (shawls, hats, and long dresses) parodies expectations and their merriment destabilizes power. The Grannies create community with each other and strengthen social ties wherever they meet to sing and make their causes known. Networked around the world, they share strategies and songs, and form a significant social movement for older feminists.

THEMES ARISING

Indeed, groups like the Grannies have inspired this book's focus on the diversity of ways feminists organize and learn in community—both in terms of the issues addressed and of the practices enacted. In Chapter 2, we looked at learning through activities in women's resource centres and nonprofit organizations, stressing that the nonprofit provides space for much needed critique and analysis, and a rethinking of the meaning of leadership. Chapter 3 examined how an understanding of health in the community is influenced not only by disease but by the social determinants. In Chapter 4, we focused on how the arts can be infused into our adult education practice and exploration of social justice issues. This was followed by Chapter 5's review of the evolving landscape of social movement learning through ICTs. In Chapter 6, we examined how women encounter religious movements, especially religious fundamentalism, and how they enact identities because of and in relationship to these religious movements. In Chapter 7, we focused on the issues implicit in research in the community and our focus in Chapter 8 was feminist pedagogy. The link between transformative learning theories and social transformation was the subject of Chapter 9; issues of power, resistance, and informal learning were explored in Chapter 10; Chapter 11 discussed how women engage at the policy level to continue challenging global injustices. We now identify some of the themes arising from these discussions.

159

Importance of Community for Women

One of the central issues in this book about women's learning and leading in the community is the meaning of community when women are at the centre of the process. If it is true that *community* is never used in a negative sense, as Raymond Williams (1976) put it, then we might say that the word community is sacrosanct—that it conjures up notions of what is working well, in addition to notions of collegiality and belonging. Yet, this seems all too simple. When conjoined with women's learning, community may need to be nuanced considerably. Community in this sense is not bliss—it is a combination of ideas and people who work together to create new ideas and new options.

For women, community is not necessarily a place of infinite cohesion or integration; it may be a network of ideas, a loose association created through the use of ICTs, or a group of women united by a cause globally, if not in person. To use the tripartite formulation of community proposed by Smith (2001), a community is formed by (a) location or geography such as a town or village; (b) common interest or characteristic such as feminists, environmentalists, religion or political party; or (c) profound connection or spiritual bonding. Though all three forms of community might apply to feminists, the one that seems closest to what we have been talking about in this book is the community of feminists that is formed by common interest. Though there are variations in commitment, range of participation, or degree of action, the community of feminists is a large and powerful group of people. Their divergence and their commonality exist on a continuum and yet all are working in some way to enhance authority and ability for women. As we have seen, sometimes feminists work with government as is the case in the Nordic countries, which place high on any scale of inclusion of women, and at other times in opposition especially in situations where the state is oppressive for women as in Saudi Arabia (see Miles, 2013). The forms and aspirations of women vary by country, state, and individual. There may be cynicism about engaging with the state, given suspicions about their motives or the consequences of not cooperating with them.

It is difficult to think of community without thinking of the ultimate question of who is included or excluded. Ultimately, learning in the community is, as Lyn Tett (2010) says, a question of who is in and out of the community. She interprets community as a "shared lived experience" that can consist of common place, interest, or function. The tricky part here is that communities involve boundaries, groupings distinguished from others; being *in* a community implies that others are *outside* of it. The creation of categories of commonality and difference can reinforce polarization, and there is always going to be someone who is excluded. Of course, this does not make excuses for exclusion based on pervasive inequalities—gender, race, ability, and class—as a core task of feminism is to challenge exclusions entrenched dominant structures.

A key example is the multiple exclusions that women with disabilities express, as their priorities get boxed in discussions of health or disability issues and their gender is relegated to a secondary concern, if not ignored entirely (Batliwala, 2012). Some community development literature emphasises the importance of relational concepts such as hospitality, which serves as a reminder to intentionally welcome those who are regularly overlooked, ignored, excluded. As well, there are renewals of concepts like *communitas*, the interconnection to "share in collective imagining" (Westoby & Dowling, 2013, p. 8), rather than focusing on who is inside and who is outside. This is not to shy away from differences, but rather to find ways to address them and to constantly relearn the most basic of concepts.

The adaptation process is very important, especially for those of us who came of age in second wave feminism and its concerns for equality. We have been steeped in the political, cultural and social energy of the 1980s and 1990s when the women's movement in and of itself was very strong and so-called identity politics had its own sphere, way of knowing, and adherents. We recognize that there has been a shift to bury women's concerns or to subsume them under larger global conversations and transnational concerns (Walby, 2011). As exemplified in this book, however, we remain committed to women as an identifiable group and community, and as an important sector in learning and teaching. Our concern has led us to interpret our own concerns.

Focus on Learning and Education for Women

In reviewing the contexts of women's collective engagement, we have highlighted diversity of creative opportunities to learn together. Working in community allows women to include an interpersonal and political dimension to the development of solidarity and support for each other—the overall goal is personal and social transformation. Community and its development have a strong learning dimension in this regard: learning about change, enacting change, and resisting undesirable change. The intersection of learning, power, and resistance is central to women's causes and projects. Adult education brings this learning dimension into sharp relief, and allows for transformation, both personal and social, as well as the possibility of substantive renewal and reinvigoration. An understanding of a women-specific focus on adult learning and development is essential to understanding women's lives and actions on the continuum from local to international contexts.

It is puzzling that a particular focus on feminists and learning has not been widely taken up, though learning for citizen participation and action has been an area of growing interest among adult educators (Mayo & Annette, 2010). Yet, feminist learning and citizen learning are intertwined: both involve the ways people come together to create a collective understanding of social conditions in order to claim and open up spaces for participation and to change power relations. The obscuring of a distinctive feminist identity in social movement work, for example, has hurt the advancement of theorizing about women's social movement learning in the 21st century. Gita Sen and Marina Durano's (2014) call for strengthening an explicit human rights agenda, including feminism, in development work is needed to bring issues of discrimination back into focus. While acknowledging that the evolving context of neoliberal economics continues to undermine social progress, Sen and Durano call for revitalized policy engagement to fix what has come undone over the past decade. They point out that getting bogged down in development benchmarks, such as the MDGs, has undermined the long view of human rights and dignity. This is where women's organizations and feminist learning have a crucial role to play.

The effects of the privatization of civic space, the erosion of public services, and the offloading of responsibility to community groups are quite apparent both locally and globally. There is no doubt that this neoliberal landscape affects teaching practice. This situation calls for a reinvigoration of the political and economic focus that hallmarked the heyday of second wave feminism. We are encouraged by the increasing sophistication of power analysis by activists to keep pace with the increasing influences of neoliberalism. Negotiating creative ways of leading and working in organizations for change has always been central to women's learning and activism, especially through nonprofit women's resource centres, which were often formed as safe havens for women to learn, heal, and challenge oppression collectively. In response, we are advocating a continued interplay of adult education, women's learning, and community learning, not only in these centres but in the community generally, as a way to address key critical and political issues.

To accomplish such resistance and creativity, community educators know that a focus on actions that involve co-learning and co-knowledge, from the bottom up, is needed. In the words of Lyn Tett (2010): "if local people are engaged in using their own knowledge then they can develop a capacity for self-determination" (p. 51). Such knowledge, which comes from the hearts and minds of the people most affected, is really useful knowledge; it is "knowledge calculated to make you free" (Johnson, 1988, p. 22), and is integral to increased quality of life for women. It is clear from the preceding chapters that taking the time for analysis and the collective creation of knowledge and of learning is of the essence.

A key way of tapping into this knowledge is through informal learning in the community. Rachel Gorman (2007) underscores the value of this learning for women because it resists the isolated and atomized kinds of learning that are highly individualized and masculinist. Informal learning in community provided space for women in groups such as the Women's Institutes, WCTU, and Chautauqua to gather and organize, and to dream possibilities for themselves that were not possible in the larger society (English & Mayo, 2012). Informal learning in these organizations and through practices and interactions in women's situated lives is learning that is borne of women's impulses and beliefs. It may be face to face but it also may be virtual and connected through social media. Whatever the space, such learning is infused by Freirean epistemology and is oriented to increased freedom and quality of life for women. In building and creating learning opportunities in the community, women connect their local practices to the public and global sphere.

Social Transformation as a Goal of Feminism

As noted in Chapter 2, the purpose of feminist organizing and leadership is not simply job creation, but part of the feminist movement's goals to end gender-based discrimination and oppression. The action of the movement travels from local to global, and back again, as activists work to educate, improve conditions, and support victims of violence. At the national and international level the focus may be changing laws that discriminate, and at the local level it may be integrating these laws into everyday life through an ongoing cycle of small gains, backlash, and further gains. Progress is slow. In no way can we say that things are worse for women in industrialized countries than a century ago, but media attention to ongoing violence, discrimination, and horrific conditions such as the use of rape as a weapon of war, show there is still far to go. In Canada, as we write this, there are renewed calls for a national public inquiry into the many cases of murdered or missing Aboriginal women, or *Stolen Sisters*. Indeed, *Stolen Sisters* was the title of the Amnesty International (2004) report that put a human face on the tragedies—a human face that is often missing from the discussion (Eberts, 2014). Over the past decade, collaboration among various organizations and international pressure from Amnesty and UN bodies, has tried to keep the issue of VAW, especially among Aboriginal women, in public discussions (Eberts). Activists know these are not just random acts of violence, but are representative of a deep, systemic web of gender injustice, colonialism and racism.

Change of a societal nature involves concomitant change in community and with individuals. The community is where issues are felt most keenly and where the energy for women's activism resides. Consequently, social movements are located in the communal spaces that have the potential to "become free spaces, breeding grounds for democratic change ... popular movements with enduring power and depth always find their strength in community-based associations" (Evans & Boyte, 1992, p. 187).

Yet, we cannot forget that local and global issues are intricately connected, and international governance creates a reciprocal relationship between local and international agencies, making policy work and legal reform possible. On the spectrum, one can imagine a women's centre offering workshops for women interested in becoming involved in local councils, and on the other end of the spectrum, the various components of UN Women researching conditions and monitoring implementation of conventions and protocols. The points on this spectrum are not fixed, given that the issues flow back and forth as feminists locally and internationally seek to enact alternative forms of power to overcome oppression. Local and international community involvement in policy work is essential to changing the system.

FINAL NOTE

A focus on women's learning and community is integral to the future of adult education in the 21st century. Along with learning, we need strong support in the form of policy and governance to strengthen feminism's goals. Policy needs to pay attention to women's learning and to include the full spectrum, from children to older adults. As well, global policies that govern adult education ought to fully acknowledge issues of gender (Stromquist, 2013).

At the beginning of this book we evoked Mary Oliver's (2005) suggestion that we need to be "ignited or be gone." Clearly, this book has been about being ignited about learning in the community, with women and for women. Without passion for change, we will not accomplish the collective feminist project at any time. The consolation is that feminism, especially community-based feminism, is a lifelong project for all of us, and most importantly, is a multi-generational project that honours those before us and makes way for those who follow us. May we all be ignited with passion for change.

REFERENCES

Accardi, M. T. (2013). *Feminist pedagogy for library instruction*. Sacramento, CA: Library Juice Press.

Addams, J. (1910/1912). *Twenty years at hull-house with autobiographical notes*. New York, NY: MacMillan Company.

Ahmed, S. (2002). This other and other others. *Economy and Society, 31*(4), 558–572.

All India Bakchod. (2013). *It's your fault* [Video]. Retrieved from https://www.youtube.com/watch?v=8hC0Ng_ajpY

Allen, J. K., Dean, D. R., & Bracken, S. J. (Eds.). (2008). *Most college students are women: Implications for teaching, learning and policy*. Stirling, VA: Stylus.

Allman, P. (2001). *Revolutionary social transformation: Democratic hopes, political possibilities, and critical education*. Westport, CT: Bergin and Garvey.

Allman, P. (2010). *Critical education against global capitalism: Karl Marx and revolutionary critical education* (Revised paperback version). Rotterdam, The Netherlands: Sense Publishers.

Amadahy, Z. (2003). The healing power of women's voices. In K. Anderson & B. Lawrence (Eds.), *Strong women stories: Native vision and community survival* (pp. 144–155). Toronto, ON: Sumach Press.

Amnesty International. (2004). *Stolen sisters: A human rights response to discrimination and violence against Indigenous women in Canada* (AMR 20/003/2004). Ottawa, ON: Author. Retrieved from http://www.amnesty.ca/sites/default/files/amr200032004enstolensisters.pdf

Appadurai, A. (1996). *Modernity at large: Cultural dimensions of globalisation*. Minneapolis, MN: University of Minnesota Press.

Archer, D., & Cottingham, S. (1996). *REFLECT mother manual: Regenerated Freirean literacy through empowering community techniques*. London, England: ActionAid.

Armacost, L. K. (2005). Menogogy: The art and science of becoming a crone: A new perspective on transformative learning. *Proceedings of the sixth international transformative learning conference*, Michigan State University. Retrieved from http://transformativelearning.ning.com/page/proceedings-1

Arnot, M. (2006). Gender equality, pedagogy and citizenship: Affirmative and transformative approaches in the UK. *Theory and Research in Education, 4*(2), 131–150.

Association for Progressive Communications. (2015). *How technology issues impact women's rights: 10 points on Section J*. Retrieved from http://www.genderit.org/node/4262

Association of Universities and Colleges in Canada (AUCC). (2005). *Momentum: The 2005 report on university research and knowledge transfer*. Ottawa, ON: AUCC.

Atleo, M. (2012). Health care professional working with aboriginal: Canadian adult education and practice. In L. M. English (Ed.), *Adult education and health* (pp. 90–106). Toronto, ON: University of Toronto Press.

Audet, F., Paquette, F., & Bergeron, S. (2013). Religious nongovernmental organisations and Canadian international aid, 2001–2010: A preliminary study. *Canadian Journal of Development Studies/Revue canadienne d'études du développement, 34*(2), 291–320. doi:10.1080/02255189.2013.794721

Australian Research Council. (2012). *Special research initiative for an aboriginal and Torres Strait islanders' research network*. Retrieved from http://www.arc.gov.au/ncgp/sri/atsirn_selrpt.htm

Ayed, N. (2013, January 16). *Delhi's voices, women and rape in India* [CBCnews]. Retrieved from http://www.cbc.ca/news/world/story/2013/01/15/f-vp-ayed-delhi.html

Baker, C. R. (2007). *Hybrid church in the city: Third space thinking*. Aldershot, Hants, England: Ashgate.

Barnacle, R. (2009). Gut instinct: The body and learning. *Educational Philosophy and Theory, 41*(1), 22–33.

Barndt, D. (Ed.). (2011). *¡Viva!: Community arts and popular education the Americas*. Albany, NY: SUNY Press & Toronto, ON: Between the Lines.

Barton, C. (2005). Where to for women's movements and the MDG. *Gender and Development, 13*(1), 25–34. doi:10.1080/13552070512331332274

Bashevkin, S. (2009). *Women, power, politics: The hidden story of Canada's unfinished democracy*. Toronto, ON: Oxford University Press.

165

Batliwala, S. (2011). *Feminist leadership for social transformation: Clearing the conceptual cloud.* New Delhi, India: CREA. Retrieved from http://web.creaworld.org/files/f1.pdf

Batliwala, S. (2012). *Changing their world: Concepts and practices of women's movements* (2nd ed.). Toronto, ON: AWID. Retrieved from http://www.awid.org/content/download/147805/1631969/file/Changing%20Their%20World%202ED%20ENG.pdf

Batliwala, S., with Rosenhek, S., & Miller, J. (2013). *Women moving mountains: The collective impact of the Dutch MDG3 fund.* Toronto, ON: Association of Women in Development. Retrieved from http://www.awid.org/Library/Women-Moving-Mountains3

Bauch, P. A. (2007). Jane Addams (1860–1935). In G. L. Anderson & K. G. Herr (Eds.), *Encyclopedia of activism and social justice* (Vol. 1, pp. 37–40). Thousand Oaks, CA: Sage.

Baum, H. S. (2000). Fantasies and realities in university–community partnerships. *Journal of Planning Education and Research, 20*(2), 234–246. doi:10.1177/0739456X0002000208

BBC. (2012, October 10). Malala Yousafzai: Portrait of the girl blogger. *BBC news magazine.* Retrieved from http://www.bbc.com/news/magazine-19899540

Beaulac, J., Kristjansson, E., & Cummins, S. (2009). A systematic review of food deserts, 1966–2007. *Preventing Chronic Disease, 6*(3), A105.

Beck, U. (1986). *Risk society: Towards a new modernity.* New Delhi, India: Sage. (Translated from the German *Risikogesellschaft*)

Belenky, M. F., & Stanton, A. V. (2000). Inequality, development and connected knowing. In J. Mezirow & Associates (Eds.), *Learning as transformation: Critical perspectives on a theory in progress* (pp. 71–102). San Francisco, CA: Jossey-Bass.

Belenky, M. F., Clinchy, B. M., Goldberger, N. R., & Tarule, J. M. (1986). *Women's ways of knowing: The development of self, voice, and mind.* New York, NY: Basic Books.

Benseman, J. (2005). Participation. In L. M. English (Ed.), *International encyclopedia of adult education* (pp. 455–460). Basingstoke, England: Palgrave Macmillan.

Berkley Center. (2011). *Practitioners and faith-inspired development.* Retrieved from http://berkleycenter.georgetown.edu/projects/practitioners-and-faith-inspired-development

Bhabha, H. K. (1994). *The location of culture.* New York, NY: Routledge.

Bhabha, H. K. (1995). Translator translated. *Artforum International, 33*(7), 88–119.

Bhabha, H. K. (1998). On the irremovable strangeness of being different. *Publications of the Modern Language Association of America, 113*(1), 34–39.

Bhatt, E. R. (2006). *We are poor but so many: The story of self-employed women in India.* New York, NY: Oxford University Press.

Bhattacharjya, M., Birchall, J., Caro, P., Kelleher, D., & Sahasranaman, V. (2013). Why gender matters in activism: Feminism and social justice movements. *Gender & Development, 21*(2), 277–293. doi:10.1080/13552074.2013.802150

Bier, S. (Director). (2010). *In a better world* [Feature Film]. Directed by Susanne Bier (Denmark), 113 min.

Birden, S. (2004). Theorizing a coalition-engendered education: The case of the Boston women's health book collective's body education. *Adult Education Quarterly, 54*(4), 257–272. doi:10.1177/0741713604266141

Blaney, F. (2003). Aboriginal women's action network. In K. Anderson & B. Lawrence (Eds.), *Strong women stories: Native vision and community survival* (pp. 156–170). Toronto, ON: Sumach Press.

Block, S. R., & Rosenberg, S. (2002). Toward an understanding of founder's syndrome: An assessment of power and privilege among founders of nonprofit organizations. *Nonprofit Management and Leadership, 12*(4), 353–368.

Blunt, K. (2007). Social work education: Achieving transformative learning through a cultural competence model for transformative education. *Journal of Teaching in Social Work, 27*(3/4), 93–114.

Bly, L., & Wooten, K. (Eds.). (2012). *Make your own history: Documenting feminist and queer activism in the 21st century.* Los Angeles, CA: Litwin Books.

Boal, A. (1974/1985). *Theatre of the oppressed* (A. C. McBride & M.-O. L. McBride, Trans.). New York, NY: Theatre of Communications Group.

Bouvard, M. (1994). *Revolutionizing motherhood: The mothers of the Plaza de Mayo*. Lanham, MD: Rowman and Littlefield.

Bracken, S. (2008). Submerged feminism(s)? In J. K. Allen, D. R. Dean, & S. J. Bracken (Eds.), *Most college students are women: Implications for teaching, learning and policy* (pp. 159–172). Stirling, VA: Stylus.

Bracken, S. (2011). Understanding program planning theory and practice in a feminist community-based organization. *Adult Education Quarterly, 61*(2), 121–138. doi:10.1177/0741713610380446

Braithwaite, R., Cockwill, S., O'Neill, M., & Rebane, D. (2007). Insider participatory action research in disadvantaged post-industrial areas. *Action Research, 5*(1), 61–74. doi:10.1177/1476750307072876

Brookfield, S. D. (2005). *The power of critical theory: Liberating adult learning and teaching*. San Francisco, CA: Jossey-Bass.

Brookfield, S. D. (2010). Theoretical frameworks for understanding the field. In C. E. Kasworm, A. D. Rose, & J. M. Ross-Gordon (Eds.), *Handbook of adult and continuing education* (pp. 71–81). Thousand Oaks, CA: Sage.

Brooks, A. K. (2000a). Cultures of transformation. In A. L. Wilson & E. R. Hayes (Eds.), *Handbook of adult and continuing education* (pp. 161–170). San Francisco, CA: Jossey-Bass.

Brooks, A. K. (2000b). Transformation. In E. Hayes, D. D. Flannery, A. K. Brooks, E. J. Tisdell & J. M. Hugo (Eds.), *Women as learners: The significance of gender in adult learning* (pp. 139–153). San Francisco, CA: Jossey-Bass.

Brown, M. (1997). The cultural saliency of radical democracy: Moments from the Aids Quilt. *Ecumene: A Journal of Cultural Geographies, 4*(1), 27–45. doi:10.1177/147447409700400103

Buck, M. A. (2009). Discovering the transformative learning potential in the spirituality of midlife women. *Proceedings of the Eighth International Transformative Learning Conference*, College of Bermuda. Retrieved from http://transformativelearning.ning.com/page/proceedings-1

Bunyan, P. (2013). Partnership, the big society and community organizing: Between romanticizing, problematizing and politicizing community. *Community Development Journal, 48*(1), 119–133. doi:10.1093/cdj/bss014

Burge, L. (2011). *Women social activists of Atlantic Canada: Profiles of wisdom*. Fredericton, NB: University of New Brunswick Scholarly. Retrieved from https://womenactivists.lib.unb.ca

Burke, P. J., & Jackson, S. (2007). *Reconceptualising lifelong learning: Feminist interventions*. London, England: Routledge.

Buskens, I. (2013). Open development is a freedom song: Revealing intent and freeing power. In M. L. Smith & K. M. A. Reilly (Eds.), *Open development: Networked innovations in international development* (pp. 327–351). Ottawa, ON: IDRC.

Buskens, I., & Webb, A. (Eds.). (2009). *African women and ICTs: Investigating technology, gender and empowerment*. London, England: Zed Books.

Buskens, I., & Webb, A. (Eds.). (2014). *Women and ICT in Africa and the Middle East: Changing selves, changing societies*. London, England: Zed Books.

Butler, J. (1994). Contingent foundations: Feminism and the question of postmodernism. In S. Seidman (Ed.), *The postmodern turn: New perspectives on social theory* (pp. 153–170). Cambridge, England: Cambridge University Press.

Butler, J. (1999). *Gender trouble: Feminism and the subversion of identity* (2nd ed.). New York, NY: Routledge.

Buttala, S. (2004). *Keynote address: Narrative matters conference*. Fredericton, NB: University of St. Thomas and University of New Brunswick.

Butterwick, S. (2005). Feminist pedagogy. In L. M. English (Ed.), *International encyclopedia of adult education* (pp. 257–262). Basingstoke, England: Palgrave Macmillan.

Butterwick, S. (2012). The politics of listening: The power of theatre to creative dialogic spaces. In L. Manicom & S. Walters (Eds.), *Feminist popular education in transnational debates: Building pedagogies of possibility* (pp. 59–73). Basingstoke, England: Palgrave Macmillan.

Butterwick, S., & Harper, L. (2006). An "inter-cultural" view of community-academic partnerships: Tales from the field. *Proceedings of the 36th annual SCUTREA conference*. Retrieved from http://www.leeds.ac.uk/educol/documents/155187.doc

Butterwick, S., & Jubas, K. (2006). The organic and accidental IT worker: Women's on-the-job teaching and learning experiences. In *Proceedings of the national conference of the Canadian association for the study of adult education*. Toronto, ON: York University. Retrieved from http://www.casae-aceea.ca/sites/casae/archives/cnf2006/cnf2006.html

Butterwick, S., & Selman, J. (2003). Deep listening in a feminist popular theatre project: Upsetting the position of audience in participatory education. *Adult Education Quarterly, 54*(1), 7–22. doi:10.1177/0741713603257094

Caglar, G., Prügl, E., & Zwingel, S. (Eds.). (2013). *Feminist strategies in international governance.* London, England: Routledge.

Calas, M., & Smircich, L. (2006). From the "woman's point of view" ten years later: Towards a feminist organization studies. In S. Clegg, C. Hardy, T. Lawrence, & W. Nord (Eds.), *The SAGE handbook of organization studies* (2nd ed., pp. 284–347). London, England: Sage. doi:10.4135/9781848608030.n9

Cameron, P. (2011). Using zines in research to help express young women's experiences of depression. In C. Maclean & R. Kelly (Eds.), *Creative arts in research for community and cultural change* (pp. 177–206). Calgary, AB: Detselig.

Cameron, P. (2014). Learning with a curve: Young women's 'depression' as transformative learning. In V. C. X. Wang (Ed.), *Handbook of research on adult and community health education: Tools, trends, and methodologies* (pp. 100–122). Hershey, PA: IGI Global.

Carleton, S. (2012, December 26). #IdleNoMore: A longer view. *Canadian Dimension.* Retrieved from https://canadiandimension.com/articles/view/idlenomore-a-longer-view1

Carpenter, S. (2012). Centering Marxist-feminist theory in adult learning. *Adult Education Quarterly, 62*(1), 19–35. doi:10.1177/0741713610392767

Carpenter, S., & Mojab, S. (Eds.). (2011). *Educating from Marx: Race, gender, and learning.* New York, NY: Palgrave Macmillan.

Carson, R. (1962). *Silent spring.* Boston, MA: Houghton Mifflin.

Carty, L. E., & Mohanty, C. T. (2015). Mapping transnational feminist engagements: Neoliberalism and the politics of solidarity. In R. Baksh & W. Harcourt (Eds.), *The Oxford handbook of transnational feminist movements* (pp. 82–115). Oxford, England: Oxford University Press.

Chapman, V.-L. (2003). On "knowing one's self" selfwriting, power, and ethical practice: Reflections from an adult educator. *Studies in the Education of Adults, 35*(1), 35–53.

Chigudu, H. (2014). Hope Chigudu's thoughts on 'Riding the waves of activist leadership'. *News from AWDF.* Retrieved from African Women Development Fund web site: http://www.awdf.org/hope-chigudus-thoughts-on-riding-the-waves-of-activist-leadership/

Choudry, A., & Kapour, D. (Eds.). (2010). *Learning from the ground up: Global perspectives on social movements and knowledge production.* New York, NY: Palgrave Macmillan.

Chovanec, D. M. (2009). *Between hope and despair: Women learning politics.* Halifax, NS: Fernwood Publishing.

Chovanec, D. M., Cooley, M., & Smith Díaz, R. (2010). *How to catch a penguin: Generating women's activism in the Chilean student movement* [Documentary video, 23 mins]. Edmonton, AB: University of Alberta.

Clandinin, D. J., & Connelly, F. M. (2000). *Narrative inquiry: Experience and story in qualitative research.* San Francisco, CA: Jossey-Bass.

Clark, C. (2001). Off the beaten path: Some creative approaches to adult learning. *New Directions for Adult and Continuing Education, 2001*(89), 83–91.

Clark, C., & Dirkx, J. (2008, Winter). The emotional self in adult learning. *New Directions for Adult and Continuing Education, 2008*(120), 89–95. doi:10.1002/ace.319

Clover, D. E. (2006a). Culture and antiracisms in adult education: An exploration of the contributions of arts-based learning. *Adult Education Quarterly, 57*(1), 46–61.

Clover, D. E. (2006b). Out of the dark room: Participatory photography as a critical, imaginative, and public aesthetic practice of transformative education. *Journal of Transformative Education, 4*(3), 275–290. doi:10.1177/1541344606287782

Clover, D. E. (2007a). Tapestries through the making: Quilting as a valuable medium of feminist adult education and arts-based inquiry. In D. E. Clover & J. Stalker (Eds.), *The arts and social justice: Re-crafting adult education and community cultural leadership* (pp. 83–101). Leicester, England: National Institute of Adult Continuing Education.

Clover, D. E. (2007b). Feminist aesthetic practice of community development: The case of myths and mirrors community arts. *Community Development Journal, 42*(4), 512–522. doi:10.1093/cdj/bsm041

Clover, D. E. (2010). A contemporary review of feminist aesthetic practices in selective adult education journals and conference proceedings. *Adult Education Quarterly, 60*(3), 233–248.

Clover, D. E. (2012). Feminist artists and popular education: The creative turn. In L. Manicom & S. Walters (Eds.), *Feminist popular education in transnational debates: Building pedagogies of possibility* (pp. 193–208). Basingstoke, England: Palgrave Macmillan.

Coady, M. J. (2013). Adult education for health and wellness. In T. Nesbit, S. Brigham, N. Taber, & T. Gibb (Eds.), *Building on critical traditions: Adult education and learning in Canada* (3rd ed., pp. 173–183). Toronto, ON: Thompson Educational Publishers.

Coates, K. (2015). *#IdleNoMore and the remaking of Canada*. Regina, SK: University of Regina Press.

Cobb, P. D., & Rubin, B. A. (2006). Contradictory interests, tangled power and disorganized organization. *Administration and Society, 38*(1), 79–112.

Conti, G., & Fellenz, R. (1986). Myles Horton: Ideas that have withstood the test of time. *Adult Literacy and Basic Education, 10*(1), 1–18.

Cooke, B. (2004). Rules of thumb for participatory change agents. In S. Hickey & G. Mohan (Eds.), *Participation: From tyranny to transformation?* (pp. 42–55). London, England: Zed Books.

Cooke, B., & Kothari, U. (Eds.). (2001). *Participation: The new tyranny.* London, England: Zed Books.

Cooks, L., & Isgro, K. (2005). The "cyber summit" and women: Incorporating gender into information and communication technology UN policies. *Frontiers, 26*(1), 71–89.

Cooley, L. A. (2007). Transformational learning and third-wave feminism as potential outcomes of participation in women's enclaves. *Journal of Transformative Education, 5*(4), 304–316.

Coombs, P. H. (1973). *New paths to learning for rural children and youth.* New York, NY: International Council for Education and Development.

Coontz, S. (2011). *A strange stirring: The feminine mystique and the American women at the dawn of the 1960s.* New York, NY: Basic Books.

Cornwall, A. (2004). Spaces for transformation? Reflections on issues of power and difference in participation in development. In S. Hickey & G. Mohan (Eds.), *Participation: From tyranny to transformation?* (pp. 75–91). London, England: Zed Books.

Cornwall, A., & Edwards, J. (2014). Introduction. In A. Cornwall & J. Edwards (Eds.), *Feminist empowerment and development: Changing women's lives* (pp. 1–31). London, England: Zed Books.

Cornwall, A., Harrison, E., & Whitehead, A. (Eds.). (2007). *Feminisms in development: Contradictions, contestations and challenges.* London, England: Zed Books.

Cornwall, A., Harrison, E., & Whitehead, A. (Eds.). (2008). *Gender myths and feminist fables: The struggle for interpretive power in gender and development.* Malden, MA: Wiley-Blackwell.

Cottrell, B., & Parpart, J. L. (2006). Academic-community collaboration, gender research, and development: Pitfalls and possibilities. *Development in Practice, 16*(1), 15–26.

Cranton, P. (2006). *Understanding and promoting transformative learning* (2nd ed.). San Francisco, CA: Jossey-Bass.

Cranton, P., & Wright, B. (2008). The transformative educator as learning companion. *Journal of Transformative Education, 6*(1), 33–47.

CREA. (2014). CREA: Who we are – history & founders. Retrieved from http://creaworld.org/who-we-are/history-founders

Crenshaw, K. W. (1991). Mapping the margins: Intersectionality, identity politics, and violence against women of color. *Stanford Law Review, 43*(6), 1241–1299.

Crenshaw, K. W. (2010). Close encounters of three kinds: On teaching dominance, feminism, and intersectionality. *Tulsa Law Review, 46*, 151–189.

Crowther, J., & Tett, L. (2012). Learning literacy for citizenship and democracy. In L. Tett, M. Hamilton, & J. Crowther (Eds.), *More powerful literacies* (pp. 117–128). Leicester, England: National Institute of Adult Continuing Education.

Cueva, M., & Cueva, K. (2008). Cancer education through dance: From taproot to grace. *Convergence, 41*(2–3), 135–142.

David, R., & Mancini, A. (2004). *Going against the flow: The struggle to make organisational systems part of the solution rather than part of the problem.* Sussex, England: Institute of Development Studies, University of Sussex.

Davies, B., & Gannon, S. (2005). Feminism/poststructuralism. In B. Somekh & C. Lewin (Eds.), *Research methods in the social sciences* (pp. 318–325). Thousand Oaks, CA: Sage.

De Kadt, E. (2009). Should god play a role in development? *Journal of International Development Studies, 21*(6), 781–787.

Deerchild, R. (2003). Tribal feminism is a drum song. In K. Anderson & B. Lawrence (Eds.), *Strong women stories: Native vision and community survival* (pp. 97–105). Toronto, ON: Sumach Press.

Deneulin, S., & Bano, M. (2009). *Religion in development: Rewriting the secular script.* London, England: Zed Books.

Denning, S. (2006). Effective storytelling: Strategic business narrative techniques. *Strategy & Leadership, 34*(1), 42–48. doi:10.1108/10878570610637885

Dodaro, S., & Pluta, L. (2012). *The big picture: The antigonish movement of Eastern Nova Scotia.* Montreal, QC: McGill-Queens University Press.

Donnelly-Cox, G., Donoghue, F., & Hayes, T. (2001). Conceptualising the third sector in Ireland, North and South. *Voluntas: International Journal of Voluntary and Nonprofit Organizations, 12*(3), 195–204.

Drexler, P. (2013, March 2–3). The tyranny of the queen bee. *The Wall Street Journal*, C1–C2.

Dreyfus, H., & Rabinow, P. (1982). *Michel Foucault: Beyond structuralism and hermeneutics, with an afterword by Michel Foucault.* Chicago, IL: University of Chicago Press.

Dullea, K. (2006). Women shaping participatory research to their own needs. *Community Development Journal, 41*(1), 65–74. doi:10.1093/cdj/bsi041

Eberts, M. (2014). Victoria's secret: How to make a population of prey. In J. Green (Ed.), *Indivisible: Indigenous human rights* (pp. 144–165). Halifax, NS: Fernwood.

Ehrenreich, B. (2009). *Bright-sided: How the relentless promotion of positive thinking has undermined America.* New York, NY: Holt.

Ehrenreich, B., & English, D. (1978). *For her own good: 150 years of the experts' advice to women.* New York, NY: Anchor Press.

Eichler, M. (2005). The other half (or more) of the story: Unpaid household and care work and lifelong learning. In N. Bascia, A. Cumming, A. Datnow, K. Leithwood, & D. Livingstone (Eds.), *International handbook of educational policy* (Vol. 13, pp. 1023–1042). Dordrecht, The Netherlands: Springer.

Eichler, M., Albanese, P., Ferguson, S., Hyndman, N., Liu, L. W., & Matthews, A. (2010). *More than it seems: Household work and lifelong learning.* Toronto, ON: Women's Press.

Eimhjellen, I. S. (2014). Internet communication: Does it strengthen local voluntary organizations? *Nonprofit and Voluntary Sector Quarterly, 43*(5), 890–909.

Elabor-Idemudia, P. (2002). Participatory research: A tool in the production of knowledge in development discourse. In K. Saunders (Ed.), *Feminist post-development thought: Rethinking modernity, postcolonialism & representation* (pp. 227–242). London, England: Zed Books.

Ellsworth, E. (1989). Why doesn't this feel empowering? Working through the repressive myths of critical pedagogy. *Harvard Educational Review, 59*(3), 297–323.

Elmborg, J. (2006). Critical information literacy: Implications for instructional practice. *The Journal of Academic Librarianship, 32*(2), 192–199.

English, L. M. (2005a). Foucault, feminists and funders: A study of power and policy in feminist organizations. *Studies in the Education of Adults, 37*(2), 137–150.

English, L. M. (2005b). Third-space practitioners: Women educating for civil society. *Adult Education Quarterly, 55*(2), 85–100. doi:10.1177/0741713604271851

English, L. M. (2006a). A Foucauldian reading of learning in feminist nonprofit organizations. *Adult Education Quarterly, 56*(2), 85–101. doi:10.1177/0741713605283429

English, L. M. (2006b). Women, knowing, and authenticity: Living with contradictions. In P. Cranton (Ed.), *Authenticity in teaching. New Directions for Adult and Continuing Education, 2006*(111), Fall, 17–25. San Francisco, CA: Jossey-Bass. doi:10.1002/ace.224

English, L. M. (2011). Power, resistance and informal pathways: Lifelong learning in feminist nonprofit organizations. In S. Jackson, I. Malcolm, K. Thomas (Eds.), *Gendered choices: Learning, work, identities in lifelong learning* (pp. 209–225). London, England: Springer.

English, L. M. (2012). A critical theory of adult health learning. In L. M. English (Ed.), *Adult education and health* (pp. 13–25). Toronto, ON: University of Toronto Press.

English, L. M., & Irving, C. J. (2008). Reflexive texts: Issues of knowledge, power and discourse in researching gender and learning. *Adult Education Quarterly, 58*(4), 267–283. doi:10.1177/0741713608322019

English, L. M., & Irving, C. J. (2012). Women and transformative learning. In E. W. Taylor & P. Cranton (Eds.), *Handbook of transformative learning* (pp. 245–259). San Francisco, CA: Jossey-Bass.

English, L. M., & Irving, C. J. (2015). Feminism and adult education: The nexus of policy, practice, and payment. *Canadian Journal for the Study of Adult Education, 27*(2), 16–30.

English, L. M., & Mayo, P. (2012). *Learning with adults: A critical pedagogical introduction.* Rotterdam, The Netherlands: Sense Publishers.

English, L. M., & Peters, N. (2011). Founders' syndrome in women's nonprofit organizations: Implications for practice and organizational life. *Nonprofit Management and Leadership, 22*(2), 159–171. doi:10.1002/nml.20047

English, L. M., & Peters, N. (2012). Transformative learning in feminist organizations: A feminist interpretive inquiry. *Adult Education Quarterly, 62*(2), 103–119. doi:10.1177/0741713610392771

English, L. M., & Tisdell, E. J. (2010). Spirituality and adult education. In C. E. Kasworm, A. D. Rose, & J. M. Ross-Gordon (Eds.), *Handbook of adult and continuing education* (pp. 285–293). Thousand Oaks, CA: Sage.

English, L. M., McAulay, K., & Mahaffey, T. (2012). Financial literacy and academics: A critical discourse analysis. *Canadian Journal for the Study of Adult Education, 25*(1), 17–25. Retrieved from http://journals.msvu.ca/index.php/cjsae/issue/current

Eubanks, V. (2011). *Digital dead end: Fighting for social justice in the information age.* Cambridge, MA: MIT Press.

Evans, S., Perricci, A., & Roberts, A. (2013). "Why archive?" and other important questions asked by occupiers. In M. Morrone (Ed.), *Informed agitation: Library and information skills in social justice movements and beyond.* Sacramento, CA: Library Juice.

Evans, S. M., & Boyte, H. C. (1992). *Free spaces: The sources of democratic change in America* (2nd ed.). Chicago, IL: University of Chicago Press.

Eyben, R. (2012). *The hegemony cracked: The power guide to getting care onto the development agenda.* IDS Working Paper, 411. Brighton, England: Institute of Development Studies, University of Sussex. Retrieved from http://www.ids.ac.uk/publication/the-hegemony-cracked-the-power-guide-to-getting-care-onto-the-development-agenda

Eyben, R. (2014). Subversively accommodating: Feminist bureaucrats and gender mainstreaming. In A. Cornwall & J. Edwards (Eds.), *Feminisms, empowerment and development: Changing women's lives* (pp. 159–174). London, England: Zed.

Facio, A. (2013a). Confronting globalization: Feminist spirituality as political strategy. In A. Miles (Ed.), *Women in a globalising world: Transforming equality, development, diversity and peace* (pp. 37–48). Toronto, ON: Inanna.

Facio, A. (2013b, November). Political motherhood vs violence against mothers 25. *Open Democracy.* Retrieved from https://www.opendemocracy.net/5050/alda-facio/political-motherhood-vs-violence-against-mothers

Fahlander, F. (2007). Third space encounters: Hybridity mimicry and interstitial practice. In P. Cornell & F. Fahlander (Eds.), *Encounters/materialities/confrontations: Archaeologies of social space and interaction* (pp. 15–41). Newcastle, England: Cambridge Scholars Press.

Fairclough, N. (1992). *Discourse and social change.* Cambridge, England: Polity Press.

REFERENCES

Fairclough, N. (2000). *New labour, new language?* London, England: Routledge.

Fairclough, N., & Wodak, R. (1997). Critical discourse analysis. In T. A. van Dijk (Ed.), *Discourse as social interaction* (Vol. 1, pp. 258–284). London, England: Sage.

Fayé, O. N. (Ed.). (2013). *For the elimination and a prevention of all forms of violence against women and girls in West Africa: Report of a study conducted in 10 countries.* Dakar, Senegal: AAWORD. Retrieved from http://www.afard.org/allfichiers/PublicationWomenViolence.pdf

Fejes, A. (2011). Confession, in-service training and reflective practices. *British Educational Research Journal, 37*(5), 797–812. doi:10.1080/01411926.2010.500371

Fejes, A., & Dahlstedt, M. (2013). *The confessing society: Foucault, confession and practices of lifelong learning: Governing the subject.* London, England: Routledge.

Ferree, M. M., & Martin, P. Y. (1995). Doing the work of the movement: Feminist organisations. In M. M. Ferree & P. Y. Martin (Eds.), *Feminist organisations: Harvest of the new women's movement* (pp. 3–23). Philadelphia, PA: Temple University Press.

Ferris, H., & Walters, S. (2012). Heartfelt pedagogy in the time of HIV and AIDS. In L. Manicom & S. Walters (Eds.), *Feminist popular education in transnational debates: Building pedagogies of possibility* (pp. 75–91). Basingstoke, England: Palgrave Macmillan.

FIDH - Fédération internationale des ligues des droits de l'Homme. (2014). *Egypt: Keeping women out: Sexual violence against women in the public sphere.* Report number: 630a. Paris, France: FIDH. Retrieved from http://www.fidh.org/IMG/pdf/egypt_sexual_violence_uk-webfinal.pdf

Fiedler, M. (Ed.). (2010). *Breaking through the stained glass ceiling: Women religious leaders in their own words.* New York, NY: Seabury Books.

Filliponi-Berardinelli, J. (2013). Exploring efficacy in negotiating support: Women re-entry students in higher education. *College Quarterly, 16*(2). Retrieved from http://collegequarterly.ca/

Fletcher, J. K. (1998). Relational practice: A feminist reconstruction of work. *Journal of Management Inquiry, 7*(2), 163–186.

Fletcher, J. K. (2003). *The paradox of post heroic leadership: Gender matters.* Working Paper 17, Center for Gender in Organizations, Simmons School of Management, Boston. Retrieved from http://www.simmons.edu/som/docs/cgo_wp17_DNC.pdf

Foertsch, J. (2000). The circle of learners is a vicious circle: Derrida, Foucault, and feminist pedagogic practice. *College Literature, 27*(3), 111–129.

Foley, G. (1999). *Learning in social action: A contribution to understanding informal education.* London, England: Zed Books.

Ford, J. (2006). Discourses of leadership: Gender, identity and contradiction in a UK public sector organization. *Leadership, 2*(1), 77–99. doi:10.1177/1742715006060654

Forest, C. (2009). Transformative development in U.S. women living in poverty. *Proceedings of the eighth international transformative learning conference,* College of Bermuda. Retrieved from http://transformativelearning.ning.com/page/proceedings-1

Foroughi, B. (2013). Toronto community housing: Tenant participation and informal learning. *Canadian Journal for the Study of Adult Education, 25*(2), 35–52. Retrieved from http://journals.msvu.ca/index.php/cjsae/issue/view/126

Foroughi, B., & English, L. M. (2013). ICTs and adult education. In P. Mayo (Ed.), *Learning with adults: A reader* (pp. 153–160). Rotterdam, The Netherlands: Sense Publishers.

Foucault, M. (1977). *Discipline and punish: The birth of the prison* (A. Sheridan, Trans.). New York, NY: Vintage.

Foucault, M. (1978). *The history of sexuality: An introduction* (Vol. 1). Harmondsworth, England: Penguin.

Foucault, M. (1980). *Power/knowledge: Selected interviews and other writings 1972–1977* (R. Hurley, Trans.). New York, NY: Pantheon.

Foucault, M. (2003). In P. Rabinow & N. Rose (Eds.), *The essential Foucault: Selections from the essential works of Foucault 1954–1984.* New York, NY: The New Press.

Frank, F., & Smith, A. (2000). *The partnership handbook.* Hull, Quebec, Canada: Human Resources and Development Canada, Government of Canada.

Franklin, U. (1999). *The real world of technology*. Toronto, ON: House of Anansi.

Fraser, N. (2005). Reframing justice in a globalizing world. *New Left Review, 36*, 69–88.

Fraser, N. (2007). Feminist politics in the age of recognition: A two-dimensional approach to gender justice. *Studies in Social Justice, 1*(1), 23–35.

Freire, P. (1970). *Pedagogy of the oppressed*. (M. B. Ramos, Trans.). New York, NY: Continuum.

Freire, P. (1994/2004). *Pedagogy of hope: Reliving pedagogy of the oppressed* (R. R. Barr, Trans.). New York, NY: Continuum.

Friedan, B. (1963). *Feminine mystique*. New York, NY: W. W. Norton and Co.

Fuller, L., & Meiners, E. (2005). Reflection: Empowering women, technology and (feminist) institutional change. *Frontiers: A Journal of Women's Studies, 26*(1), 168–180.

Gahlot, M. (2014, June 17). Despite tougher laws, India can't shake rape culture. *USA Today*. Retrieved from http://awid.org/Library/Despite-tougher-laws-India-can-t-shake-rape-culture

Gajjala, R., & Oh, Y. J. (Eds.). (2012). *Cyberfeminism 2.0*. New York, NY: Peter Lang.

Gerbaudo, P. (2012). *Tweets and the streets: Social media and contemporary activism*. London, England: Pluto Press.

Gilchrist, A. (2009). *The well-connected community: A networking approach to community development*. Bristol, England: Policy Press.

Gilligan, C. (1982). *In a different voice*. Cambridge, MA: Harvard University Press.

Ginsberg, M. B., & Wlodkowski, R. J. (2010). Access and participation. In C. E. Kasworm, A. D. Rose, & J. M. Ross-Gordon (Eds.), *Handbook of adult and continuing education* (pp. 25–34). Thousand Oaks, CA: Sage.

Glasgow Women's Library. (2014). *Badges of honour: How badge-wearing women changed the world*. Retrieved from http://womenslibrary.org.uk/whats-on/badges-of-honour/

Gokal, S., Barbero, R., & Balchin, C. (Eds.). (2011). *Key learnings from feminists on the frontline: Summaries of case studies on resisting and challenging fundamentalisms*. Toronto, Mexico City and Capetown: Association of Women in Development. Retrieved from http://www.awid.org/Library/Feminists-on-the-Frontline-Case-Studies-of-Resisting-and-Challenging-Fundamentalisms

Goldberger, N., Tarule, J., Clinchy, B., & Belenky, M. (Eds.). (1996). *Knowledge, difference and power: Essays inspired by women's ways of knowing*. New York, NY: Basic Books.

Gorman, R. (2007). The feminist standpoint and the trouble with "informal learning": A way forwards for Marxist-feminist educational research. In A. Green, G. Rikowski, & H. Raduntz (Eds.), *Renewing dialogues in Marxism and education: Openings* (pp. 183–199). New York, NY: Palgrave Macmillan.

Gorman, S. (2008). Bursting the bubble: Internet feminism and the end of activism. *Feminist Media Studies, 8*(2), 220–223.

Gouthro, P. A. (2005). A critical feminist analysis of the homeplace as learning site: Expanding the discourse of lifelong learning. *International Journal of Lifelong Education, 24*(1), 5–19.

Gouthro, P. A. (2009). Neoliberalism, lifelong learning and the homeplace: Problematizing the boundaries of 'public' and 'private' to explore women's learning experiences. *Studies in Continuing Education, 31*(2), 157–172.

Gouthro, P. A. (2013). Neoliberalism, lifelong learning and the homeplace. In M. Murphy (Ed.), *Social theory and education research* (Vol. II). London, England: Sage.

Green, J. (Ed.). (2007). *Making space for Indigenous feminism*. Halifax, NS: Fernwood.

Greene, M. (1995). *Releasing the imagination: Essays on education, the arts, and social change*. San Francisco, CA: Jossey-Bass.

Grodach, C. (2010). Art spaces, public space, and the link to community development. *Community Development Journal, 45*(4), 474–493. doi:10.1093/cdj/bsp018

Groen, J., & Kawalilak, C. (2014). *Pathways of adult learning: Professional and education narratives*. Toronto, ON: Canadian Scholars' Press.

Guttentag, B., & Sturman, D. (2009). *Soundtrack for a revolution* [Motion picture]. New York, NY: Louverture Films.

Hafkin, N. J., & Huyer, S. (Eds.). (2006). *Cinderella or cyberella? Empowering women in the knowledge society*. Bloomfield, CT: Kumarian Press.

REFERENCES

Hakim, C. (2003). *Models of the family in modern society.* Aldershot, England: Ashgate.

Hall, B. L., & Clover, D. E. (2005). Social movement learning. In L. M. English (Ed.), *International encyclopedia of adult education* (pp. 584–589). Basingstoke, England: Palgrave Macmillan.

Hall, B. L., & Clover, D. E. (2006). Social movement learning. In R. Veira de Castro, A.V. Sancho, & P. Guimarães (Eds.), *Adult education: New routes in a new landscape* (pp. 159–166). Braga, Portugal: University of Minho.

Hamp, J. (2007). Voice and transformative learning. *Proceedings of the seventh international transformative learning conference,* University of New Mexico. Retrieved from http://transformativelearning.ning.com/page/proceedings-1

Hango, D. (2013, December). Gender differences in science, technology, engineering, mathematics and computer science (STEM) programs at university. *Insights on Canadian Society,* Statistics Canada, Catalogue no. 75-006-X. Retrieved from http://www.statcan.gc.ca/pub/75-006-x/2013001/article/11874-eng.pdf

Hansman, C. A., & Wright, K. J. (2005). Popular education in Bolivia: Transformational learning experiences. *Proceeding of the sixth international transformative learning conference,* Michigan State University. Retrieved from http://transformativelearning.ning.com/page/proceedings-

Hanson, C. (2013). Exploring dimensions of critical reflection in activist–facilitator practice. *Journal of Transformative Education, 11*(1), 70–89. doi:10.1177/1541344613488834

Hanson, C. (2015). I learned I am a feminist: Lessons for adult learning from participatory action research with union women. *Canadian Journal for the Study of Adult Education, 27*(1), 1–15. Retrieved from http://journals.msvu.ca/index.php/cjsae/article/view/3361

Haraway, D. (1985). Manifesto for cyborgs. *The Socialist Review, 80,* 65–107.

Haraway, D. (1991). *Simians, cyborgs and women: The reinvention of nature.* New York, NY: Routledge.

Hargittai, E., & Shaw, A. (2014). Mind the skills gap: The role of Internet know-how and gender in differentiated contributions to Wikipedia. *Information, Communication & Society, 18*(4), 424–442. doi:10.1080/1369118X.2014.957711

Harouni, H. (2014). The sound of TED: A case for distaste. *The American Reader.* Retrieved from http://theamericanreader.com/the-sound-of-ted-a-case-for-distaste/

Harper, L., English, L. M., & MacDonald, T. E. (2010). Rural feminist activism and religious fundamentalism, Nova Scotia, Canada. *Resisting and challenging religious fundamentalisms: Learning from experience.* Retrieved from Association of Women in Development web site: http://www.awid.org/eng/About-AWID/AWID-Initiatives/Resisting-and-Challenging-Religious-Fundamentalisms/CF-Case_Studies

Hart, M. (2002). *The poverty of life affirming work: Motherwork, education, and social change.* Westport, CT: Greenwood.

Hasenfeld, Y., & Gidron, B. (2005). Understanding multi-purpose hybrid voluntary organizations: The contributions of theories on civil society, social movements and nonprofit organizations. *Journal of Civil Society, 1*(2), 97–112. doi:10.1080/17448680500337350

Hayes, E., & Flannery, D., with Brooks, A., Tisdell, E. J., & Hugo, J. (2000). *Women as learners: The significance of gender in adult learning.* San Francisco, CA: Jossey-Bass.

Healy, H. (2014). Is there a feminist spring? *New Internationalist, 474,* 12–17.

Hickey, S., & Mohan, G. (Eds.). (2004). *Participation: From tyranny to transformation?* London, England: Zed Books.

High, S. (2010). Telling stories: A reflection on oral history and new media. *Oral History,* spring, 101–112.

Hill Collins, P. (1998). *Fighting words: Black women and the search for justice.* Minneapolis, MN: University of Minnesota Press.

Hoggan, C., Simpson, S., & Stuckey, H. L. (Eds.). (2009). *Creative expression in transformative learning: Tools and techniques for educators of adults.* Malabar, FL: Krieger.

Hollander, J. B. (2011). Keeping control: The paradox of scholarly community-based research in community development. *Community Development Journal, 46*(2), 265–272. doi:10.1093/cdj/bsp062

Hollinshead, K. (1998). Tourism, hybridity, and ambiguity: The relevance of Bhabha's 'Third space' cultures. *Journal of Leisure Research, 30*(1), 121–156.

Holst, J. (2002). *Social movements, civil society and radical adult education*. London, England: Bergin & Garvey.

hooks, b. (2000). *Feminism is for everybody*. New York, NY: South End Press.

hooks, b. (2001). *All about love: New visions*. New York, NY: Perennial.

hooks, b. (2013). *Dig deep: Beyond lean in*. Retrieved from http://thefeministwire.com/2013/10/17973/

Hope, A., & Timmel, S. (1984/1999). *Training for transformation: A handbook for community workers* (Vol. 4). Rugby, England: Practical Action.

Horsman, J. (2012). WWW.Net: Quest(ion)ing transformative possibilities of the web. In L. Manicom & S. Walters (Eds.), *Feminist popular education in transnational debates: Building pedagogies of possibility* (pp. 147–162). New York, NY: Palgrave Macmillan.

Horton, A. I. (1989). *The highlander folk school: A history of its major programs, 1932–1961*. Brooklyn, New York, NY: Carlson.

Htun, M., & Weldon, S. L. (2012). The civic origins of progressive policy change: Combating violence against women in global perspective, 1975–2005. *American Political Science Review, 106*(3), 548–569. doi:10.1017/S0003055412000226

Hughes, C. (2000). Resistant adult learners: A contradiction in feminist terms? *Studies in the Education of Adults, 32*(1), 51–62.

Ibáñez-Carrasco, F., & Riaño-Alcalá, P. (2011). Organizing community-based research knowledge between universities and communities: Lessons learned. *Community Development Journal, 46*(1), 72–88. doi:10.1093/cdj/bsp041

Idle No More. (2012, November 10). *Idle no more is founded by 4 women*. Retrieved from http://www.idlenomore.ca/idle_no_more_is_founded_by_4_women

Ingleby, J. (2006). Hybridity or the third space and how shall we describe the kingdom of god. *Encounter Mission Ezine, 11*. Retrieved from http://www.redcliffe.org/mission

Irving, C. J., & English, L. M. (2008). Partnering for research: A critical discourse analysis. *Studies in Continuing Education, 30*(2), 107–118.

Irving, C. J., & English, L. M. (2009). Feminist network activism and education in Canada. *Proceedings of the 28th national annual conference of the Canadian association for the study of adult education* (pp.122–128). Ottawa, ON: Carleton University. Retrieved from http://www.casae-aceea.ca/?q=archives

Irving, C. J., & English, L. M. (2011). Community in cyberspace: Gender, social movement learning and the Internet. *Adult Education Quarterly, 61*(3), 262– 278. doi:10.1177/0741713610380448

Jackson, A. Y. (2004). Performativity identified. *Qualitative Inquiry, 10*(5), 673–690. doi:10.1177/1077800403257673

Jackson, S. (2003). Lifelong earning: Lifelong learning and working-class women. *Gender and Education, 15*(4), 365–376.

Jackson, S. (Ed.). (2010). *Innovations in lifelong learning: Critical perspectives on diversity, participation and vocational learning*. New York, NY: Routledge.

Jackson, S., Malcolm, I., & Thomas, K. (Eds.). (2011). *Gendered choices and transitions in lifelong learning: Part-time pathways, full time lives*. London, England: Springer.

Jacobi, T. (2012). Twenty year sentences: Women's writing workshops in US prisons and jails. In L. Manicom & S. Walters (Eds.), *Feminist popular education in transnational debates: Building pedagogies of possibility* (pp. 111–128). Basingstoke, England: Palgrave Macmillan.

Jaeger, P. T. (2012). *Disability and the Internet: Confronting a digital divide*. Boulder, CO: Lynne Rienner Publishers.

JASS. (2013). *Annual report, 2013*. Retrieved from http://www.justassociates.org/sites/justassociates.org/files/web_jass_ar_2013.pdf

JASS. (2014). *What we do*. Retrieved from http://www.justassociates.org/en/what-we-do

Jeanetta, S. (2005). Finding voice in a community-based learning process. *Proceedings of the sixth international transformative learning conference*. Michigan, MI: Michigan State University. Retrieved from http://transformativelearning.ning.com/page/proceedings-1

Jeris, L., & Gajanayake, J. (2005). Transformation on the ground in Sri Lanka: Just who is transformed? Tales from the inside/out and the outside/in. *Proceedings of the sixth international transformative learning conference.* Michigan, MI: Michigan State University. Retrieved from http://transformativelearning.ning.com/page/proceedings-1

Johnson, R. (1988). Really useful knowledge, 1790–1850. In T. Lovett (Ed.), *Radical approaches to adult education: A reader* (pp. 3–34). London, England: Routledge.

Johnson-Bailey, J. (2006). Transformative learning: A community empowerment conduit for African American women. In S. B. Merriam, B. C. Courtenay, & R. M. Cervero (Eds.), *Global issues and adult education: Perspectives from Latin America, Southern Africa and the United States* (pp. 307–318). San Francisco, CA: Jossey-Bass.

Johnson-Bailey, J. (2012). Positionality and transformative learning: A tale of inclusion and exclusion. In E. W. Taylor & P. Cranton (Eds.), *Handbook of transformative learning: Theory, research and practice* (pp. 260–273). San Francisco, CA: Jossey-Bass.

Johnson-Bailey, J., & Alfred, M. V. (2006). Transformational teaching and the practices of black women adult educators. *New Directions for Adult and Continuing Education, 2006*(109), 49–58. doi:10.1002/ace.207

Joyce, J. (1968). *A portrait of the artist as a young man: With six drawings by Robin Jacques.* London, England: Jonathan Cape. (First published 1916)

Kelly K., & Caputo, T. (2011). *Community: A contemporary analysis of policies, programs, and practices.* Toronto, ON: University of Toronto Press.

Kenix, L. J. (2008). Nonprofit organizations' perceptions and uses of the Internet. *Television and New Media, 9*(5), 407–428.

Khan, H., & Basha, O. K. M. R. (2008). *Religion and development: Are they complementary?* Global working paper series, No.006 2008. Retrieved from http://www.u21global.com/portal/corporate/pdf/wp/2008/wp_006-2008.pdf

Khan, S. (2000). *Muslim women: Crafting a North American identity.* Gainesville, FL: University of Florida Press.

Kilde, J. H. (1999). The "predominance of the feminine" at Chautauqua: Rethinking the gender-space relationship in Victorian America. *Signs, 24*(2), 449– 486.

Kilgore, D., & Bloom, L. R. (2002). When I'm down, it takes me a while: Rethinking transformational education through narratives of women in crisis. *Adult Basic Education, 12*(3), 123–133.

King, T. (2003). *The truth about stories: A native narrative* (Canadian Broadcasting Company Massey Lectures Series). Toronto, ON: Anansi.

Klassen, C. (2003). Confronting the gap: Why religion needs to be given more attention in women's studies. *Third Space: A Journal of Feminist Theory and Culture, 3*(1). Retrieved from http://journals.sfu.ca/thirdspace/index.php/journal/article/viewArticle/klassen/165

Kluge, M. A. (2007). Re-creating through recreating: Using the personal growth through adventure model to transform women's lives. *Journal of Transformative Education, 5*(2), 177–191.

Knowles, M. (1970). *The modern practice of adult education.* New York, NY: Association Press.

Kopecky, M. (2012). Foucault, governmentality, neoliberalism and adult education – Perspective on the normalization of social risks. *Journal of Pedagogy/Pedagogický časopis, 2*(2), 246–262. doi:10.2478/v10159-011-0012-2

Kraglund-Gauthier, W. L., Chareka, O., Murray Orr, A., & Foran, A. (2010). Teacher education in online classrooms: An inquiry into instructors' lived experiences. *The Canadian Journal for the Scholarship of Teaching and Learning, 1*(2), 1–13. Retrieved from http://ir.lib.uwo.ca/cjsotl_rcacea/vol1/iss2/4/

Lapp, C. A., & Carr, A. N. (2010). Storyselling. In A. J. Mills, G. Durepos, & E. Wiebe (Eds.), *Encyclopedia of case study research* (Vol. 2, pp. 895–898). Thousand Oaks, CA: Sage.

Lather, P. (1996). The politics of accessible language. *Harvard Educational Review, 66*(3), 525–545.

Lawrence, R. L. (2012). Intuitive knowing and consciousness. *New Directions for Adult and Continuing Education, 2012*(134), 5–13. San Francisco, CA: Jossey-Bass. doi:10.1002/ace.20011

Ledwith, M. (2009). Antonio Gramsci and feminism: The elusive nature of power. *Educational Philosophy and Theory, 41*(6), 684–697. doi:10.1111/j.1469-5812.2008.00499.x

Ledwith, M. (2011). *Community development: A critical approach* (2nd ed.). Bristol, England: Policy Press.

Ledwith, M., & Springett, J. (2010). *Participatory practice: Community-based action for transformative change*. Bristol, England: Policy Press.

Lee, N., Irving, C., & Francuz, J. (2014). Community-embedded learning and experimentation: fostering spaces for transformative learning online. In A. Nicolaides & D. Holt (Eds.), *Spaces of transformation and transformation of space: Proceedings of XI international transformative learning conference* (pp. 499–506). New York, NY: Teachers College, Columbia University. Retrieved from http://transformativelearning.ning.com/page/proceedings-1

Lensmire, T. J., McManimon, S. K., Tierney, J. D., Lee-Nichols, M. E., Casey, Z. A., Lensmire, A., & Davis, B. M. (2013). McIntosh as synecdoche: How teacher education's focus on white privilege undermines antiracism. *Harvard Educational Review, 83*(3), 410–431.

Lerner, J. (2010). Learning democracy through participatory budgeting: Who learns what, and so what? In E. Pinnington & D. Schugurensky (Eds.), *Learning citizenship by practicing democracy: International initiatives and perspectives* (pp. 242–251). Newcastle upon Tyne, England: Cambridge Scholars Publishing.

Lin, C. I. C., Tang, W.-H., & Kuo, F.-Y. (2012). Mommy wants to learn the computer: How middle-aged and elderly women in Taiwan learn ICT through social support. *Adult Education Quarterly, 62*(1), 73–90. doi:10.1177/0741713610392760

Livingstone, D. W. (1999). Exploring the icebergs of adult learning: Findings of the first Canadian survey of informal learning practices. *Canadian Journal for the Study of Adult Education, 13*(2), 49–72. Retrieved from http://journals.msvu.ca/index.php/cjsae/issue/view/157

Livingstone, D. W. (2012). Probing the icebergs of adult learning: Comparative findings and implications of the 1998, 2004, and 2010 Canadian surveys of formal and informal learning practices. *Canadian Journal for the Study of Adult Education, 25*(1), 47–71. Retrieved from http://journals.msvu.ca/index.php/cjsae

Lombe, M., Newransky, C., Crea, T., & Stout, A. (2012). From rhetoric to reality: Planning and conducting collaborations for international research in the global south. *Social Work, 58*(1), 31–40. doi:10.1093/sw/sws056

López, E., & Adanali, Y. (2007). *Cotacachi, Ecuador: The inclusion of indigenous women in a local participatory budgeting process*. Retrieved from United Cities and Local Governments (UCLG) website: http://www.uclg-cisdp.org/en/observatory/inclusion-indigenous-women-local-participatory-budgeting-process

Lorde, A. (1984). *Sister outsider: Essays and speeches*. Freedom, CA: Crossing Press.

Lynskey, D. (2010). *33 revolutions per minute: A history of protest songs*. London, England: Faber & Faber.

MacKeracher, D. (2004). *Making sense of adult learning* (2nd ed.). Toronto, ON: University of Toronto Press.

Maguire, P. (1987). *Doing participatory research: A feminist approach*. Amherst, MA: Center for International Education, University of Massachusets.

Malcolm, I. (2012). It's for us to change that: Emotional labor in researching adults' learning: Between feminist criticality and complicity in temporary, gendered employment. *Adult Education Quarterly, 62*(3), 252–271. doi:10.1177/0741713611402050

Manicom, A., Rhymes, J., Armour, N., & Parsons, D. (2005). *Public policy and the participation of rural Nova Scotia women in the new economy*. Research Project Report presented to Status of Women Canada, Ottawa, ON.

Manicom, L., & Walters, S. (Eds.). (2012). *Feminist popular education in transnational debates: Building pedagogies of possibility*. New York, NY: Palgrave Macmillan.

Mann, S. (2012). *Idle no more is founded by 4 women*. Retrieved from http://www.idlenomore.ca/idle_no_more_is_founded_by_4_women

Mannell, J. (2012). It's just been such a horrible experience: Perceptions of gender mainstreaming by practitioners in South African organisations. *Gender & Development, 20*(3), 423–434. doi:10.1080/13552074.2012.731753

Manuh, T., Anyidoho, N. A., & Pobee-Hayford, F. (2013). A femocrat just doing my job: Working within the state to advance women's empowerment in Ghana. In R. Eyben & L. Turquet (Eds.), *Feminists in development organizations: Change from the margins* (pp. 37–54). Rugby, England: Practical Action.

marino, d. (1997). *Wild garden: Art, education, and the culture of resistance*. Toronto, ON: Between the Lines.

Marple, L., & Latchmore, V. (2006). LGBTQ activism: Small town social change. *Canadian Woman Studies, 24*(4), 55–58.

Marshall, J. D. (1990). Foucault and educational research. In S. J. Ball (Ed.), *Foucault and education: Disciplines and knowledge* (pp. 11–28). New York, NY: Routledge.

Marshall, K., & Van Saanen, M. (2007). *Development and faith: Where mind, heart, and soul work together*. Washington, DC: World Bank.

Marsick, V., Watkins, K., Callahan, M. W., & Volpe, M. (2009). Informal and incidental learning in the workplace. In M. C. Smith & N. Defrates-Densch (Eds.), *Handbook of research on adult learning and development* (pp. 570–600). New York, NY: Routledge.

Maté, G. (2004). *When the body says no: The cost of hidden stress*. Toronto, ON: Random House.

Mayo, M., & Annette, J. (Eds.). (2010). *Taking part? Active learning for active citizenship and beyond*. Leicester, England: National Institute of Adult Continuing Education.

Mayo, M., & Rooke, A. (2006). *Active learning for active citizenship: Evaluation report*. London, England: Department for Communities and Local Government. Retrieved from http://webarchive.nationalarchives.gov.uk/20120919132719/ http://www.communities.gov.uk/documents/communities/pdf/152717.pdf

Mayuzumi, K. (2006). The tea ceremony as a decolonizing epistemology: Healing and Japanese women. *Journal of Transformative Education, 4*(1), 8–26.

McCaffery, J. (2005). Using transformative models of adult literacy in conflict resolution and peacebuilding processes at community level: Examples from Guinea, Sierra Leone and Sudan. *Compare, 35*(4), 443–462.

McCammon, H. J., & Campbell, K. E. (2002). Allies on the road to victory: Coalition formation between the suffragists and the woman's Christian temperance union. *Mobilization: An International Journal, 7*(3), 231–251.

McDermott, C. (2007). Teaching to be radical: The women activist educators of highlander. *Proceedings of the adult education research conference-Canadian association for the study of adult education joint conference* (pp. 403–407). Halifax, Nova Scotia: Mount Saint Vincent University. Retrieved from http://www.adulterc.org/Proceedings/2007/Proceedings/McDermott.pdf

McDermott, C. (2008). From cook to community leader: Women's leadership at highlander research and education center. *Proceedings of the 49th annual adult education research conference*. St. Louis, MO: University of Missouri-St. Louis. Retrieved from http://www.adulterc.org/Proceedings/2008/Proceedings/McDermott.pdf

McGivney, V. (1990). *Education's for other people: Access to education for non-participant adults: A research report*. Leicester, England: National Institute of Adult Continuing Education.

McGivney, V. (1993). *Women, education and training: Barriers to access, informal starting points and progression routes*. Leicester, England: National Institute of Adult Continuing Education.

McGivney, V. (2001). *Fixing or changing the pattern? Reflections on widening adult participation in learning*. Leicester, England: National Institute of Adult Continuing Education.

McIntosh, P. (2008). White privilege: Unpacking the invisible knapsack. In P. Rothenberg (Ed.), *White privilege: Essential readings on the other side of racism* (pp. 123–127). New York, NY: Worth.

McWilliams, M. (1995). Struggling for peace and justice: Reflections on women's activism in Northern Ireland. *Journal of Women's History, 6*(4), 7(1), 13–39.

Mehra, B., Merkel, C., & Bishop, A. (2004). The Internet for empowerment of minority and marginalized users. *New Media and Society, 6*(6), 781–802.

Mejiuni, O. (2009). Potential for transformative mentoring relationships among women in academia in Nigeria. *Proceedings of the eighth international transformative learning conference.* Paget Parish, Bermuda: College of Bermuda. Retrieved from http://transformativelearning.ning.com/page/proceedings-1

Mejiuni, O. (2012). *Women and power: Education, religion and identity.* Ibadan, Nigeria: University Press.

Merriam, S. B. (2009). *Qualitative research: A guide to design and implementation.* San Francisco, CA: Jossey-Bass.

Meyer, S. (2009). Promoting personal empowerment with women in East Harlem through journaling and coaching. In J. Mezirow, E. W. Taylor, & Associates (Eds.), *Transformative learning in practice: Insights from community, workplace, and higher education* (pp. 216–226). San Francisco, CA: Jossey-Bass.

Mezirow, J. (1978). *Education for perspective transformation; Women's re-entry programs in community colleges.* New York, NY: Teacher's College, Columbia University.

Mezirow, J., Taylor, E. W., & Associates. (Eds.). (2009). *Transformative learning in practice: Insights from community, workplace, and higher education.* San Francisco, CA: Jossey-Bass.

Michelson, E. (1998). Re-membering: The return of the body to experiential learning. *Studies in Continuing Education, 20*(2), 217–233. doi:10.1080/0158037980200208

Mies, M., & Shiva, V. (1993). *Ecofeminism.* London, England: Zed Books.

Miles, A. (1996). *Integrative feminisms: Building global visions, 1960s–1990s.* New York, NY: Routledge.

Miles, A. (Ed.). (2013). *Women in a globalizing world: Transforming equality, development, diversity and peace.* Toronto, ON: Inanna.

Miller, V., VeneKlasen, L., Reilly, M., & Clark, C. (2006). *MCH3 power: Concepts for revisioning power for justice, equality and peace.* Washington, DC: Just Associates. Retrieved from http://www.justassociates.org/en/resources/mch3-power-concepts-revisioning-power-justice-equality-and-peace

Mills, S. (1997). *Discourse.* London, England: Routledge.

Mitchell, W. J. T. (1995). Translator translated (Interview with cultural theorist Homi Bhabha). *Artforum International, 33*(7), 80–83, 110, 113.

Muthien, B. (2006). Leadership and renewal: Cite, site and sight in women's movements. *Development, 49*(1), 99–101.

Myers, C., & Colwell, M. (2012). *Our god is undocumented: Biblical faith and immigrant justice.* Maryknoll, NY: Orbis Books.

Nanibush, W. (2013). Idle No More: Strong hearts of women's indigenous leadership. In A. Miles (Ed.), *Women in a globalizing world: Transforming equality, development, diversity and peace* (pp. 503–504). Toronto, ON: Inanna.

Nash, S. T. (2007). Teaching African American women's experiences with intimate male partner violence: Using narratives as text in gender violence pedagogy. *Journal of Transformative Education, 5*(1), 93–110.

Neal, R. (1998). *Brotherhood economics: Women and co-operatives in Nova Scotia.* Sydney, Australia: University College of Cape Breton Press.

Nelson, S. (2012). *Challenging hidden assumptions: Colonial norms as determinants of aboriginal mental health.* Retrieved from National Collaborating Centre for Aboriginal Health website: http://www.nccah-ccnsa.ca/Publications/Lists/Publications/Attachments/70/colonial_norms_EN_web.pdf

Nettles, K. D. (2007). Becoming red thread women: Alternative visions of gendered politics in post-independence Guyana. *Social Movement Studies: Journal of Social, Cultural and Political Protest, 6*(1), 57–82. doi:10.1080/14742830701251336

Newman, M. (2008). The "self" in self-development: A rationalist meditates. *Adult Education Quarterly, 58*(4), 284–298. doi:10.1177/0741713608318892

Nieves, Y. (2012). Embodying women's stories for community awareness and social action. *New Directions for Adult and Continuing Education, 2008*(134), 33–42. doi:10.1002/ace.20014

Ntseane, P. G., & Chilisa, B. (2012). Indigenous knowledge, HIV, and AIDS education and research: Implications for health educators. In L. M. English (Ed.), *Adult education and health* (pp. 76–89). Toronto, ON: University of Toronto Press.

Nussbaum, M. C. (2000). *Women and human development: A capabilities approach.* New York, NY: Cambridge University Press.

O'Brien, M. (2011). Towards a pedagogy of care and well-being. In A. O'Shea & M. O'Brien (Eds.), *Pedagogy, oppression and transformation in a "post-critical" climate: The return of Freirean thinking* (pp. 14–35). London, England: Bloomsbury.

O'Neill, P., & Eyben, R. (2013). It's fundamentally political: Renovating the master's house. In R. Eyben & L. Turquet (Eds.), *Feminists in development organizations: Change from the margins* (pp. 85–99). Rugby, England: Practical Action.

Oliver, M. (2005). What I have learned so far. *New and selected poems* (Vol. 2). Boston, MA: Beacon Press.

Ollis, T. (2012). *A critical pedagogy of embodied education: Learning to become an activist.* New York, NY: Palgrave Macmillan.

Onosaka, J. R. (2006). *Feminist revolution in literacy: Women's bookstores in the United States.* New York, NY: Routledge.

Owram, D. (2004). Managing the ethical risks: Universities and the new world of funding. *Journal of Academic Ethics, 2*(3), 173–186. doi:10.1007/s10805-005-2980-0

Oyieke, L. I., Dick, A. L., & Bothma, T. (2013). Social media access and participation in established democracies and authoritarian states. *Innovation, 47*, 121–144.

Papan, A. S., & Clow, B. (2012). *The food insecurity-obesity paradox as a vicious cycle for women: A qualitative study.* Halifax, Nova Scotia: Atlantic Centre of Excellence for Women's Health. Retrieved from http://www.acewh.dal.ca/pdf/Full%20Plate-Nov12.pdf

Parviainen, J. (2010). Choreographing resistances: Spatial–kinaesthetic intelligence and bodily knowledge as political tools in activist work. *Mobilities, 5*(3), 311–329. doi:10.1080/17450101.2010.494838

Peddle, K., Powell, A., & Shade, L. R. (2012). The researcher is a girl: Tales of bringing feminist labour perspectives into community informatics practice and evaluation. In A. Clement, M. Gurstein, G. Longford, M. Moll, & L. R. Shade (Eds), *Connecting Canadians: Investigations in community informatics* (pp. 117–132). Edmonton, AB: Athabasca University Press.

Pettit, J. (2010). Multiple faces of power and learning. *IDS Bulletin, 41*(3), 25–35.

Pinnington, E., & Schugurensky, D. (Eds.). (2010). *Learning citizenship by practicing democracy: International initiatives and perspectives.* Newcastle upon Tyne, England: Cambridge Scholars Publishing.

Plett, L. S. (2008). Refashioning Kleine Gemeinde women's dress in Kansas and Manitoba: A textual crazy quilt. *Journal of Mennonite Studies, 26*, 111–131. Retrieved from http://jms.uwinnipeg.ca/index.php/jms/issue/view/40

Polletta, F. (2006). *It was like a fever: Storytelling in protest and politics.* Chicago, IL: University of Chicago Press.

Pollitt, K. (2013, March 25). Who's afraid of Sheryl Sandberg? *The Nation.* Retrieved from http://www.thenation.com/article/173238/whos-afraid-sheryl-sandberg

Porter, A. (2012). Neo-conservatism, neo-liberalism and Canadian social policy: Challenges for feminism. *Canadian Woman Studies, 29*(3), 19–31.

Prins, E. (2005). Framing a conflict in a community-university partnership. *Journal of Planning Education and Research, 25*, 57–74. doi:10.1177/0739456X04270370

Prügl, E. (2013). Gender expertise as feminist strategy. In G. Caglar, E. Prügl, & S. Zwingel (Eds.), *Feminist strategies in international governance* (pp. 57–73). London, England: Routledge.

Pui-lan, K. (2005). *Postcolonial imagination and feminist theology.* Louisville, KY: Westminster John Knox Press.

Pui-lan, K. (Ed.). (2010). *Hope abundant: Third world and Indigenous women's theology.* Maryknoll, NY: Orbis Books.

Quigley, A., & Kraglund-Gauthier, W. L. (2008). Getting beyond "just another academic exercise": Towards a new discourse on the 2006 state of the field of adult literacy and future studies in the literacy field. *Proceedings of the national conference of the Canadian association for the study of adult education* (pp. 307–313). Vancouver, Canada: University of British Columbia. Retrieved from http://www.casae-aceea.ca/~casae/sites/casae/archives/cnf2008/cnf2008.html

Rakodi, C. (2011). Revisiting religion: Development studies thirty years on. *World Development, 39*(1), 45–54. doi:10.1016/j.worlddev.2010.05.007

Reading, C. L., & Wien, F. (2009). Health inequalities and social determinants of Aboriginal peoples' health. Prince George, BC: National Collaborating Centre for Aboriginal Health.

Rebick, J. (2009). *Transforming power: From the personal to the political.* Toronto, ON: Penguin.

Rebick, J. (2013). Occupy and feminism. In A. Miles (Ed.), *Women in a globalizing world* (pp. 577–581). Toronto, ON: Inanna.

Reeve, C. (2014, March 9). One woman seeks to reclaim public space for all women in Egypt. *Community Times.* Retrieved from http://communitytimes.me/one-woman-seeks/

Revkin, A. (2012, December 18). *Two video views of science as a 'girl thing'* [web log post]. *New York Times Dot Earth Blog.* Retrieved from http://dotearth.blogs.nytimes.com/2012/12/18/two-video-views-of-science-as-a-girl-thing/?_r=0

Rhoad, J. (2012). *The return of The AIDS memorial quilt: What women have to do with it* [web log post]. Retrieved from http://www.womensorganizations.org/?p=167&option=com_wordpress&Itemid=114

Romanelli, F., Cain, J., & McNamara, P. J. (2014). Should TED Talks be teaching us something? *American Journal of Pharmaceutical Education, 78*(6), 113. doi:10.5688/ajpe786113

Rosenblum, N. L., & Lesch, C. H. T. (2011). Civil society and government. In M. Edwards (Ed.), *The Oxford handbook of civil society* (pp. 285–297). Oxford, England: Oxford University Press.

Rosser, S. V. (2005). Through the lenses of feminist theory: Focus on women and information technology. *Frontiers, 26*(1), 1–23.

Rosser, S. V. (2012). The link between feminist theory and methods in experimental research. In S. N. Hesse-Biber (Ed.), *Handbook of feminist research: Theory and praxis* (2nd ed., pp. 264–289). Thousand Oaks, CA: Sage.

Rothschild-Whitt, J. (1979). The collectivist organization: An alternative to rational bureaucratic models. *American Sociological Review, 44,* 509–527.

Roy, C. (2004). *The raging grannies: Wild hats, cheeky songs, and witty actions for a better world.* Montreal, QC: Black Rose Books.

Roy, C. (2009). Beyond the headlines: Documentary film festivals and citizenship education. In S. Carpenter, M. Laiken, & S. Mojab (Eds.), *Proceedings of the 28th annual conference of the Canadian association for the study of adult education* (pp. 241–247). Toronto, ON: OISE/University of Toronto. Retrieved from http://www.casae-aceea.ca/?q=archives

Roy, C. (2012). Why don't they show those on TV? Documentary film festivals, media and community. *International Journal of Lifelong Education, 31*(3), 293–307. doi:10.1080/02601370.2012.683610

Royal, C. (2008). Framing the Internet: A comparison of gendered spaces. *Social Science Computer Review, 26*(2), 152–169. doi:10.1177/0894439307307366

Rushdie, S. (1991). *Imaginary homelands.* London, England: Granta Books.

Ruth-Sahd, L. A., & Tisdell, E. J. (2007). The meaning and use of intuition in novice nurses: A phenomenological study. *Adult Education Quarterly, 57*(2), 115–140. doi:10.1177/0741713606295755

Ryan, A. B. (2001). *Feminist ways of knowing: Towards theorising the person for radical adult education.* Leicester, England: National Institute of Adult Continuing Education.

Sachs, J. D. (2005). *Investing in development: A practical plan to achieve the millennium development goals.* London, England: Earthscan.

Sandberg, S. (2013). *Lean in: Women, work, and the will to lead.* New York, NY: Knopf.

Sawade, O. (2014). Lessons, challenges, and successes while working on the "triangle" of education, gender, and sexual and reproductive health. *Gender and Development, 22*(1), 127–140. doi:10.1080/13552074.2014.889339

Sawer, S. (1999). EMILY's list and angry white men: Gender wars in the nineties. *Journal of Australian Studies, 23*(62), 1–9. doi:10.1080/14443059909387494

Scampini, A. (2003). Some thoughts on the conference processes. In C. Medel-Añonuevo (Ed.), *Women moving CONFINTEA V: A mid-term review*. Hamburg, Germany: UNESCO Institute for Education.

Schugurensky, D. (2011). *Paulo Freire* (Continuum library of educational thought, no. 16). New York, NY: Continuum.

Scott, A., & Page, M. (2001). Change agency and women's learning: New practices in community informatics. In L. Keeble & B. D. Loader (Eds.), *Community informatics: Shaping computer-mediated social relations* (pp. 147–174). London, England: Routledge.

Scott, J. C. (1990). *Domination and the arts of resistance: Hidden transcripts*. New Haven, CT: Yale University Press.

Scott, M. (2011). Reflections on 'The big society'. *Community Development Journal, 46*(1) 132–137. doi:10.1093/cdj/bsq057

Segalo, P. (2014). Embroidery as narrative: Black South African women's experiences of suffering and healing. *Agenda, 28*(1), 44–53. doi:10.1080/10130950.2014.872831

Selwyn, N., & Facer, K. (2007). *Beyond the digital divide: Rethinking digital inclusion for the 21st century*. Bristol, England: Futurelab. Retrieved from http://www.nfer.ac.uk/publications/FUTL55/FUTL55.pdf

Selwyn, N., Gorard, G., & Furlong, J. (2006). *Adult learning in the digital age: Information technology and the learning society*. London, England: Routledge.

Sen, G., & Durano, M. (Eds.). (2014). *The remaking of social contracts: Feminists in a fierce new world*. London, England: Zed Books.

Sen, G., & Grown, C. (1987). *Development, crises, and alternative visions: Third world women's perspectives*. New York, NY: Monthly Review Press.

Shade, L. R. (1996). *Report on the use of the Internet in Canadian women's organizations*. Ottawa, Ontario, Canada: Status of Women Canada, Government of Canada.

Shade, L. R. (2004). Bending gender into the net: Feminizing content, corporate interests, and research strategy. In P. N. Howard & S. Jones (Eds.), *Society online: The Internet in context* (pp. 57–70). Thousand Oaks, CA: Sage.

Shaw, M., & Meade, R. (2013). Community development and the arts: Towards a more creative reciprocity. In P. Mayo (Ed.), *Learning with adults: A reader* (pp. 195–204). Rotterdam, The Netherlands: Sense Publishers.

Shiva, V. (Ed.). (1994). *Close to home: Women reconnect ecology, health and development worldwide*. Gabriola Island, BC: New Society.

Skocpol, T., & Williamson, V. (2012). *The tea party and the remaking of republican conservativism*. New York, NY: Oxford University Press.

Smith, L. (2013). Towards a model of critical information literacy instruction for the development of political agency. *Journal of Information Literacy, 7*(2), 15–32. doi:10.11645/7.2.1809

Smith, L. T. (2012). *Decolonizing methodologies: Research and Indigenous peoples* (2nd ed.). London, England: Zed Books.

Smith, M. (2010). Gender, whiteness and "other others" in the academy. In S. Razack, M. Smith, & S. Thobani (Eds.), *States of race: Critical race feminism for the 21st century* (pp. 37–57). Toronto, ON: Between the Lines.

Smith, M. K. (2001). Community. *The encyclopedia of informal education*. Retrieved from http://www.infed.org/community/community.htm

Smith, M. K. (2002). Mary Parker Follett: Community, creative experience and education. *The encyclopedia of informal education*. Retrieved from http://infed.org/mobi/mary-parker-follett-community-creative-experience-and-education

Smith, M. M. (2007). Nonprofit religious organization web sites: Underutilized avenue of communicating with group members. *Journal of Media and Religion, 6*(4), 273–290.

Sousa, J., & Quarter, J. (2003). *Informal and non-formal learning in nonprofit organizations*. Nall Working paper, #72. Retrieved from http://www.oise.utoronto.ca/depts/sese/csew/nall/res/index.htm

Stalker, J. (2011). Gender analysis. In K. Rubenson (Ed.), *Adult learning and education* (pp. 231–237). Amsterdam, The Netherlands: Elsevier.

Stein, J. G. (2003). *Cult of efficiency* (The Canadian Broadcasting Corporation, Massey Lectures). Toronto, ON: House of Anansi Press.

Stoddart, J. (2014). Thérèse Casgrain. *The Canadian Encyclopedia.* Retrieved from http://www.thecanadianencyclopedia.ca/en/article/therese-casgrain (Revised by M.-E. Lambert & A. McIntosh, 2014; originally prepared in 2008)

Stromquist, N. P. (2006). Gender, education and the possibility of transformative knowledge. *Compare, 36*(2), 145–161.

Stromquist, N. P. (2013). Adult education of women for social transformation: Reviving the promise, continuing the struggle. *New Directions for Adult and Continuing Education, 2013*(138), 29–38. doi:10.1002/ace.20051

Stuckey, H. L. (2009a). The body as a way of knowing: Meditation, movement and the image. In C. Hoggan, S. Simpson, & H. L. Stuckey (Eds.), *Creative expression in transformative learning: Tools and techniques for educators of adults* (pp. 29–50). Malabar, FL: Krieger.

Stuckey, H. L. (2009b). Creative expression as a way of knowing in diabetes adult health education: An action research study. *Adult Education Quarterly, 60*(1), 46–64.

Swift, J. (1999). *Civil society in question.* Toronto, ON: Between the Lines.

Taber, N. (2012). Beginning with the self to critique the social: Critical researchers as whole beings. In L. Naidoo (Ed.), *An ethnography of global landscapes and corridors* (pp. 73–88). Rijeka, Croatia: InTech Publishing. Retrieved from http://www.intechopen.com/articles/show/title/beginning-with-the-self-to-critique-the-social-critical-researchers-as-whole-beings

Taber, N. (Ed.). (2015). A critical engagement with the current place of feminism in Canadian adult education [Special issue]. *Canadian Journal for the Study of Adult Education, 27*(2). Retrieved from http://journals.msvu.ca/index.php/cjsae

Tadros, M. (Ed.). (2011). Gender, rights and religion at the crossroads [Special issue]. *IDS Bulletin, 42*(1).

Taylor, E. W. (2008). Transformative learning theory. *New Directions for Adult and Continuing Education, 2008*(119), 5–15. doi:10.1002/ace.301

Taylor, E. W. (2009). Fostering transformative learning. In J. Mezirow, E. W. Taylor, & Associates (Eds.), *Transformative learning in practice: Insights from community, workplace, and higher education* (pp. 3–17). San Francisco, CA: Jossey-Bass.

Taylor, E. W., & Cranton, P. (2013). A theory in progress? Issues in transformative learning theory. *European Journal for Research on the Education and Learning of Adults, 4*(1), 33–47. doi:10.3384/rela.2000-7426.rela5000

Taylor, E. W., Cranton, P., & Associates. (2012). *Handbook of transformative learning: Theory, research, and practice.* San Francisco, CA: Jossey-Bass.

Te'eni, D., & Young, D. R. (2003). The changing role of nonprofits in the network economy. *Nonprofit and Voluntary Sector Quarterly, 32*(3), 397–414.

Terry, G. (2007). *Women's rights.* London, England: Pluto Press.

Tescione, S. M. (1998). A woman's name: Implications for publication, citation and tenure. *Educational Researcher, 27*(8), 38–42.

Tett, L. (2010). *Community education, learning and development* (3rd ed.). Edinburgh, Scotland: Dunedin.

Tett, L., & Maclachlan, K. (2008). Learners, tutors and power in adult literacies research in Scotland. *International Journal of Lifelong Education, 27*(6), 659–672. doi:10.1080/02601370802408316

Tett, L., Hamilton, M., & Crowther, J. (2012). *More powerful literacies.* Leicester, England: National Institute of Adult Continuing Education.

Thomas, R., & Davies, A. (2005). What have the feminists done for us? Feminist theory and organizational resistance. *Organization, 12*(5), 711–740.

Thompson, J. (2007). *More words in edgeways: Rediscovering adult education.* Leicester, England: National Institute of Adult Continuing Education.

Tisdell, E. J. (2000). Feminist pedagogies. In E. Hayes & D. Flannery (Eds.), *Women as learners* (pp. 155–183). San Francisco, CA: Jossey-Bass.

Tisdell, E. J. (2005). Emancipatory education. In L. M. English (Ed.), *International encyclopedia of adult education* (pp. 205–210). Basingstoke, England: Palgrave Macmillan.

Titterton, M., & Smart, H. (2008). Can participatory research be a route to empowerment? A case study of a disadvantaged Scottish community. *Community Development Journal, 43*(1), 52–64. doi:10.1093/cdj/bsl037

Tobin, J. A., & Tisdell, E. J. (2015). I know down to my ribs: A narrative research study on the embodied adult learning of creative writers. *Adult Education Quarterly* [Advance online publication]. doi:10.1177/0741713615574901

Toboso, M. (2011). Rethinking disability in Amartya Sen's approach: ICT and equality of opportunity. Thematic issue on ICT and the capability approach. *Ethics and Information Technology, 13*(2), 107–118. doi:10.1007/s10676-010-9254-2

Tough, A. (1979). *Adult's learning projects* (Rev. ed.). Toronto, ON: Ontario Institute for Studies in Education.

Treleaven, L. (2004). A knowledge-sharing approach to organizational change: A critical discourse analysis. In H. Tsoukas & N. Mylonopoulos (Eds.), *Organizations as knowledge systems: Knowledge, learning and dynamic capabilities* (pp. 154–180). New York, NY: Palgrave Macmillan.

Tremblay, M. (2010). *Quebec women and legislative representation*. Vancouver, Canada: University of British Columbia Press.

Turnbull, D. (1997). Reframing science and other local knowledge traditions. *Futures, 29*(6), 551–562.

UN Women. (2014). *Agreed: Conclusions of the 58th session of the commission on the status of women*. New York City. Retrieved from http://www.unwomen.org/~/media/Headquarters/Attachments/Sections/CSW/58/CSW58-agreedconclusions-advanceduneditedversion.pdf

UNESCO. (1997). Hamburg declaration on adult learning. *Adult Education and Development, 49*, 251–260. Retrieved from http://www.unesco.org/education/uie/confintea/declaeng.htm

UNESCO. (2009). *Confintea VI: Belém framework for action*. Belém, Brazil. Retrieved from http://www.unesco.org

United Nations. (1981). *The convention on the elimination of all forms of discrimination against women*. Retrieved from http://www.un.org/womenwatch/daw/cedaw/text/econvention.htm

Van Dijk, J. A. G. M. (2005). *The deepening divide: Inequality in the information society*. Thousand Oaks, CA: Sage.

Van Zoonen, L. (2001). Feminist Internet studies. *Feminist Media Studies, 1*(1), 67–72.

Vehviläinen, M., & Brunila, K. (2007). Cartography of gender equality projects in ICT: Liberal equality from the perspective of situated equality. *Information, Communication & Society, 10*(3), 384–403.

Vella, J. (2002). *Learning to listen: Learning to teach* (Rev. ed.). San Francisco, CA: Jossey-Bass.

VeneKlasen, L., & Miller, V. (2002). *A new weave of power, people and politics: The action guide for advocacy and citizen participation*. Oklahoma City, OK: JASS.

Ver Beek, K. A. (2000). Spirituality: A development taboo. *Development in Practice, 10*(1), 31–43.

Vivek, A., & Antony, M. J. (2014). Information and communication technology for women empowerment. *Women's Link, 20*(3), 26–29.

Wadud, A. (2008). *Inside the gender Jihad: Women's reform in Islam*. Oxford, England: Oneworld.

Wainaina, N. (2012). Her story, our journey: Advocating for the rights of African women. Nairobi, Kenya: FEMNET. Retrieved from http://femnet.co/index.php/en/other-publications/item/download/125_ee74699d26308431b071906509b3acb1

Walberg, B. (2008). Responding to the needs of post-secondary aboriginal education: The development of the indigenous leadership and community development program. In K. Knopf (Ed.), *Aboriginal Canada revisited* (pp. 100–120). Ottawa, ON: University of Ottawa Press.

Walby, S. (2011). *The future of feminism*. Cambridge, England & Malden, MA: Polity Press.

Walker, P. E., & Shannon, P. T. (2011). Participatory governance: Towards a strategic model. *Community Development Journal, 46*(suppl 2), ii63–ii82. doi:10.1093/cdj/bsr011

Wallerstein, N., & Duran, B. (2006). Using community-based participatory research to address health disparities. *Health Promotion Practice, 7*(3), 312–323. doi:10.1177/1524839906289376

Walsh, S., & Brigham, S. (2007). Internationally educated female teachers who have immigrated to Nova Scotia: A research/performance text. *International Journal of Qualitative Methods, 6*(3), 1–28.

Walter, P. (2007). Adult learning in new social movements: Environmental protest and the struggle for the Clayoquot sound rainforest. *Adult Education Quarterly, 57*(3), 248–263.

Walters, S., & Manicom, L. (Eds.). (1996). *Gender in popular education: Methods for empowerment* (pp. 1–22). London, England: Zed Books.

Waterhouse, P., & Scott, M. (2013). *Here we stand: An inquiry into local activism and dissent.* Retrieved from National Coalition for Independent Action website: http://www.ioe.mmu.ac.uk/caec/docs/ NCIA%20Here%20We%20Stand.pdf

Welton, M. (1997). In defense of civil society: Canadian adult education in neo-conservative times. In S. Walters (Ed.), *Globalization, adult education and training: Impacts and issues* (pp. 27–38). London, England: Zed Books.

Westoby, P., & Dowling, G. (2013). *Theory and practice of dialogical community development: International perspectives.* Abingdon, Oxon, England: Routledge.

Whitmore, E., Wilson, M. G., & Calhoun, A. (Eds.). (2011). *Activism that works.* Halifax, Nova Scotia: Fernwood.

Wieringa, S. E. (Ed.). (2008). *Traveling heritages: New perspectives on preserving and sharing women's history.* Amsterdam, The Netherlands: Aksant.

Wiessner, C. (2009). Noting the potential for transformation: Creative expression through music. In C. Hoggan, S. Simpson, & H. L. Stuckey (Eds.), *Creative expression in transformative learning: Tools and techniques for educators of adults* (pp. 103–127). Malabar, FL: Krieger.

Wiggins, N. (2012). Popular education for health promotion and community empowerment: A review of the literature. *Health Promotion International, 27*(3), 356–371. doi:10.1093/heapro/dar046

Williams, G. (2004). Towards a repoliticization of participatory development: Political capabilities and spaces of empowerment. In S. Hickey & G. Mohan (Eds.), *Participation: From tyranny to transformation?* (pp. 92–106). London, England: Zed Books.

Williams, I. D. (2006). Southern community women teach a new generation lessons of leadership for social change. *Journal of Transformative Education, 4*(3), 257–274.

Williams, R. (1976). *Key-words: Vocabulary of culture and society.* London, England: Fontana.

Wilson, K. (2008). Reclaiming "agency", reasserting resistance. *IDS Bulletin, 39*(6), 83–91. doi:10.1111/j.1759-5436.2008.tb00515.x

Wohlsen, M. (2012, June 4). Women engineers trace tech gender gap to childhood. *The Huffington Post.* Retrieved from http://www.huffingtonpost.com/2012/06/04/women-engineers_n_1568695.html

World Bank. (2012). *World development report 2012: Gender equality and development.* Washington, DC: The Bank.

World Health Organization. (1986). *The Ottawa charter for health promotion.* First international conference on health promotion, Ottawa, 21 November 1986. Retrieved from http://www.who.int/ healthpromotion/conferences/previous/ottawa/en/#

World Health Organization. (2011). *Social determinants of health: Key concepts.* Retrieved from http://www.who.int/social_determinants/thecommission/finalreport/key_concepts/en/

Wotherspoon, T., & Hansen, J. (2013). The "Idle no more" movement: Paradoxes of first nations inclusion in the Canadian context. *Social Inclusion, 1*(1), 21–36.

Young, J. R. (2012, April 3). For archivists, 'occupy' movement presents new challenges [Blog post]. *The Chronicle of Higher Education Wired Campus Blog.* Retrieved from http://chronicle.com/ blogs/wiredcampus/for-archivists-%e2%80%98occupy%e2%80%99-movement-presents-new-challenges/35929

Yousafzai, M., with Lamb, C. (2013). *I am Malala: The girl who stood up for education and was shot by the Taliban.* New York, NY: Little, Brown & Co.

Zaghloul, N. S. (2013). Day 8/16 of activism against gender violence: Fighting back-reclaiming the 'public.' *Women living under Muslim laws.* Retrieved from http://w2ww.wluml.org/ar/node/8392

185

REFERENCES

Zarzar, A. L. B., Meneses, J., & Azavedo, M. (2002). Gender and the participatory budget in Recife. *BRIDGE Gender and Development in Brief, 12*. Retrieved from http://www.bridge.ids.ac.uk/dgb12.html#3

Zerehi, S. S. (2014, August 19). Michael Brown's shooting in Ferguson lost on social media: Filters used by Facebook helped to bury news about Michael Brown's shooting. *CBC News: Technology & Science*. Retrieved from http://www.cbc.ca/news/technology/michael-brown-s-shooting-in-ferguson-lost-on-social-media-1.2740014

ABOUT THE AUTHORS

Leona M. English is Professor of Adult Education at St. Francis Xavier University, Canada. She is the co-author, with Peter Mayo, of *Learning with Adults: A Critical Pedagogical Introduction* (Sense, 2012), which was presented with the C.O. Houle Award for Outstanding Literature in Adult Education by the American Association for Adult and Continuing Education. She has served as president of the Canadian Association for the Study of Adult Education and was editor of the *International Encyclopedia of Adult Education.* She is presently co-editor of *Adult Education Quarterly.*

Catherine J. Irving is responsible for the Marie Michael Library at the Coady International Institute of St. Francis Xavier University, Antigonish, Nova Scotia, Canada. She combines her library work with research on feminism and women's learning. Her passion is for unearthing the many ways that libraries inform adult education. Over the past number of years she has contributed her research findings to publications such as *Adult Education Quarterly, Studies in Continuing Education,* and the *Journal of Adult and Continuing Education.* She has presented at the Adult Education Research Conference, the Canadian Association for the Study of Adult Education, and SCUTREA.

SUBJECT INDEX

NAME INDEX

CPSIA information can be obtained at www.ICGtesting.com
Printed in the USA
BVOW06s1346220116

433921BV00009B/52/P

9 789463 002004